INDIVIDUALIZING VOCATIONAL AND TECHNICAL INSTRUCTION

DAVID J. PUCEL
Professor, University of Minnesota

WILLIAM C. KNAAK
Superintendent, Special Intermediate Vocational School District 916
White Bear Lake, Minnesota

CHARLES E. MERRILL PUBLISHING COMPANY
A Bell & Howell Company
Columbus, Ohio

THE MERRILL SERIES
IN CAREER PROGRAMS

Published by
Charles E. Merrill Publishing Company
A Bell & Howell Company
Columbus, Ohio 43216

International Standard Book Number: 0-675-08743-0

Library of Congress Catalog Card Number: 74-18613

1 2 3 4 5 6—79 78 77 76 75
Printed in the United States of America

**This book is dedicated to our wives,
Virginia and Delores.**

THE
MERRILL SERIES
IN CAREER
PROGRAMS

In recent years our nation has literally rediscovered education. Concurrently, many nations are considering educational programs in revolutionary terms. They now realize that education is the responsible link between social needs and social improvement. While traditionally Americans have been committed to the ideal of the optimal development of each individual, there is increased public appreciation and support of the values and benefits of education in general, and vocational and technical education in particular. With occupational education's demonstrated capacity to contribute to economic growth and national well being, it is only natural that it has been given increased prominence and importance in this educational climate.

With the increased recognition that the true resources of a nation are its human resources, occupational education programs are considered a form of investment in human capital—an investment which provides comparatively high returns to both the individual and society.

The Merrill Series in Career Programs is designed to provide a broad range of educational materials to assist members of the profession in providing effective and efficient programs of occupational education which contribute to an individual's becoming both a contributing economic producer and a responsible member of society.

The series and its sub-series do not have a singular position or philosophy concerning the problems and alternatives in providing the broad range of offerings needed to prepare the nation's work force. Rather, authors are encouraged to develop and support independent positions and alternative strategies. A wide range of educational and occupational experiences and perspectives have been brought to bear through the Merrill Series in Career Programs National Editorial Board. These experiences, coupled with those of the authors, assure useful publications. I believe that this title, along with others in the series, will provide major assistance in further developing and extending viable educational programs to assist youth and adults in preparing for and furthering their careers.

Robert E. Taylor
Editorial Director
Series in Career Programs

PREFACE

Individualized instruction has long been a goal of the effective educator. Students are individuals who learn in varied ways and at different speeds. Yet an instructor is required to provide instruction to a group of students and not just to isolated individuals. This book explains and describes procedures that allow an instructor to manage the learning activities of a group while accounting for the needs of individuals.

What is individualized instruction? Much time is wasted when individuals argue about means of achieving individualized instruction without specifying the educational goals they wish to achieve. The methods and procedures used to individualize a program are quite different depending upon the goal to be achieved. This book addresses a number of individualized instruction models for achieving various goals and suggests one as being most appropriate for vocational education.

Methods and procedures for individualizing vocational and technical instruction are discussed with examples taken from a variety of vocational and technical fields. Some of the key topics covered are (1) establishing the need for a program, (2) identifying program content, (3) identifying the students to be served, (4) developing objectives, (5) developing instructional strategies, and (6) monitoring student progress.

The book concludes with important considerations for managing an individualized program or series of programs since the failure of such programs is often due to management problems and not to the curriculum.

CONTENTS

Progress, 190; Summary, 190; References, 190.

7   **Managing the Individualized Learning
           System**   **192**

Goals and Objectives, 192; Ingredients
of a Successful System, 193; To Buy
or Build a System of Individualized
Instruction, 197; Materials Production,
Quality, and Quantity, 202; The Process of Educational Change, 204; The
Instructional Materials Center, 207;
Differentiated Staffing, 209; Scheduling, 210; Summary, 216; References,
216.

Chapter 1   INDIVIDUALIZED INSTRUCTION— AN IDEA WHOSE TIME HAS COME

Instruction and the System

"Why should I individualize vocational instruction?" is the question often raised by vocational instructors when they are asked by supervisors and others to consider individualizing their instructional programs. They ask the question primarily because they assume that the instructional system which may have served their needs and in which they have acquired some confidence should also be capable of serving current vocational instructional needs. This assumption is highly questionable. Society and societal expectations have changed, and the effective vocational educator is one who is willing to recognize and adapt to these changes.

Currently, people are demanding access to all facets of public instruction, academic and occupational. This access is being demanded by the children of the affluent as well as the poor, the disadvantaged, and the handicapped. Upon gaining original access to education, people are also demanding a flexible educational system which will allow them to return in the future to pursue more study pertaining to their original goal or some new goal. When they do return, they are requesting that the new instruction be built upon those skills they have already developed and not to have to start as though they knew nothing about the subject.

In this country there has not been a serious commitment to an open-access curriculum design which will provide people with the flexibility they

1

desire. For example, the student who has already made a commitment to "college preparatory" curriculum has typically been denied access to work experience programs or vocational courses while in high school. A nonacademically oriented student typically has been denied an opportunity for genuine school support and respect for the technical and vocational curriculum within the high school program. Few programs have been developed which allow people to return to the educational system in such a way that they can gain credit for the prior knowledge they have acquired through earlier education or experience.

The cry for accountability has also been heard throughout the land, and there is no evidence that that cry is going to diminish. Accountability means many things to many people, but as applied to vocational instruction programs, it usually means (1) public assurances that the training will be effective and that the participants in such training programs will be able to be employable in the occupations for which training is being given and (2) the cost to the public and to the student will be reasonable in relationship to the training benefit being derived.

The thrusts for access and accountability along with other strong motivators are forcing changes in all educational structures including the many arenas of vocational-technical instruction.

In order to understand how the educational system might be changed to make it more effective, we must first understand the functions which education has been asked to fulfill in the past and in the future. Our society was built upon the democratic concept that the governed should select those who govern. It appeared logical to our founding fathers that those who had to select representatives to govern them should be knowledgeable and educated, and, therefore, they should have at least a minimum of education. This belief is still evident in the requirements which immigrants must meet in obtaining citizenship within the United States; people wishing to become citizens of the United States must demonstrate knowledge of our way of government and be able to read and write English.

Since all people could not afford to send their children to school, yet they were given an opportunity to participate in determining who would govern, public education was initiated and funded through public monies. The first subjects included in the curriculum were reading, writing, and arithmetic. The abilities to read, write, and compute were viewed as basic skills which everyone needed. Later other courses were included on the belief that they would facilitate citizenship development and because they were needed by students who wished to prepare for the professions by attending colleges and universities. With the exception of the basic courses in reading, writing, and arithmetic, little emphasis was placed upon how the material contained in the curriculum related to what people would do once they left the educational system and entered society.

Schools were not asked to show how the material taught would benefit students once they left school. Much of what the elementary and secondary schools taught was included in the curriculum because it was required for college entrance, and it was assumed that the colleges and universities had established how the material related to what students would need once they left college. In most cases this was not true. Most college and university programs included requirements in their curricula based as much upon tradition as upon relevance to what students would do upon leaving college.

This condition was allowed to persist because society had other mechanisms, besides the schools, for training people in the skills which were required to become employed after they left school. Most industries needed large numbers of unskilled and semiskilled personnel. In those industries where skilled personnel were required, the demand was small enough so that apprenticeship and on-the-job training programs could fulfill most of the need. Therefore, those people who left the educational system after developing minimal basic skills found many opportunities to enter the labor market after leaving schools, and society welcomed them because there was always a large demand for such people. Relatively few people were needed in the professions which required a college education. Therefore, little attempt was made to develop an educational system which was designed to encourage all people to remain in school and to develop their maximum potential. If people did not wish to continue in the educational system they were advised to leave and take a job. In providing all people with a minimal level of reading, writing, and arithmetic skills and then selectively educating those people needed in the professions, the educational system fulfilled the needs of society.

Instructional practices in the schools were developed consistent with these societal expectations. The system was designed to selectively educate people and, therefore, to selectively eliminate people from the schools. Students were taught as groups. Courses were developed with highly structured content and were presented within the school year or some other fixed period of time. Teachers presented the content to the students as a group when the majority of the students were ready for it. Those students who were ready earlier and those students who were not ready received the content with the majority. All students progressed at the speed of the majority. Students were looked upon as either having "aptitude" to learn a particular type of content or not having it. A student who was not succeeding in an area was often told that he or she lacked aptitude in that area. This condition was viewed as a fact which was not worth trying to change. Aptitude was defined in terms of a person's potential or capacity to learn. It was assumed that if a student could not grasp the material within the time period allotted by the instructor, his aptitude or potential to deal with that type of material was low. There-fore, it was not worth continuing to work with the individual on that sub-ject matter. The student could always leave school and find a job. Stu-dents were given another chance at learning the material if they wished to repeat a grade. Most students, especially older ones, felt that repeating a grade was humiliating and, therefore, they left school if they were above the minimum mandatory age for staying in the school. If students did wish to repeat a grade they were required not only to repeat the subject or subjects with which they experienced difficulty, but also they were re-quired to repeat all of the material for a particular grade.

Since the majority of students proceeded through the system satis-factorily, the system was not changed for the few people who did not make it. Whether or not a student was progressing satisfactorily was de-termined by how well he or she was progressing as compared with others in the class. If the student was at the top of the class he was given an A. If the student was at the middle of the class he was given a C. If the student was at the bottom of the class he was given an F. No one paid a great deal of attention to the exact competency level the students had achieved. Typ-ically, the students who received A's had developed a sufficient level of competency to use the skills and knowledge which they learned effec-tively. However, students with grades lower than an A generally lacked some of the fundamental skills and knowledge in the subject matter area being taught.

Besides not being capable of adequately reflecting the competencies which students had mastered and could perform, this type of evaluation tended to eliminate students who did not grasp the material the first time from dealing with it in the future. Students who got F's were viewed as having "failed" to develop as much knowledge and skills as the other members of the class. Therefore, rather than being assisted in the devel-opment of these competencies they were eliminated by being "failed." For example, if Mary experienced difficulty in learning addition and sub-traction, she might fail math in the fourth grade. The basis for determin-ing whether she did poorly in math was to compare her math progress with the progress of others in the class. Since math was viewed as a basic subject, she might have to repeat the entire fourth grade even though she may have done very well in reading, writing, and other subjects. To many, this process of being selected out affected their perceptions of them-selves throughout their lives.

The educational system accepted the assumption that people would learn varying amounts of a given subject matter area because they had different aptitudes in the subject matter area. Therefore, it was reasonable for different people to develop different levels of competence in a subject matter area. This philosophy of aptitude and its implications for how people viewed competency development led to large numbers of people completing formal schooling with C's and D's who really did not possess a sufficient amount of competence in many of the skills they had been taught in the school to be able to use them effectively.

Figure 1-1 shows the general continuing enrollment of people remaining in this educational system. It shows a hypothetical group that started together in kindergarten and progressed through post-high school education in the past. The educational system and the grading system accompanying it continually excluded people from the educational system, so that only the most able or most persistent individuals continued their education at the higher levels. Those people who were not able to progress as fast as the majority of the people in their group were "failed" out of the system.

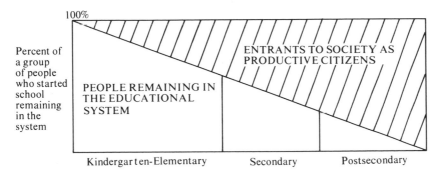

EDUCATIONAL LEVEL

FIGURE 1—1

EXPECTED RETENTION RATE OF
THE EDUCATIONAL SYSTEM
IN THE PAST

The following is an example of how the process operated. Of the group that entered the fourth grade, some of the people were failed and did not go on to the fifth grade. Of those people who did go on to the fifth grade, some were failed and, therefore, did not go on to the sixth grade. The elimination of people was repeated at each grade level, causing fewer and fewer people to continue to remain in the educational system. When a person did leave the system, reentering the system to continue one's education was very difficult. Administrative procedures in the schools were not developed to readily facilitate continuing education once that education was interrupted. Social stigma was attached to an older person's reentering school and being in classes with younger students.

In the past this system worked well since those who left the educational system could find work in the largely unskilled labor market and if the job they had was eliminated, they could readily find another. As society determined that more and more people should be educated at higher levels, minimum age laws were enacted to keep people in schools. It was assumed that mandatory education would better prepare people for citizenship and would allow them to become more productive in the growing technological society. Many students remained in schools because it was mandatory and did receive some benefit from the additional education, but they continued to question the relevancy of school to what they would do after leaving school. These students tended to leave school upon reaching the minimum age. With mandatory education came the adoption of other options into the educational curriculum. As the technological advancements in the society continued to increase, it became obvious that it would no longer be possible to rely on the informal educational system outside of schools to prepare all of the skilled personnel needed in business and industry. The numbers of craftsmen and other trained personnel required demanded that new mechanisms be established to prepare people to enter business and industry. The schools were encouraged to include programs aimed at helping people to develop salable skills. The federal government encouraged this development through the passage of federal legislation which provided incentive money to develop vocational programs. Such incentive monies continue to exist today. Money became available in meaningful quantities with the passage of the Smith-Hughes Act in 1917 and was used to develop vocational programs which were incorporated into the high schools as technology developed. Some students did not wish to go on to college or to learn a salable skill. However, mandatory attendance laws required them to continue their education. Therefore, a general education curriculum was developed to provide students with a broad general educational background. As society continued to apply increasing pressure for students to remain in high schools, large numbers of students enrolled in the general education curriculum to obtain a high school diploma which had increasing value as a ticket to future employment. A student could elect (1) the college preparatory option, (2) the option aimed at helping him or her develop a salable skill, or (3) the general education option, which did not lead to college or a salable skill.

The addition of the mandatory minimum age and opening of other options, in addition to the college preparatory track, fulfilled the societal needs for another period of time. The mode of instruction during this period was the same as the mode of instruction during the earlier period. Students were taught as groups, student aptitude was viewed as potential to achieve in a given subject matter area, people were graded based upon how well they did as compared with other people in the class, and people completed schooling having achieved widely different levels of competence in the subjects they studied. This system continued to eliminate people from additional education if they were not able to perform at the same level as the majority of the group. Once they did leave school, re-entering continued to be difficult.

But we can no longer afford to have our educational system provide students with an education that has minimal relevance to them. Educational programs must be designed to address needs which individuals and society understand. In some cases this may mean changing the program, and in others, it may mean informing people of the relevance of what currently exists. Society can no longer afford to have large numbers of students leaving the educational system without the skills they need to survive and to progress. These skills include general skills such as human relations, computational, reading, writing, and citizenship skills, as well as salable skills. Automation and technological developments have eliminated vast numbers of the jobs which unskilled or semiskilled individuals could hold in the past; jobs are available, but few are available to the untrained.

During the twenty-year period, 1947-1967, our national manpower composition changed rapidly, due largely to technological development.

> Farm employment declined by 4¼ million (that is, by more than half), railroad employment by 850,000 (more than half), textile employment by 360,000 (more than one-quarter), mining employment by 330,000 (more than one-third), employment in the lumber products industry by 230,000 (more than one-quarter), and in the leather, tobacco, and petroleum industries together 140,000 jobs were lost. In these eight industries the total job loss was over 6 million, in the face of a rapid expansion of the total economy over a 20-year period. (*Vocational Education: The Bridge Between Man and His Work* 1968, p. 163)

However, during the same period there was a rapid expansion in the demand for professional, technical, and service personnel. This demand has continued to expand, and students who leave the educational system today without a salable skill are likely to face unemployment or employment in "dead end" jobs which do not lead to advancement.

In the past those people who left the educational system before completing high school were welcomed into the labor market; they are now termed dropouts. They are viewed as an undesirable product of the educational system, and society has invested large sums of money in remedial programs to try to prepare them to become productive members of society. These programs have addressed general skills as well as salable skills.

As the dropout problem became more severe, programs were established outside of the educational system to help dropouts develop skills which they were not able to develop within the regular educational system. Congress looked toward the Bureau of Labor for assistance in developing these programs.

Some of the remedial programs for dropouts and other individuals who could not find employment were funded under the Area Redevelopment Act, the Manpower Development and Training Act, the Youth Employment Act, the Neighborhood Youth Corps, the Job Corps, and the Economic Opportunity Act. The National Advisory Council for Vocational Education reported, "The Manpower Development and Training Act, the Job Corps, and other training, as well as the work programs, are designed primarily to compensate for earlier educational deficiencies. These acts serve primarily a remedial function and were not aimed at elimination of the causes of the problem" (*Vocational Education: The Bridge Between Man and His Work*, pp. 181-82). Certainly a partial solution to this problem would be the development of an educational system capable of helping all people develop salable skills, including good work attitudes.

To this point we have shown that the educational system has been encountering difficulties during recent years. These difficulties apparently are due to a change in the role which education is being called upon to play in our modern society. No longer is it appropriate to educate only a small portion of the total population beyond the minimum literacy level and to assume that others will be absorbed into society as productive citizens. The system must adopt new procedures that will allow for the wide variety of individual desires, learning styles, and learning rates. The National Advisory Council on Vocational Education suggested a number of trends they felt should be included in an educational system that would lend itself to fulfilling the needs of modern society. Some of these trends are: (1) greater individualization of instruction, (2) planning which accepts the fact that not all students learn in the same way, nor will they learn the same things under the same circumstances, (3) program planning based upon the assumption that school fails students rather than students fail school, (4) teachers becoming managers of the learning environment rather than purveyors of information, and (5) recognition that education can no longer be planned within the confines of the school but must coordinate with community resources and agencies (*Vocational Education: The Bridge Between Man and His Work*, p. 191).

Figure 1-2 pictorially presents the retention rate which society expects the educational system to have in the future. We can see that the expectations for the educational system in the future are quite different than those shown in figure 1-1 as being the expectations for the educational system in the past.

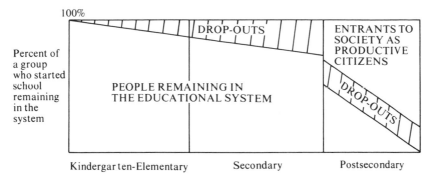

FIGURE 1—2

EXPECTED RETENTION RATE OF
THE EDUCATIONAL SYSTEM
IN THE FUTURE

In the future, society will expect the educational system to develop techniques for assisting all individuals to prepare to become productive citizens. The informal educational opportunities of the past will not be as readily available to individuals in the future. Provisions must be made for the development of general basic skills as well as for the development of skills which allow an individual to obtain employment. If a person wishes to prepare for employment during high school, programs should be available to allow him or her to do so. If a person wishes to obtain employment after receiving additional education beyond high school, the high school experience or the experience beyond high school should prepare the person with a salable skill. If one wishes to leave school and to return later, the program should allow him/her to continue from where he/she left off. If a person completes a program and finds employment, but later becomes unemployed, he/she should be allowed to reenter for retraining and to receive credit for skills he/she has already developed. The accomplishment of these objectives requires that programs be flexible enough to meet the needs of individuals. If programs are not meeting the needs of individuals, students will leave the educational system and become dropouts and they will not want to reenter the educational system. Students are no longer willing to accept whatever the educational system puts before them as being of value. They are asking questions about the value of the experiences that they obtain in school. If relevance is not shown, many of them are not willing to participate in the educational experience. They not only ask "what do you want me to do?" but also "why?" Schools are not only being asked to dispense knowledge and to provide a learning environment, but they are also being called upon to sell it.

Currently, society views dropouts as being undesirable due to the lack of employment possibilities available to people with insufficient skills. Dropouts are viewed as a failure of the educational system rather than as a failure of the individuals who drop out. Figure 1-2 indicates that dropouts can occur not only from the high school program but also from the postsecondary program. Postsecondary dropouts are those people who did not develop salable skills during their high school experience because they planned on developing them in a post-high school experience, but who later drop out of the post-high school experience before developing the salable skill.

In light of these and other changing expectations for education, new educational methodologies and strategies must be developed. Educators must develop mechanisms which will allow them to change their educational programs as the needs of society change. They must also allow for dealing with individual differences in ways that these differences become an asset to the student rather than a liability. The objective of preparing people as productive citizens requires that the educational system adjust to the needs of society. If it cannot, the products of the system—students—will find they are not adequately prepared to become productive citizens, and, therefore, the educational system will have failed.

One mechanism or approach to revitalizing the educational system is individualized instruction. Individualized instruction attempts to adapt the educational program to the specific needs of a student. It is aimed at assisting the student to develop from the point he is at currently to a place where he would like to be in the future. This characteristic makes it very compatible with the philosophy that people should be able to enter and exit the educational system throughout their lifetimes. The particular competencies which the student lacks in order to achieve the objective that he has for the future become the basis for developing an instructional program for the student. A student and the educational system are then judged in terms of how well the student is able to attain the goals which they have set for the student. If the goals are not accomplished, not only the student fails but the educational system also fails. If we review the trends described by the National Advisory Council on Vocational Education discussed earlier, we can see that such individualized instruction is consistent with those trends.

Individualized Instruction

PROGRAM DEFINITION

Few educators would disagree with the need for individualizing instruction to allow students to achieve relevant goals. There is considerable disagreement, however, in how educators define individualizing instruction and in how they define relevant goals. Some define individualized instruction in terms of the development of a variety of different methods of presenting content to students so that they can select a method that best suits their personal learning styles. Although this certainly could be used as a method of defining individualized instruction, it does not provide a basis for making a meaningful distinction between what are considered to be individualized and nonindividualized programs. This definition relates primarily to method of presentation rather than to the basic structure of an individualized program as compared to a nonindividualized program. Therefore, a discussion of alternative modes of presenting content to students based on individual differences will be discussed later in chapter 5 but is not used here as the basis for defining an individualized program. The present discussion will concentrate on basic goals or functions of programs as a method for defining individualized instruction. The distinction between types of individualized instructional models based upon program goals is important to the vocational educator. Many of the publications that have been available on individualized instruction have been developed with nonvocational programs in mind. Therefore, some of the methods of individualized instruction which are presented in these publications do not work very well in vocational education. However, once the instructor sees how various individualized programs differ depending on their goals, it becomes easier for the instructor to modify methods developed by others to his or her program.

In some cases, a relevant program goal is to help students prepare for an occupation by developing prescribed amounts of competency in a set of prescribed skills and knowledge. In other cases, the relevant goal is to provide students with a general understanding of a subject matter area. If the objective of a particular course is to provide a person with competency in specific areas, the individualized instruction model used is quite different than the model that would be used with a course aimed at presenting students with a general acquaintance with these areas. Therefore, the key to determining the type of individualized instruction model to be used is not the subject matter to be taught, but the context within which a particular subject matter is taught. One can teach metal working in an industrial arts program or in a trade and industrial education program. Usually the trade and industrial education metal working program would be aimed at developing certain prescribed skills related to metal working, based on the needs of industry. The industrial arts program might have the objective of acquainting students with metal working skills. Although both of these programs are dealing with the same subject matter content, they would be taught from two quite different individualized instruction models.

This book relates primarily to the implementation of individualized instruction in vocational programs. The American Vocational Education Association defines a vocational program as follows. Vocational programs are

> ... designed to prepare individuals for gainful employment as semi-skilled or skilled workers or technicians or sub-professionals in recognized occupations and in new and emerging occupations, or to prepare individuals for enrollment in advanced technical education programs, but excluding any program to prepare individuals for employment in occupations generally considered professional or which require a baccalaureate or higher degree. (American Vocational Association 1971)

The key portions of this definition are (1) vocational programs are designed to prepare individuals for gainful employment, and (2) vocational programs are designed to prepare individuals for employment in occupations requiring less than a baccalaureate or higher degree. Using this definition, a two-year post-high school program designed to prepare practical nurses would be considered as a vocational program, but a four-year nursing baccalaureate degree provided by a university would not be considered a vocational program.

This definition provides a basis for judging the primary relevance of vocational programs. Relevance should be judged on the extent to which the program adequately prepares individuals to enter those occupations which the program is designed to serve. This is not to say that this is all that vocational programs should be concerned with. They should also be concerned with preparing people to advance in the occupations and with assisting students to develop other skills, such as citizenship and social skills; however, these are not the bases for judging primary relevance. Therefore, the content for vocational programs should be derived from business and industry. For years, vocational educators have established advisory committees made up of representatives of business and industry to advise them in the development of vocational programs. When these advisory committees have been adequately utilized, programs have tended to be relevant. Vocational educators have also developed analysis techniques which allow them to analyze the businesses or industries for which they hope to prepare individuals for employment as a basis for curriculum development. Some of these techniques will be discussed in a later chapter.

The identification of the content to be included in a program provides the raw materials to be included in courses. The next step is to determine how these raw materials should be processed to make them most easily understood by the students in a manner consistent with the goals of the course. A number of general instructional models are available which outline different strategies that can be used to plan courses. Many of them can be categorized as individualized instruction models, but only one of them is totally consistent with vocational education philosophy.

INSTRUCTIONAL MODELS AND STRATEGIES

Individualized instruction is a global term used to designate any instructional methodology or strategy which attempts to make a program responsive to the unique needs of individuals. The following discussion describes the major individualized instruction models and the basic strategies which define each of them. It also contrasts the individualized instruction models with the "traditional" model of instruction. Each of the models is useful, depending upon how we view content, time, and proficiency level within the instructional setting (see figure 1-3). Content refers to what is presented to students during a course or program, time refers to the length of time students are given to learn the content, and proficiency level refers to how much skill or knowledge a person is expected to develop relative to a task before the task is completed. An instructional program can be developed to try to insure that all students learn similar content, or it can be developed to allow students to select their own content. An instructional program can be developed to insure that all students work on a task for the same period of time, or it can be developed to allow students to work on a task for different periods of time. An instructional program can be developed to insure that all students develop a minimal level of proficiency on a task (master the task), or it can be developed to allow different students to develop different levels of proficiency. Figure 1-3 presents the eight basic instructional models categorized by content, time, and expected level of proficiency.

The content dimension is viewed quite differently depending upon the purpose for teaching the content within a course or program. If it is felt that the content to be taught is composed of basic skills which all students *must* study in order to successfully function in the future, then the fixed-content scheme is used. Fixed-content means that the students are not allowed to select what they are going to study. They may elect to study the content in various ways, but they must study the same content. The content is fixed by the educational system. Courses contained in a program for preparing medical doctors are generally fixed-content courses. Once students indicate that they wish to become a doctor and enter the pro-

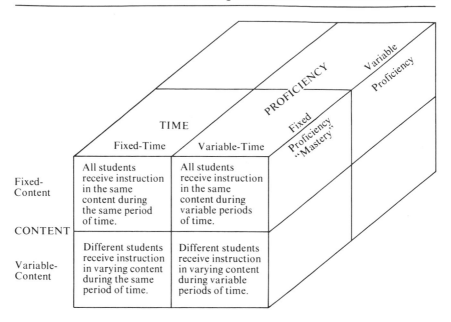

FIGURE 1–3

EIGHT BASIC INSTRUCTIONAL MODELS

gram, they must study the courses included in the program and the content contained in each course which has been specified by the medical profession. These tasks are determined by examining what a medical doctor is expected to be able to do.

If the exact content students should study is not important, the variable-content mode can be used. Since it is not essential that students study specifics from the body of content but that they achieve some general familiarity with the content, students are allowed to select content from a wide range of content related to the program or course being taught. An example can be drawn from a career education course aimed at familiarizing students with a variety of occupations. The purpose is to familiarize students with a variety of occupations, but it is not important that all students study the same occupations. Therefore, students are allowed to select the occupations they wish to study.

Since the fixed-content versus variable-content dimension refers to the way in which content in a particular course is selected and not to the way in which courses are selected, a student could select a course which included highly prescribed content from a variety of courses, and the content dimension for that particular course would be a fixed-content mode. Another student might enter a program with a highly specific list of courses which must be completed to finish the program, but he or she is given freedom to select content once in a course. This student would be participating in a course designed with a variable-content mode.

Since vocational programs are designed primarily to prepare people for gainful employment and program relevancy is determined by the extent to which people are prepared to enter the occupations the program is designed to prepare them to enter, most vocational education programs use the fixed-content mode. The total vocational curriculum has a great number of alternative options that students might select, but upon entering a particular course within an option, the content is usually prescribed based upon the industries or businesses to which the course is related. For example, a student might have options available in the health fields, trade and industrial fields, home economics fields, agricultural fields and distributive education fields, but upon selecting the fashion merchandising course within the distributive education field, the student is expected to learn the techniques and practices used in fashion merchandising.

The time dimension refers to the amount of time a student is allowed to complete a particular portion of content, regardless if the content is selected by the student or is prescribed by the educational system. If the student is given a prescribed amount of time to study a particular task, a fixed-time mode is being used. If the student is given as much time as needed to study a particular task, a variable-time mode is being used. Traditionally, educational programs have been developed using the fixed-time mode of instruction. Students were given a prescribed amount of time to learn a task. For example, students were given six weeks to learn how to arc weld before they were asked to move on to oxyacetylene welding. It is obvious that this mode would lead to variable levels of proficiency being developed by the students studying arc welding. Some would master the skill within the six-weeks period, and others would develop varying levels of the skill.

If the students were allowed to study arc welding either until they had developed a minimal level of skill or the level they wished to develop, they would be experiencing the variable-time mode. We will be defining individualized vocational instruction in terms of the variable-time mode, which acknowledges that students learn at different rates of speed. It is assumed that students should not be required to move on to a new task unless they are ready.

The last dimension useful in categorizing basic instructional models is the proficiency level dimension. Instructional programs can be developed to allow different students to develop different levels of proficiency relative to a given task. Such programs can be described as variable-proficiency programs. Variable-proficiency programs allow people to explore a content area where the primary function of the program or course is not skill or knowledge mastery. The following example is from a career education program aimed at familiarizing people with occupations. Students who are studying about farmers and what they do may have different interests in farming. Those with a strong interest may spend a lot of time studying farming, while those with a slight interest may spend a much shorter period of time. The students with more interest will probably develop a greater proficiency in their knowledge of farming than those who are less interested.

If a student is required to develop a prescribed amount of proficiency on a task before leaving that task, a fixed-proficiency or "mastery" mode is used. "Mastery" implies that a student has developed the expected or prescribed level of proficiency in a task. An example is the case where students in a foods preparation class must be able to prepare 100 fruit salads within an hour before leaving the fruit salads task. If they can only prepare ninety-eight salads within an hour, they have not mastered the task, but if they can prepare 100 or more per hour they have mastered the task. Individualized vocational instruction is usually organized around the fixed-proficiency or mastery mode. This is based on the assumption that business and industry expect to employ people who are not only familiar with a task, but who also have developed a minimal level of proficiency in the task so that they can perform on the job. The owner of a garage employing auto mechanics does not want to hire a transmission specialist who has a slight familiarity with automatic transmissions. He wants to hire a person whom he can count on to repair automatic transmissions.

The way a person views both the time and expected proficiency dimensions is related to a person's perception of how people learn. As we have seen, in the past many educators believed that a person had a certain amount of potential to learn a given type of content. Therefore, if a person could not learn the content within the prescribed period of time, he was viewed as not having sufficient aptitude for that content, and therefore, was discouraged from continuing to study that content in the future. This point of view led educators to develop teaching strategies which were based on a fixed-time, variable-proficiency mode. All students were given a certain number of weeks in which to study a topic; after that time was up, they were tested and the class moved on to the next topic. If a student did not understand the topic, he or she was expected to move on to the next topic with the rest of the class. The teacher tended to feel that if the student did not master the topic in the time allotted, the student would not master it. Students were not given additional time, and grades were assigned based upon the level of proficiency developed by each student.

Today, many educators view a person's aptitude not in terms of potential but in terms of the speed at which a person learns. They assume that most people can learn almost any content to a specified level of competence given a sufficient amount of time. John B. Carroll, in an article presented in the *Teachers College Record* (1963), defines an aptitude in terms of the speed at which a person learns a particular task. If one accepts the premise that most people can learn any content given a sufficient amount of time, it is apparent that instructional strategies based upon a fixed-time model are no longer always appropriate. It is also apparent that most students can attain a specified level of proficiency, and therefore, it is not reasonable to assume that students will necessarily attain different levels of proficiency. If a student does not master a task within a certain period of time, more time should be allotted. One would expect that most interested students could master the content if they are given a sufficient amount of time and do not have any severe physical or mental handicaps.

It is possible to organize an instructional program using any of the eight instructional models indicated in figure 1-3 and listed below, which result from all possible combinations of the content, time, and proficiency levels.

	*1. Fixed-content, fixed-time, fixed-proficiency
("Traditional" model)	2. Fixed-content, fixed-time, variable-proficiency
(Model recommended for vocational education)	3. Fixed-content, variable-time, fixed-proficiency
	4. Fixed-content, variable-time, variable-proficiency
	5. Variable-content, fixed-time, fixed-proficiency
(Individualized instruction models)	6. Variable-content, fixed-time, variable-proficiency
	7. Variable-content, variable-time, fixed-proficiency
	8. Variable-content, variable-time, variable-proficiency

*Model is not feasible.

The first model (fixed-content, fixed-time, fixed-proficiency) is not feasible or practical because it provides no means of accounting for individual differences which are always present. The only circumstance under which such models would work is if all students learned a particular task at the same speed and to the same level of proficiency. Since students are different and have different aptitudes, they will learn the same task at different rates of speed. If the time to learn a specific task is fixed, it is not possible for all students who wish to study the task to reach the same level of proficiency unless the time is set at the time it would take the slowest student to master the task. This is not reasonable because everyone else would have to be idle while they waited for that person.

The second model is generally considered to be the "traditional" instructional model. The same content is presented to all students during a specified period of time, resulting in variable proficiency among individuals. This model produces a continual group of failures as a by-product because it does not allow for individual differences; it just describes them and magnifies them.

Models 3 through 8 are feasible individualized instruction models because they all provide for combinations of content to be studied, time to study the content, and proficiency levels which allow for individual student differences. If a fixed-time mode is used, it is only meaningful to accompany that model with a variable-proficiency mode, or a variable-content mode as described earlier. If students are given a prescribed amount of time to study a task, different individuals will develop different levels of proficiency. If a variable-time mode is used, it may be accompanied by either a fixed- or variable-proficiency mode. If students are allowed to study a task until they wish to move to another task, the variable-proficiency mode is being used. If students are told they should study the task until it is mastered, a fixed-proficiency or mastery mode is being used.

The variable-time mode can be used with either variable- or fixed-content. If it is used with the variable-content mode, students select the content that they wish to study and study it until they master it or until they wish to move on to something else. If it is used with the fixed-content mode, students study the prescribed content until they master it or until they wish to move on to something else. Since the school year is fixed for most elementary and secondary education programs, they use a combination of these two models in their individualized instruction programs. Selected basic skills are identified which all students are expected to master. The numbers and types of skills selected to be mastered are such that even the slowest students can master them during the normal school year. Beyond this group of basic skills, the students are allowed to select other learning activities aimed at supplemental skill development, which they can study until they wish to move on to something else. They are allowed to complete as many of these tasks as they can during the normal school year.

Model number 3 (fixed-content, variable-time, fixed-proficiency) is the model used most often in vocational education. The main objective of such a model is to assist all students who wish to enter a particular occupation with the development of the skills and knowledge required to enter the occupation, regardless of the amount of time it takes each individual to master the tasks. The tasks contained in the instructional program are identified by examining what people must know and be able to do in order to perform at entry level jobs in the occupation. These tasks then become the content for the program and the courses included in the program. Since the content is derived from the occupation and it is assumed that people enrolled in the program wish to enter the occupation, the content is fixed. Students who enter the vocational program to prepare for the occupation do so with the expectation that upon completing the program they will be competent to perform at entry level jobs in the occupation. Therefore, it is not only essential to provide experience with each of the tasks or acquaintance with the knowledge, but it is important to be able to certify that the students have mastered the skills and knowledge and are able to perform satisfactorily.

Implications for the
Traditional Classroom

The traditional classroom setting is characterized by a group of students coming into the classroom during a class period, studying the topic of the day, being examined as a group, and then moving on to the next topic. This procedure is repeated throughout the length of a course which is expected to last for a prescribed period of time, such as nine months. The adoption of any of the individualized instruction models necessitates many changes in this highly regimented and controlled learning environment. The most obvious change is that students will be studying different tasks at different points in time. This will be true in all cases. It is obviously true if a variable-content instructional model is adopted. It is also true if a variable-time, mastery model is adopted. In the first case students select different content to study, and in the second, students will be studying different content because it will take some students longer to master a task than others. Once a student has mastered a task it is only reasonable to allow him or her to move on to another task. Therefore, natural individual differences will quickly spread the students over the many tasks being taught in a course or program.

With different students studying different tasks at the same time, group instruction where all students are presented the same content at the same time has limited application. Few topics will be meaningful to all students at the same time because they will be studying different tasks. Therefore, the instructional methods adopted by the teacher have to be such that most tasks can be studied by individual students when they are ready to study them. If a teacher is to be able to provide meaningful learning experiences for students in such an environment it will not be possible for the teacher to act as the primary source of all information. The teacher would not be able to keep up with twenty students who are all working on different tasks.

Therefore, the teacher's role in the classroom must change and the methods used in the past must be adapted. The teacher must develop alternative methods of dispensing information to students so that he or she does not have to provide all information. Instructional resources in the forms of people, audio-visual aids, and written instructional materials must be available to students as they proceed through a task. These materials are not meant to replace the teacher, but they are resources to expand the teacher's ability to deal with many students working on many different tasks.

The task of developing materials to implement such a program is further compounded if the instructor wishes to recognize different student learning styles. Different students not only learn at different rates of speed but they learn best under different circumstances. Some students learn best through reading, others through films, others through demonstrations. This requires an instructor to develop alternative sets of learning materials for the same task if he wishes to further facilitate a student's learning.

In this environment the teacher is but one of a large number of resources available to the student. The primary role of the teacher becomes one of managing the learning environment and developing methods of presenting the materials to students in meaningful ways.

The management and development of materials in such a learning environment are based on the assumption that what is to be learned can be precisely specified so that the teacher will know what to teach and the student will know what is expected and when a task has been mastered. As indicated earlier, the question of what to teach in vocational programs is answered by observing what people must know and be able to do in order to perform in the occupation the program is designed to serve. The process of describing what students have to know and do is called task analysis. The procedures used in conducting a task analysis will be discussed in chapter 4.

Once the tasks have been identified they have to be described in behavioral terms that will give guidance to both the teacher and the student. Describing a task in behavioral terms means describing it in such a way that one can observe if a person can perform the task. For example, a task analysis of dry cleaning occupations might indicate that dry cleaning shop operators should be able to tell one fabric from another. A behavioral statement of this task would be: the student will be able to differentiate fabrics. The key word in this statement is the verb "differentiate" which tells us which behavior we expect students to be able to exhibit. Such a behavioral statement is a behavioral objective. Once the behavior is stated, the objective must be expanded further in order to make it an effective instructional objective. The conditions under which the behavior is to take place must be specified (givens), as well as the level of performance desired (standard). Details on how to write such objectives and their functions are presented in chapter 4.

Once the task has been precisely specified, learning activities must be developed which will facilitate the development of the specified behaviors. Since the instructor will not be able to spend a lot of time with individual students as they study the task, these activities must be designed and organized in a way that students can proceed through them with the aid of learning resources. Learning resources, as defined earlier, are those people, audio-visual aids, and other materials that are designed to assist the student to master a task as he proceeds through the learning activities.

The stated behavioral objective, and the learning activities and resources which are designed to assist the student to achieve the objective are included in a *learning package* along with evaluation instruments. The learning package is a self-contained package which defines the behavorial objective to be mastered, the activities in which the student might engage to reach the objective, the resources that are available to assist the student to complete the activities, and devices which allow the student and the teacher to assess if the objective has been mastered.

Assessment of whether the student has mastered the objective requires the development of assessment instruments such as tests and checklists. Once the instruments have been developed, the teacher must determine what score students must achieve on each instrument in order for the teacher to be able to say that the student has mastered the content. The mastery level score, or *criterion score,* is generally set at the score a person should get in order to indicate that he or she has sufficient knowledge or skill to perform satisfactorily at entry level jobs in the occupation. These instruments are then used to certify whether or not a person has mastered a task. How such instruments should be developed and interpreted will be presented in chapter 6.

Teachers develop learning guides to assist them in managing the learning environment with students working on many different learning packages at the same time. Learning guides are written documents specifying the behavior to be developed (the behavioral objective), how to develop the behavior (learning activities), resources available (learning resources), and the level of proficiency desired (mastery as defined by achieving a certain score on an instrument which reflects entry level job proficiency).

Some students may feel they have sufficient experience relative to the task, and therefore have mastered it, without proceeding through the learning package. In such instances students should be encouraged to demonstrate their proficiency by performing satisfactorily on the instruments designed to certify mastery of the task. For example, if a student has a hobby of repairing automobiles, he may feel that he has mastered the task of changing spark plugs. If this student can demonstrate mastery knowledge and skill associated with changing spark plugs, he should be certified as having mastered the task and should not be required to complete that learning package.

Necessary Conditions for a Successful Program

In order for such an individualized instructional program to work, we must make a number of assumptions about the students who are enrolled in the program. One assumption is that the students who attempt to complete a learning package are ready for it, both in terms of motivation and prerequisite skills and knowledge.

Motivation refers to whether a person wants to do something or is willing to do it. Most educators assume that all students want to learn and will take advantage of learning materials and activities if they are available. Experience with modular scheduling has proven that this is not true. The modular scheduling approach was designed to allow students flexibility in terms of the amount of time they wished to spend on different subjects and to allow teachers flexibility in organizing learning activities. Students were given freedom to utilize their time in ways they felt would meet their needs best. It was assumed that they would use their time to more efficiently study the content of the courses they were taking. Scott D. Thomson has reviewed how the modular scheduling approach has been succeeding. He points out the contradiction in human behavior which results from a desire for freedom and an unwillingness to assume responsiblity. A careful analysis of modular scheduling revealed that many students responded well to the freedoms of modular scheduling and achieved well. However, "Those who achieved poorly under a traditional class schedule tend to achieve even more poorly today under the modular schedule . . ." (Thomson 1971).

It appears that we cannot assume that just because the learning materials are available, students will use them and learn. Any individualized instructional program must be developed with student motivation in mind. One source of motivation that has been used by vocational educators is to continually relate what the student is studying to how it will be useful on the job. Most students who enroll in vocational programs are preparing themselves to enter an occupation. This goal is implicit in their enrollment in the program. If they can be shown that what they are studying will help them develop the skills and knowledge necessary to succeed in the occupation, they will enter the learning experience with intrinsic motivation (motivation from within). People who tend not to succeed well in the traditional classroom setting tend to lack intrinsic motivation, but the classroom setting is controlled enough to keep them at the learning activities, due to the structure of the program. When these people are removed from the structured classroom, they tend to do more poorly unless they can be motivated to learn. Therefore, one challenge to vocational instructors who individualize their programs is to develop intrinsic motivation. It is possible, as will be shown later, but it must be built into the program. One way to do it is to include a brief paragraph which describes why a student should master a task along with the learning guide for the task. Therefore, the student will be able to see the relevance of the task to his or her goal.

Another assumption that must be made when designing individualized vocational programs is that students who wish to study a task have the necessary skills and knowledge to study it. Learning activities and materials are always developed for students with certain prerequisite skills and knowledge in mind. For example, we would assume people could walk before we would teach them to run. One of the more frustrating experiences students can have is to be expected to master a task without having a sufficient amount of skills and knowledge to even begin studying it. Therefore, in the designing of an individualized instruction program the instructor must be very clear as to what the student should be able to do and know before attempting to study a task. If the learning materials for a task on "how to give an injection" are developed on the assumption that students understand the muscle structure of the body, that assumption should be made clear to the students. Those who do not understand the muscle structure of the body could then obtain that knowledge before attempting to study the task.

We have discussed the situation where a student does not have the particular skills or knowledge to undertake a specific task. At times students wish to enter programs when they lack even the basic skills necessary in reading, writing and arithmatic. Just as the learning activities and materials associated with a particular task are developed assuming certain prerequisite skills and knowledge, the entire program or course is designed assuming certain basic skills levels. For example, people entering an auto mechanics program are expected to be able to read an auto manufacturers repair manual. Without sufficient reading ability to do so, the student would be at a great disadvantage. Therefore, it is important to be able to specify the basic skills levels which are assumed during the development of a program and to develop methods that allow students to determine if they possess these basic skills to the expected levels. We are not suggesting that students who do not have sufficient basic skills be eliminated from the programs, but rather that they be assisted in developing their basic skills so they can receive maximum benefit from the program.

Summary

This chapter has been an introduction to the need for changing our ways of thinking about our educational system, alternative individualized instruction models, and some of the major assumptions which must be accounted for in order for these models to work. Society has changed greatly since our educational system was established. The educational system originally was expected to assist students with the development of basic skills in reading, writing, and arithmetic and to help people who wished to enter the professions to do so. Since few people were needed in the professions, people were selectively educated after they developed minimal basic skills. The educational system was developed to accomplish this selective education. The majority of the people were expected to become employed and to develop job-related skills and knowledge through mechanisms other than the formal educational system. Today the educational system is not only expected to provide students with basic skills, but it is also expected to help the majority develop salable skills relevant to modern society.

The accomplishment of this new educational goal is dependent upon the development of an educational system that meets individual needs, both in terms of desired ends of education and means to arrive at these ends. Students have different interests, learn at different rates of speed, and learn using different methods. The meeting of these individual needs requires individualized instruction. But what is individualized instruction? We have seen a number of instructional models which can be called individualized instruction models. The one that seems to be most appropriate for use with vocational programs is the fixed-content, variable-time, mastery model. Vocational programs are developed to assist individuals with the development of skills and knowledge required to succeed at entry level jobs in an occupation. Therefore, the content the individuals should study should be fixed by that required in the occupation; the level of proficiency a student should attain should be set at what people in the occupation define as "mastery level," and students should be given as much time as they need to study the content to develop the mastery level.

Operating such a program poses many challenges to the teacher in areas such as classroom management, organization of learning activities, identification and development of learning resources, and classroom evaluation. The remaining chapters of this book will show that these challenges can be met.

REFERENCES

1. Carroll, John B. "A Model of School Learning," *Teachers College Record* 64 (1963): 722-33.

2. Thomson, Scott D. "Beyond Modular Scheduling," *Phi Delta Kappan,* 52 (April 1971): 484-87.

3. Venn, Grant. *Man, Education, and Manpower.* Washington, D.C.: The American Association of School Administrators, 1970, p. 281.

4. *Vocational Education: The Bridge Between Man and His Work.* Report of the Advisory Council on Vocational Education. Washington, D.C.: U.S. Department of Health, Education and Welfare, 1968.

5. *Vocational-Technical Terminology.* Washington, D.C.: American Vocational Association, March 1971.

Chapter 2

ESTABLISHING AND JUSTIFYING PROGRAM CONTENT

Employment Markets

What vocational technical programs should be offered? A vocational educator contemplating starting a new or expanded vocational technical program must consider carefully three basic questions:

1. Will the employment market have the ability to absorb the output, or graduates of the new program?
2. Will the program or programs in which training is contemplated provide jobs for which training could be justified?
3. Are there qualified students who are willing and able to take the training?

Depending on the circumstances of the vocational education planner, the data collected relative to feasibility of student employment might be local, regional, state, national, or international in character. The vocational educator must also be aware of whatever constraints there might be on the development of new programs at the national, state, or local level.

In the past, state-wide planning of programming for vocational-technical and continuing education programs in the United States was, at best, haphazard and fragmentary. For example, for a number of years more than 75 percent of the trade and industrial education enrollments were in several highly skilled crafts, namely machine shop, electricity, printing, auto mechanics, pattern making, carpentry, cabinetmaking, and drafting. The continuing demands in these fields for many years were readily identified and accepted. Hence new or expanded local programs generally established one or more of these training offerings without so much as a local study. The same general situation existed in agriculture, homemaking, distribution, and office practice.

This situation was understandable in the past due to limited funds to plan, establish, and operate programs beyond the several basic occupations. Except for the general promotion of vocational education in the early years of federally aided programs, local initiative largely determined the establishment of a program and the choice of occupational offerings. Very little planning was initiated at the state level and then only after a local community expressed its desire to initiate a program. Program planning consisted chiefly of looking at other programs and deciding to do likewise.

As the labor force has grown and diversified, the needs have become more identifiable. The philosophy and practices of vocational education have broadened to take into account the growing demands in agriculture-related jobs, homemaking-related jobs, technician jobs, health, sales, service, and office jobs. Local, state, and federal funding has also increased substantially during the last few years.

The purposes of vocational education, as stated in the Vocational Education Amendments of 1968, clearly suggest the data needed to answer questions relative to identifying programs to be offered. The act indicates that programs should be offered in those areas suited to the needs, interests, and abilities of individuals who require training to obtain gainful employment in occupational areas in which there is an actual or anticipated demand for employees. Therefore, in justifying the creation of a new program or the continued existence of an old program, vocational educators should attempt to gather information on the demand of employees in various occupations and on the population of persons needing vocational training or retraining. Three basic types of information are necessary to justify the continuation of a currently operating program or the creation of a new program:

1. the needs of individuals for training or retraining;
2. the demand or anticipated demand for employees in various occupations;
3. modifying factors such as the resources available for operating vocational programs and political activity in the community.

These three basic pieces of information considered together allow decision makers to weigh alternatives and to select one or more programs for continued or initial implementation.

With broader federal and state participation in funding vocational programs, interest in vocational program development and control has also increased at those levels. As people have become more mobile, in terms of commuting both to training facilities and to jobs, there has been increasing state interest in restricting the development of certain programs for which the *state* may have ample supply even though a local need for the program can be justified. Similarly though, there has been increased state interest in encouraging and promoting the development of programs for which there is a perceived economic or learner need in that state.

In states where postsecondary technical institutes or community colleges are state-owned and operated, occupational training programs designated by state occupational study as "necessary" can be started quite easily if the legislature recognizes the needs and provides the funds. In states where there is dependency on part-time secondary level training for occupational needs or where postsecondary institutions are locally operated and controlled, starting state-promoted programs may be somewhat more complex. In these situations the state must lead or encourage the local component agencies to begin the needed programs.

Determining Individual Needs

There are two basic ways to determine the needs of individuals for training or retraining when planning or justifying a vocational program. First, one can assess the actual expressed demand of individuals for training in a given area or areas. Second, one can assume that all of the people who need vocational education have not made their needs known and that methods of projecting the needs must be adopted. There is little doubt that this assumption is correct. However, in practice, most local vocational educational planners develop information concerning individual needs around the first method, not because they necessarily believe it to be most philosophically correct, but because they believe it to be more practically implemented. It is very difficult to initiate programs on the basis of some theoretical group of people whom societal planners assume to require vocational training. *They may not want it.* But this is not to say that attempts should not be made to encourage them to enter training.

This discussion assumes that most local planners will not be in a position to dictate or modify the social structure or to justify their programs based upon the hypothetical demand of those who they feel need training; these societal needs are generally beyond the control of local planners. Therefore, the present discussion of individual training needs will be limited to a discussion of the needs expressed by individuals.

A number of methods have been used to determine the needs of individuals in the geographic area serviced by a vocational-technical school. One method is to ask all students currently enrolled in the high schools of the area what they would like to be when they get out of school. Based upon an indication of what they would like to be, one can hypothesize the demand for training in the future. Such a practice has a number of limitations. The greatest limitation is the assumption that the expressed occupational choice of a student in school is an accurate reflection of what he will do when he leaves school. This assumption appears reasonable if you ask a student what his occupational choice is at a point very close to the time that he will enter the work force. However, if you ask a ninth grade student what he plans to be, it is unlikely that his response will be closely related to his eventual occupation. The reliability of the above procedure has been refined to some extent by a number of people. Instead of asking students an open-ended question requiring them to fill in a blank such as, "What would you like to be when you get out of school?", the student is [...] ons, such as the listing found in the [...] nal Program Classification System [...] 69). Each occupational title is ac- [...] the occupation, and the student is [...] which he is interested. The latter [...] al's response more precise. It out- [...] the student can select. It also pro- [...] n to minimally test the job against [...] ither of the two above approaches [...] o vocational program planners in [...] sing interests in different occupa- [...] r justifying new programs as well

[...] of an ongoing program or the ex- [...] ethodology is available. Accurate [...] on the number of people who apply to a given program as contrasted with the number of training stations available. As the number of people who wish to enter a program grows as contrasted with the number of stations available, the justification for program expansion or continuation increases. Data can be obtained directly from records available in most schools through the counselor or admissions person who processes applications. Actual enrollment data will become part of the normal school records as soon as the class begins. As indicated, however, this latter technique does not provide information indicative of the need for program expansion in areas other than those currently being offered. It might, however, indicate that programs in a similar occupational area should be considered.

Determining the Demand
in Occupations

The second major type of information needed to justify a current program or the implementation of a new program is the demand or anticipated demand for employees in occupations related to the program. As indicated in the Vocational Amendments of 1968, training or retraining should be provided in areas where there is a demand or an anticipated demand. Training in these areas insures both the individual and society that participation in a given program will yield a return. Since vocational programs are established to help individuals achieve employment, training in areas where there is a demand provides some assurance that an individual who is trained will actually find employment opportunities available to him when he leaves the training program.

Several methodologies are open to program planners who wish to assess the current or anticipated demands in different occupations. The simplest methodology available is to interview industrial representatives in the geographic area to determine what their current and future needs for employees will be. This can be done by asking potential employers what jobs they see having continued or increasing demand and having them provide job descriptions of these occupations. Besides providing job descriptions, estimates can also be made of the number of people they anticipate needing in each occupation in the future. The data would then be summarized over all the firms which were contacted and the data would be made available to decision makers. With labor markets as widely diverse as they are today and with the mobility characteristics of our society, the above methodology is of limited value because it allows for a view of only a limited portion of the total labor market available to graduates of any program.

Another more refined method of assessing the demand for employees in a given occupation can be found in the publication *Planning Vocational Education Programs in Pennsylvania: Guidelines for the Use of Labor Market Information* (McNamara and Franchak 1970). The system was developed to provide program planners with not only information on demand in a given occupational area but also information on the residual demand. The residual demand is calculated after the total demand is reduced by the anticipated supply. With the current vocational system as extensive as it is, it would be naive for program planners to attempt to implement new programs in an area based only upon knowledge of demand. They must also assess the output or supply of trained manpower being provided by other institutions. Using the Pennsylvania model, data are gathered on a regional basis for each of 142 different occupational areas. The data include supply information gathered from those institutions that are currently providing training in each of the occupational areas and anticipated demand information assembled by the Pennsylvania Department of Labor and Industry. Table 2-1 is a sample of the type of information provided by such a system; it shows examples of the ways in which the information concerning clerical workers could be presented to program planners. The number of people employed in each of the various occupations as of the 1970 census is reported along with the projected 1985 employment in those occupations. The annual withdrawal rate from the

TABLE 2-1

SAMPLE MANPOWER AND TRAINING DATA
(Summary of Clerical Workers 1970)

Occupational Classification	Census (1970) (1)	Projected Employment (1985) (2)	Annual Withdrawal (3)	Annual Growth (4)	Annual Demand (5)	Annual Supply (6)	Unmet Demand (7)
CLERICAL	141266	204900	7251	4242	11493	6398	5095
Accounting, Clerks and Bookkeepers.	10370	13926	431	237	668	1073	405*
Secretaries	22449	37176	1560	982	2452	1793	749
Other Clerical Workers	108447	153798	5260	2023	8283	3532	4346

*Excess Supply

occupations due to retirement and other reasons is calculated and the withdrawal rate and the anticipated annual growth in the occupations are added together to arrive at the anticipated annual demand. The annual supply of trained persons for these occupations is obtained by summarizing information gathered through a survey of all of the institutions training people for these occupations in the geographic area. The annual supply is then subtracted from the annual demand to obtain an estimate of the residual or unmet demand. The residual demand is then used by decision makers to determine the need for workers in the occupations. This system can be operationalized using data currently gathered for other purposes. The labor market data is available through most state employment service offices or their counterparts. These offices gather their data using the approach described in the U.S. Department of Labor's publication *Tomorrow's Manpower Needs: National Manpower Projections and a Guide to Their Use as a Tool in Developing State and Area Manpower*

Projections (1971). State offices of education gather statistics on the number of graduates from each of the vocational programs throughout the state. If these two pieces of information are gathered over the same geographical area it is possible to adopt the Pennsylvania system with relatively little effort.

Meaningful Jobs

It is possible to identify job opportunities where employers may be quite anxious to obtain trained persons, find students who are interested in being trained for those positions, and still have a situation where there are serious questions about whether the training should be offered. Some of these questions follow.

Does the proposed occupational training stand a reasonable test of "cost-benefit"?   For example, if a program to train certain individuals in the data processing field *requires* on-line access to a very expensive large computer and this computer is not available except for lease or purchase, can the program justify consumption of a major part of the total budget for the training of a relatively few people at very high cost?

Does the proposed program have a broad range of tasks and skill levels?   A program for training "grease rack" attendants might be eliminated because of having insufficient scope. A program for training auto mechanics, however, might encompass the lubrication attendant and many other facets of the mechanics field as well.

Does the occupation have a reasonable quality of stability?   Nearly all occupations are changing, but there are a few in which the changes are so dramatic that it is very difficult to plan either curriculum or facilities until they stabilize. It might be well, in these instances, to wait on that program until more stability occurs or graduates may find themselves outdated upon graduation and unemployable.

Is the estimated training time period appropriate?   If the training time for the position is short-term, such as three months, cycling new enrollees through the short program rapidly would tend to fill the job market very soon and the program would have to be shut down. This does not mean that such kinds of occupational training should not be done. It does mean that the permanent resources spent on a program of this type should be limited and the facilities kept flexible so that they could be converted to other occupational training programs. Similarly, programs can get too long. Many vocational-technical enrollees tend to be very work oriented. If the program exceeds two years, the probability of losing the student from the program prior to graduation will increase unless the program has particularly attractive potential.

Do employers in that occupation respect training?   Will the graduates of such training programs be given the advantage of preference in hiring for available positions and also preference in compensation? If program graduates find that they must start with unskilled persons hired off the street or transferred from the laboring division of the organization, it will be demoralizing, and such a program is not usually an appropriate use of training funds. It might be better to develop more favorable attitudes of the employers in that occupation before proceeding with training.

Weighing Alternatives

Having considered the anticipated demand for new employees in various occupations, the needs of individuals for training, and other variable factors, this information plus other modifying information must be combined in order to determine which of the alternative programs should be offered. A systems approach derived from the Pennsylvania study and used in the Minneapolis-St. Paul metropolitan area for making these determinations is illustrated in figure 2-1. Statistical data were collected on seventy-two major occupational clusters representing many hundreds of occupations for the five-county metropolitan area as illustrated on the first information block of the flowchart. This data included numbers of workers currently employed in those occupations.

Using Manpower Department formulas, workers leaving due to death, retirement, and disability were subtracted and a modest industry growth factor added as illustrated in the second block. This provided a projection of a five year need for new trained workers which, when divided by five, gave an average annual need for new trained workers.

Simultaneously, as indicated in the lower block, the graduate output of vocationally trained workers in the five-county metropolitan area from area vocational-technical institutes, secondary schools, private trade schools, and junior or community colleges was computed to ascertain how much of this average annual need for new trained workers was currently being provided. This comparison was made for each of the occupational fields being considered. When the data were compared in the first decision triangle, those occupations for which there was a low new worker demand and/or a high current training output from existing programs were rejected from program planning for the new facility being considered. For example, drafting was one occupation for which there was a massive training output in the metropolitan area, both from private and public sources. In the next round of data comparison the matters of program cost benefit, complexity, and expense were considered. An advisory committee for each program area under study was appointed to provide additional data not found in the Manpower Department studies.

FIGURE 2–1

VOCATIONAL PROGRAMS DECISION MODEL

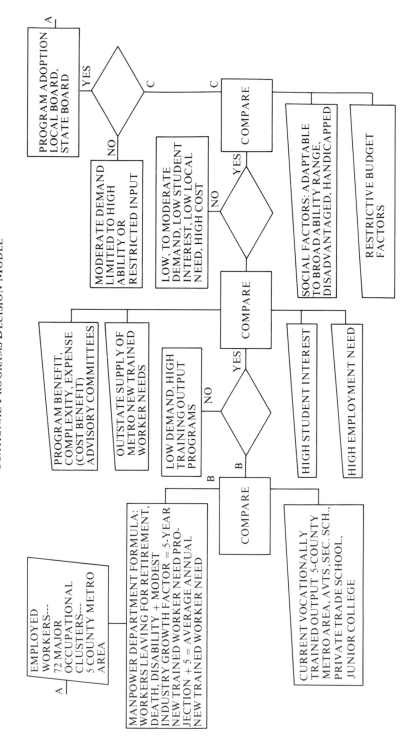

Also considered at this point was the out-of-metropolitan area supply of new trained workers who were moving into the metropolitan area and were not included in the previous figures. For example, the study showed an average annual unmet need for fifty-nine new trained aircraft plant mechanics. However, it was ascertained that one out-of-metropolitan area aircraft and power plant program was graduating forty students annually, about thirty-five of whom were moving to the metropolitan area. Another school was graduating twenty per year, fifteen of whom were moving into the metropolitan labor market. Concurrently, the advisory committee from the industry was uncertain what the impact of the jumbo jets would be on the employment of mechanics and suggested that this program might be considered in later expansion plans.

Along with this examination two other areas of interest were being considered, namely, programs in which there might be high student interest and programs in which there might be high local employment need. In this process, programs in machine shop and aircraft and power plant mechanics were delayed for reasons previously specified. Programs in cosmetology, auto mechanics, and truck mechanics were included because of high student interest and high local employment need, even though statewide demand was modest. In this elimination process, low to moderate demand, low student interest, low local need, and high cost programs were eliminated in the decision triangle. Considered in the next decision round were the social factors. The institution had a strong commitment to the training of the handicapped and wanted to include programs which might lend themselves to that purpose. They were also reluctant to reject large numbers of students because of ability and hence wanted some programs for which viable occupational training could be offered but that did not require an exceptionally high ability level. Since this was the last major exclusion in the selection process, the question of restrictive budget factors also had to be considered. There were still more programs left from those drawn from the original seventy-two occupational clusters than the mandated budget could support, and the whole process had to be reviewed once more. At this decision point, the moderate demand programs which were limited to high ability or restricted input were excluded.

Thereafter, the proposed instructional program for the new institution was submitted for program adoption through the political process of approval by the local board of education, the state Higher Education Coordinating Commission, and the State Board for Vocational Education.

The decision-making process described above is further delineated in figure 2-2, which illustrates the numerical process of considering the occupational instruction field, potential enrollment, estimated entrance into the labor force, the annual need, operating and capital costs. The process scores all of these under selection criteria, and arrives at a total rating and final selection.

FIGURE 2−2

CANDIDATE COURSE/RESOURCE COMBINATIONS

NOTE:
THE FOLLOWING ARE DEFINITIONS OF THE FACTORS USED IN THE COST ANALYSIS IN COLUMNS 24 THRU 34:

"A" IS 1 + % NON-INSTRUCTIONAL FLOOR SPACE.
"B" IS ARCHITECTURAL ESTIMATE OF COST PER SQ. FT.
"C" IS LIFE OF BOND APPLICABLE TO BUILDING (USUALLY 20 YRS.)
"D" IS LIFE OF BOND APPLICABLE TO EQUIPMENT (USUALLY 10 YRS).

LINE NUMBERS (FROM FORM 3)	17 (FLOW DIAGRAM NUMBER) OCCUPATIONAL FIELD CANDIDATE COURSE OF OCCUPATIONAL INSTRUCTION — NOTE: CANDIDATE COURSES MAY INCLUDE COMBINATIONS OR SUB-DIVISIONS OF OCCUPATIONS LISTED ON FORM 3.	18 RESOURCE REQUIREMENTS PER COURSE — TYPE OF SCHOOL (EXISTING OR PROPOSED)	19 TRAINING MEDIUM GRADES OF INSTRUCTION	20 FULL TIME STUDENT EQUIV. EXISTING / PROPOSED	21 MALE-FEMALE F.T. ANNUAL ENROLLMENT EXISTING / PROPOSED	22 ESTIMATED ENTRANTS INTO LABOR FORCE
A 4	AUTOMOTIVE SERVICE AND TECHNOLOGY	Area Voc. Tech. School	Full-time Day-Sec.	0	0	60
			11 and 12	60/120	120-0	
		Area Voc. Tech. School	Full-time Day-P. S.	0	0	50
			13 and/or 14	100	100-0	
		Area Voc. Tech. School	Full-time Day-Coop	0	0	10
			12 and/or 13 and/or 14	20	20-0	
				160/220	220-0	110

(18) (19) (20) (23)

36

A 5	AGRICULTURE RELATED TECHNOLOGY	Area Voc. Tech. School	Full-time Day-Sec.	0	0	10
			11 and 12	10/20	20-0	
		Area Voc. Tech. School	Full-time Day-P. S.	0	0	20
			13 and/or 14	40	40-0	
		Area Voc. Tech. School	Full-time Day-Coop	0	0	5
			12 and/or 13 and/or 14	10	10-0	
				50/60	60-0	30
A 6	DIESEL MECHANICS	Area Voc. Tech. School	Full-time Day-Sec.	0	0	20
			11 and 12	20/40	40-0	
		Area Voc. Tech. School	Full-time Day-P. S.	0	0	30
			13 and/or 14	60	60-0	
		Area Voc. Tech. School	Full-time Day-Coop	0	0	5
			12 and/or 13 and/or 14	10	10-0	
				80/100	100	50

FIGURE 2–2 — CONTINUED

(CONSIDER ALL FEASIBLE RESOURCE ALTERNATIVES)

	23	24	25	26	27	28	29	30	31	32	33	34	35	36	37	38	39	40	41	42	43
	(FROM COLUMN 9)	NUMBER OF TEACHING Equiv. (18)	ANNUAL OPER. COST TEACHER SALARY (COL. 24 × AVERAGE + 30% OVERHEAD)	INSTRUCTIONAL FLOOR SPACE (SQ. FT.) (18)	INSTRUCTIONAL & ARCHITECTURAL FLOOR SPACE SQ. (COL. 26 × "A")	FLOOR SPACE COST FT. (COL. 27 × "B")	ANNUAL FLOOR SPACE COST $30.00 (COL. 28 ÷ "C")	INSTRUCTIONAL EQUIPMENT COST (18)(23)	ANNUAL INSTRUCTIONAL EQUIPMENT COST (COL. 30 ÷ "D")	TOTAL ANNUAL RESOURCES COST (COL. 25 + COL. 29 + COL. 31)	PROPOSED FULL TIME STUDENT EQUIV. (FROM COL. 20)	TOTAL ANNUAL RESOURCES COST PER STUDENT (COL. 32 ÷ COL. 33)	RATING OF SOCIO ECONOMIC VALUE (FROM COL. 15) (25)	RATING OF COST PER STUDENT RESOURCES (USE COL. 34)	FUNDING AVAILABILITY	FUTURE CAREER POSSIBILITIES	ACCEPTANCE BY EMPLOYERS	SUITABILITY TO NEEDS OF DISADVANTAGED PERSONS	ADVISORY COMMITTEE ACTION	TOTAL RATING	FINAL SELECTION (26)
		3	14,000 / 54,600	200 / 1,200	14,400	432,000	21,600	42,000	4,200	80,400	60	1,360.	15	*	10	7	8	8			7
		5	15,000 / 97,500	200 / 20,000	24,000	720,000	36,000	75,100	7,500	141,000	100	1,410.	15		10	7	8	8			
		½	14,000 / 9,100	800	960	28,800	1,440	14,000	1,400	11,940	20	597.	15		10	7	8	8			
		8	152,100	21,200	38,400	1,105,000	57,600	117,000	11,700	221,400	160	1,381.	15	15	10	7	8	8		63	

Column group labels: (24)(25) OPERATING COSTS · CAPITAL COSTS — FLOOR SPACE · EQUIPMENT · RESOURCES COST ANALYSIS · TOTAL COSTS · SELECTION CRITERIA · TRADE-OFFS

Col 1	Col 2	Col 3	Col 4	Col 5	Col 6	Col 7	Col 8
7				8			
			63				59
7	7	7	7	5	5	5	5
7	7	7	7	7	7	7	7
7	7	7	7	5	5	5	5
10	10	10	10	10	10	10	10
			17				15
				17	17	17	17
1,200.	1,307.	970.	1,286.	1,340.	1,385.	106.	1,375.
10	40	10	50	20	60	10	80
12,000	52,300	9,700	64,300	26,900	83,100	10,640	111,000
600	1,500	100	2,100	1,500	3,000	100	4,500
6,000	15,000	1,000	21,000	15,000	30,000	1,000	45,000
3,600	14,400	1,800	18,000	7,200	21,600	1,440	28,800
7,200	288,000	36,000	360,000	14,400	432,000	28,800	576,000
2,400	9,600	1,200	12,000	4,800	14,400	960	19,200
200 / 2,000	200 / 8,000	1,000	10,000	200 / 4,000	200 / 12,000	500	16,000
12,000 / 7,800	14,000 / 36,400	12,000 / 7,800	44,200	14,000 / 18,200	15,000 / 58,500	7,000 / 9,100	76,700
½	2	½	2 ½	1	3	½	4

* (HIGH COST GIVES A LOW RATING)

39

Student Populations

There are a number of important considerations to account for while answering the question raised earlier about the availability of qualified students willing to take part in a program. These considerations involve decisions about the types of student populations a program is designed to serve. In chapter 3, we will discuss the establishment of program prerequisites, which are those things a student is expected to bring with him to the learning situation. The prerequisites required are determined to a large extent by the definition of the group to be served.

Programs can be designed to serve one population or many (e.g., typical students, disadvantaged, handicapped). Programs designed to serve one particular population generally require less funds to operate and less curriculum development time because the programs can be geared to one "type" of student. However, programs designed to serve a number of different groups are more costly and require more effort to develop the variety of materials needed to serve the different groups. For example, materials developed for students with one arm missing in a machine shop course may need to be different than the materials developed for a person with two arms. Procedures to teach the handling of many materials and tools typically are developed with the assumption that students will have two arms. A student probably could perform many of the same tasks with one arm, if materials were developed for him. The development of these materials takes time and resources.

The point made above also relates to decisions about the ability levels of students that a program is designed to serve. A program can be designed for students with a very narrow range of ability levels, or it can be designed for a wide range. However, a person with a great deal of reading ability and a person with little reading ability usually will not be satisfied using the same learning materials. If a program is designed to serve students with a wide range of ability levels, the materials may have to be written at a variety of levels.

Usually the question of whom to serve with a program is answered by first identifying who could be served and then reviewing the resources available and finally arriving at a compromise. The compromise attempts to serve the most people with the limited resources available.

Determining who can benefit and profit from instruction offered in a program is always a very difficult task. Legislation indicates that people should be allowed to enter programs based upon their needs, interests, and ability to benefit from training. Some information has been shown to have a high relationship with potential success in all types of further education. But these measures in many cases are not consistent with the philosophical position underlying the statement that students should be allowed to enter vocational programs based on their needs, interests, and ability to benefit from training. Table 2-2 lists some potential measures which might be useful in describing the groups to be served that are consistent with vocational education philosophy and other measures which have potential but are *not consistent* with vocational education philosophy.

TABLE 2-2

POTENTIAL COUNSELING MEASURES

Potential and Consistent	*Potential But Not Consistent*
1. Aptitudes	1. Scholastic aptitude tests to the degree that they are affected by prior academic performance
2. Measures of needs individuals would like to have satisfied by jobs	
	2. High school rank
3. Interests	3. Prior academic record
4. Vocational maturity (readiness to make occupational choices)	4. Sociological data
	5. Sex

The major objection with the "potential but not consistent" measures is that they are past-oriented or categorical variables. Individuals should be considered for inclusion in vocational programs on the basis of their potential to succeed in the occupation for which the training program is preparing them to enter, and not on the basis of past performance or their socioeconomic status. Categorical variables such as disadvantaged, minority groups, sex, and handicapped are satisfactory if one wishes to describe a group of people, but they are not truly relevant to define the types of people a program is designed to serve. The groups of individuals contained in such categories are not homogeneous enough to use such categories to specify who can benefit and who cannot benefit from instruction. For example, a program developed for rural black high school dropouts implies that rural black high school dropouts have some characteristics in common which result in all of them benefiting from the same type of instruction. Rural black high school dropouts are just as heterogeneous as any other category of people, and just because they fall into this socially defined category does not mean that they are all the same or can benefit from the same type of instruction.

Problems are also encountered if measures of past performance such as high school rank and prior academic record are used in preenrollment counseling. Such measures may be the best empirical predictors of future performance, but they penalize people based upon their past rather than allowing them to be judged based on their future potential. When people are admitted and counseled toward vocational programs based upon their past record, they are not truly being given the opportunity to enter vocational programs based upon their interests, needs, and abilities. Most of us can think of examples of individuals who could not see the relevance of education during their high school years, who went into the military service and upon coming out of the service recognized the importance of additional education, and who have succeeded where their past record would have condemned them to failure. Also, many individuals who do not do well in the academic programs in high schools because of lack of interest may find meaningful educational experiences in vocational programs. Their admission to the vocational program should not be biased by past academic performance.

The measures in the "potential and consistent" list tend to be *less* affected by past performance. Therefore, they are more appropriate measures for assessing the abilities, interests, and capabilities of an individual to benefit from instruction in a particular program.

Over the years, a great deal of research has been done to try to determine which student characteristics might be helpful in assisting students to select among the many alternative occupational training programs available to them. One of the more comprehensive studies in this area has been Project MINI-SCORE. The results of this study, as well as empirically developed normative data which can be used in counseling students in regard to post-high school vocational programs, can be found in a series of final technical reports and the final report (Pucel, Nelson, Asche, and Faurot 1972; Pucel, Nelson, and Faurot 1972; Pucel, Nelson, and Mohamed 1972; Pucel and Nelson, a, b 1972; Nelson and Pucel 1972). The results of this study indicate that measures, such as those in the "potential and consistent" list, can be useful in assisting a person to decide which of a number of alternative vocational programs to enter. The results also show that such measures are not very effective in predicting a person's probability of success in a given occupation.

Another source of normative data which can be useful in counseling students relative to vocational programs is *The Career Data Book: Results From Project TALENT's Five-Year Follow-Up Study* (Flanagan et al. 1973). This publication provides normative data developed from information gathered from high school students. Such data might also be useful when trying to determine the types of students that could realistically be served by a program.

Justifying the Continuation of a Program

Continuation of a program is generally decided based on the past success of the program. The major problem is to define "success." Program success is usually defined in terms of effectiveness (is the program accomplishing what it should be accomplishing?) and efficiency (are the costs of the production reasonable?).

If the purpose of vocational education is to help people gain skills related to employment which will aid them in becoming satisfactorily employed, vocational program effectiveness should be judged in terms of the extent to which the training program actually helps students become employed in satisfying occupations related to training.

Such an assessment of effectiveness is usually made at two points in time, upon initial placement and after the students have been on the job for a period of time. Initial placement information is obtained by determining how many people who graduated from the program actually became employed in related occupations immediately after graduation or within some short specified time after graduation. Although this criterion has been used for years to judge the effectiveness of vocational programs, it is insufficient. When initial placement is used to judge the effectiveness of programs, studies, such as "The Process and Product of Vocational Education" (Eninger 1968), find that the placement service is the major component of the instructional program that makes a difference. If the placement service is good, students tend to get placed in related jobs. If the placement service is bad, students tend not to get placed.

The objectives of vocational education are not only to get a person initially placed in an occupation related to training but also to prepare a person for continued employment. Continued employment in an occupation is achieved if the occupation continues to require personnel, if the person is satisfied enough with the occupation to remain in it, and if employers in the occupation are satisfied enough with the ability of the person to perform on the job. This concept has been studied by the Work Adjustment Project at the University of Minnesota (Dawis et al. 1968) and others in the field of industrial psychology. Unpublished investigations have found that tenure in an occupation of over six months implies a minimum of employer and employee satisfaction. If an employee is very unsatisfied with a job he will typically leave before six months and if an employer is very unsatisfied with the employee he will typically ask him to leave before six months. Therefore, a more appropriate criterion to use in judging the effectiveness of a vocational program is a follow-up taken at some point when past students have been out on the job long enough to determine if they like the kind of employment they have entered, and also long enough for employers to determine if the employees have sufficient skills related to the occupation for which they were trained.

It appears that a follow-up conducted approximately one year after students graduate would be an appropriate vehicle for gathering information concerning the effectiveness of vocational programs in light of the above discussion. If the follow-up is to provide the information needed to judge whether or not the program is effective plus diagnostic information concerning why the program might not be effective, it should gather information on the following. Follow-up should provide information on whether or not graduates are employed in related occupations, whether they are satisfied with their employment, whether their employers are satisfied with their performance, and diagnostic information which might be used to determine why individuals were not placed in related occupations, are not satisfied, or are unsatisfactory to their employers.

In any discussion of the overall effectiveness of a program one should also examine the efficiency of the program. If one agrees with the purposes of vocational education specified earlier, the efficiency of a program is judged in terms of the cost of preparing individuals who become employed in occupations related to the training program. The efficiency of a program is obtained by dividing the total cost of the program by the number of people who graduate, enter related jobs, and are successful. A program can be inefficient if the costs involved in operating the program are very high or if the output from the program is very low. The number of dropouts from the program will greatly affect this efficiency as will the quality of training of those who complete the program. If a large number of people drop out, the program will operate inefficiently because all of the instructional costs will be allocated to a few graduates. If the program is not doing a good job of training, the program would also be inefficient because many of the graduates would not be successful on the job. In each of the above cases the costs of the dropouts or the unsuccessful graduates would be allocated to those who were successful, raising further the cost per successful graduate.

Care must always be exercised in interpreting efficiency information because some programs may be high cost programs but other social values may offset the costs. For example, programs to train handicapped may be expensive per graduate but they should not necessarily be eliminated.

If the effectiveness and efficiency of a program continue to be reasonable in terms of the goals and resources of an institution, the program is usually continued. Additional information on judging program effectiveness can be found in *The Minnesota Vocational Follow-Up System: Rationale and Methods* (Pucel 1973).

Summary

Chapter 2 describes those things that must be considered in determining which vocational and technical programs to offer and those things that must be considered when deciding which programs that are now being offered should be continued. The decision to start a program is made after assessing the demand for trained people in occupations the program is designed to serve and the number of people requesting that training. In addition, the amount of resources available and the political climate surrounding the program must be assessed.

After a program has been operating, the decision about whether or not it should be continued is usually made on the basis of its effectiveness and efficiency.

REFERENCES

1. Dawis, R.V., Lofquist, L.H., and Weiss, D.J. *A Theory of Work Adjustment (A Revision).* Minneapolis, Minnesota: Work Adjustment Project, Industrial Relations Center, University of Minnesota, 1968.

2. Eninger, M.U. *The Process and Product of T & High School Level Vocational Education in the United States, the Process Variables.* Pittsburgh, Pennsylvania: Educational Systems Research Institute, April 1968.

3. Flanagan, J.C., Tiedeman, D.V.; Willis, M.B.; and McLaughlin, D.H. *The Career Data Book: Results From Project TALENT's Five-Year Follow-Up Study.* Palo Alto, California: AIR, 1973.

4. McNamara, J.F., and Franchak, S.J. *Planning Vocational Education Programs in Pennsylvania.* Harrisburg, Pennsylvania: Research Coordinating Unit, Bureau of Educational Research, Pennsylvania Department of Education, 1970.

5. Nelson, H.F., and Pucel, D.J. *Project MINI-SCORE Final Report.* Minneapolis, Minnesota: Project MINI-SCORE, Department of Industrial Education, University of Minnesota, 1972.

6. Pucel, D.J. *The Minnesota Vocational Follow-Up System: Rationale and Methods.* Minneapolis, Minnesota: University of Minnesota, Division of Vocational and Technical Education, February 1973.

7. Pucel, D.J., and Nelson, H.F. Project MINI-SCORE Final Technical Report: *General Aptitude Test Battery Training Success Norms and Employment Success Norms.* Minneapolis, Minnesota: Project MINI-SCORE Department of Industrial Education, University of Minnesota, 1972. (a) RS 003-655, ED 064 523

8. _____.Project MINI-SCORE Final Technical Report: *Minnesota Scholastic Aptitude Test and Vocational Development Inventory Training Success Norms and Employment Success Norms.* Minneapolis, Minnesota: Project MINI-SCORE, Department of Industrial Education, University of Minnesota, 1972. (b) RS 003-653, ED 064 524

9. Pucel, D.J.; Nelson, H.F.; Asche, F.M.; and Faurot, L. Project MINI-SCORE Final Technical Report: *The Ability of Standardized Test Instruments to Differentiate Membership in Different Vocational-Technical Curricula.* Minneapolis, Minnesota: Project MINI-SCORE, Department of Industrial Education, University of Minnesota, 1972. RS 003-652, ED 064 521

10. Pucel, D.J.; Nelson, H.F.; and Faurot, L. Project MINI-SCORE Final Technical Report: *Minnesota Vocational Interest Inventory Training Success Norms and Employment Success Norms.* Minneapolis, Minnesota: Project MINI-SCORE, Department of Industrial Education, University of Minnesota, 1972. RS 003-654, ED 064 522

11. Pucel, D.J.; Nelson, H.F.; and Mohamed, D.M. Project MINI-SCORE Final Technical Report: *The Ability of Standardized Tests to Predict Training Success and Employment Success.* Minneapolis, Minnesota: Project MINI-SCORE, Department of Industrial Education, University of Minnesota, 1972. RS 003-651, ED 064 525

12. U.S. Department of Health, Education and Welfare: Office of Education, and U.S. Department of Labor: Manpower Administration. *Vocational Education and Occupations.* Washington, D.C.: U.S. Government Printing Office, 1969.

13. U.S. Department of Labor. *Tomorrow's Manpower Needs: National Manpower Projections and a Guide to Their Use as a Tool in Developing State and Area Manpower Projections.* (Bureau of Labor Statistics Bulletin 1737, Volume 4) Washington, D.C.: U.S. Government Printing Office, Revised 1971.

Chapter 3   PREREQUISITE STUDENT SKILLS

Prerequisites are those things which an instructor assumes a student will bring with him to the learning situation. There is a great deal of controversy over the role and purposes of instructional program prerequisites. Some people argue that all vocational programs should be open to all individuals regardless of the previous background and skills which they have. Others argue that only people who are most likely to succeed in an occupation should be allowed to enter training programs for that occupation. Both of these arguments appear to be extreme, and many vocational educators believe in a position somewhere between these two extremes. If one reviews the federal legislation which provides funds for reimbursing vocational education, the acts indicate that the purpose of vocational education is to provide all persons with

> . . . ready access to vocational training or retraining which is of high quality, which is realistic in light of actual or anticipated opportunities for gainful employment, and which is suited to their needs, interests, and ability to benefit from training. (U.S. Government Printing Office 1968, p. 12)

The key portion of this definition that is related to the assessment of prerequisite student skills is the portion dealing with needs, interests, and ability to benefit from training. All individuals are not equally bestowed

47

with talent and learning abilities, and all individuals have not developed their abilities to the same level. Therefore, it is reasonable to assume that some people who wish to enter a vocational program may not be capable of benefiting from the instruction contained in that program. On the other hand, educators have shown over the years that most people can benefit from most types of training. The problem facing the instructor is to determine which skills, knowledge, and work-related attitudes are essential prerequisites in the occupation. There is no doubt that the overall productivity of a vocational program will be increased if people entering the program are highly selected. However, selecting only those who can be maximally successful in the occupation excludes many individuals who can benefit from the instruction and, therefore, is in conflict with the purposes of vocational education. The following discussion of the assessment and development of prerequisite student skills is in terms of those prerequisites which are essential to a person's progressing through an instructional program and becoming satisfactorily employed on a job. The discussion should *not* be put into the framework of trying to impose selection criteria which will optimize the output of a program by only allowing highly selected individuals to enter the program.

Vocational educators have been developing programs for clusters of occupations which include groups of occupations requiring similar job duties. A machine shop cluster program might contain elements which allow for the training of individuals for a variety of different occupations rather than only one. For example, a student might graduate from the program as a tool crib attendant, a machine operative, a machinist, a machine set-up man, a tool and die maker, or a tool designer. Each of these levels represents a more technical occupational level within the general machinist area. But even in programs operating under this type of framework, there are some minimum prerequisite skills, knowledge, and attitudes that allow people to develop skills as a tool crib attendant, which is the most elementary level occupation in the cluster. Therefore, regardless which program organization a school is using there is no way to avoid the establishment of prerequisites for a course or for the various learning guides contained in a course. The specification of the expected student prerequisites provides the school, the instructor, and the student with indications of the extent to which the student is ready to participate in and benefit from the instruction offered by the program.

The remainder of this chapter is organized into four sections. The first discusses the concept of instructional readiness and factors which can affect it. The second deals with identifying prerequisites. The third deals with assessing identified prerequisites, and the fourth relates to strategies for developing prerequisites that a student lacks.

Instructional Readiness

Instructional readiness refers to a student's ability to benefit from instruction at a certain point in time. Unless a student is ready to accept instruction, the effectiveness of the instruction will be diminished. A person's instructional readiness can be affected by a number of factors: (a) physical condition, (b) learning abilities, (c) basic skills, (d) attitudes, (e) prerequisite knowledge, and (f) prerequisite psychomotor skills. If the student enters a learning situation lacking sufficient levels of any of these prerequisites, it is possible that learning will be impaired. Let us discuss each factor.

It is easy to see how a severe physical handicap might affect a person's ability to perform a task or to perform in a particular occupation. Equally as important are physical conditions which are not quite so obvious such as hearing difficulties or sight difficulties. Generally, such problems should be detected among students prior to their enrolling in vocational programs. Most students come directly to vocational programs from other educational programs. However, if adults enroll in the programs they may have undetected physical handicaps. Some schools require students who are entering the vocational programs to have a physical examination prior to entry so the school is aware of any possible physical condition which might impair learning. If the school is aware of such conditions, it will be possible to develop a more appropriate program for the individual.

A student's learning abilities are his abilities to learn, think, react, and remember what is learned. These abilities are partially inherited and partially learned. People who are successful in different occupations require varying amounts of these abilities. A person who wishes to become a nurse will be expected to update herself continually after she is on a job. She will also be required to respond quickly to situations that could result in life or death. It is important that a nurse not only have the abilities to learn quickly and remember but also have the ability to react quickly to new situations. On the other hand, a nurse's aide is generally called upon to learn fewer new tasks after leaving the vocational program, and the decisions that she has to make do not have to be made as urgently. Therefore, it is possible for people with less learning ability to become nurse's aides and still be successful on the job. We are not trying to imply that one type of person is better than another type of person—only that different occupations place different demands upon people working in the occupations. A typical nurse's aide student need not be intellectually ready to engage in the types of learning activities designed for the typical nurse, although certainly some are. The tasks that the typical nurse's aide will be asked to perform on the job will require different amounts of ability than the tasks that a nurse would be required to perform on the job. Notice that reference is made to the level of learning abilities required of students to perform *in an occupation.* The level should not be based upon the learning ability requirements of the curriculum. A common problem in many education programs is that the curriculum is designed for people with higher learning abilities than those required on the job. If this is so, it is possible to have overly qualified people enter the job market who will leave the occupation because they do not find sufficient challenge. It is also likely that people who could succeed in the occupation will be excluded from the program. Instructors must always be very conscious of developing their programs in light of actual job requirements, rather than developing them in terms of some theoretical requirement of the learning situation.

Although the extent of a person's learning abilities might affect his possibilities of becoming a successful employee in a particular job, it should not affect his ability to prepare for a job in the occupational area. There are many different jobs requiring different levels of learning abilities in any major educational area, as indicated earlier. Each of these different jobs requires different types and levels of ability, and it should be possible for an instructor working in an individualized vocational program to help a person achieve an occupational level consistent with his ability in any occupational area.

Closely related to learning abilities are basic skills. Where learning abilities relate to a person's ability to learn, basic skills relate to the extent to which a person has developed skills in the basic areas of reading, writing, and arithmetic. All instructional programs assume some level of development of basic skills when the programs are developed. Unlike learning abilities, basic skills are primarily developed through education and other experiences. Since it is assumed that most people will develop sufficient amounts of basic skills to be able to pursue additional education while they are in elementary school, the development of basic skills in older people is sometimes referred to as remedial education. The education is thought to be remedial because students should have developed these skills at an earlier time. Whether students should have or should not have is really not relevant—many students have not. It is the function of the educational system to help the students *develop from the point where they are,* and therefore, the term "remedial" becomes meaningless.

Another important dimension related to success in an occupation is attitude. If a person has attitudes that are consistent with the majority of individuals in the occupation, the individual will tend to feel more comfortable in that occupation. There is a controversy in the educational system over whether a person's attitudes should be modified or whether they are outside of the domain of the educational system. In vocational education a person is preparing to enter a particular occupational area. It would seem just as appropriate to assist a person who wishes to enter that area with the development of appropriate occupationally related attitudes as it is to assist the person with the development of doing and knowing skills. This is not to say that schools should attempt to modify all students' attitudes so that students all leave the instructional program possessing the same attitudes. It does say, however, that students who complete the program should not possess work-related attitudes which would make them unemployable. An example of a work-related attitude would be the attitude toward children of someone enrolled in a child development assistant program. In many occupations a person's attitude toward children should not affect his employability. However, since a child development assistant will constantly be working with children, it would not be appropriate to continue a person in a program if that person frequently exhibited cruelty to children. Another work-related attitude would be the attitude of a student in a machinist program toward the expensive equipment which he is being taught to operate. If a student handled equipment in a destructive manner so that the equipment was continually breaking down, his attitude toward the care of equipment might need to be discussed with him. Even though such a person might be able to produce for an employer, the employer would not stand for the destruction of equipment.

The point of these examples is to indicate that we are not advocating that the instructor attempt to modify a person's social attitudes or nonessential work-related attitudes. Each person is unique and has unique attitudes which are personal. If the attitudes do not directly relate to an ability to perform the job, they should not be modified. This means that if a person can successfully perform the tasks of an occupation, the instructor should not attempt to change the individual's attitudes.

If a student does have an attitude which might conflict with his ability to perform in the occupation, he should be informed about it. It could tend to be a barrier to effective learning in the program and to successful entry to the occupation. If the student is willing to adjust this critical work-related attitude based upon the advice of school personnel, the institution should have an appropriate instructional program available to help him modify his attitude. If the person does not wish to modify the work-related attitude, he should be informed of the potential problems he might have during the vocational program as well as out on the job. The instructor and other personnel in the school must then judge the extent to which they can reasonably accommodate the individual within the occupational training program. If the attitude problem is severe enough, the student may have to be asked to leave the program. This decision to exclude a student should never be made without consultation with appropriate administrative personnel in the school and without checking appropriate federal and state laws.

The factors that might affect instructional readiness discussed to this point generally require the instructor to obtain assistance in determining the extent to which they might affect the learning of a student. They relate to the readiness of a student in terms of the overall program. The next two factors discussed must be judged in relation to each learning guide, and this judgment can be most appropriately made by people, like the instructor, who are specialists in the occupational area. The two factors are the prerequisite knowledge (knowing components) and prerequisite motor skills (doing components) which a student is assumed to possess before undertaking the learning activities related to a particular learning guide. Every time we attempt to teach a student something new, we build this new knowledge upon the student's prior knowledge. In doing so, we assume that the student has certain minimal skills. For example, if we asked a student to read some information on how to repair a typewriter, we assume that the student can read. If we ask the student to turn a screw with a screwdriver, we assume that the student knows what a screwdriver is and how it should be used. A student's ability to learn the materials contained in the learning guide is therefore dependent not only on the materials included in that guide but also upon the extent to which he has developed the prerequisite knowledge and skills which are assumed.

Many beginning instructors tend to assume students have more prerequisite knowledge and skill than they actually have. This is usually due to the fact that most beginning vocational instructors have recently come from business and industry. While they were working in the occupation, they were constantly talking and associating with people who were very familiar with the occupation and who had developed a large amount of prerequisite knowledge and skill. When they first encounter students who are attempting to develop these knowledges and skills, they have a tendency to overestimate what the students actually know.

Identifying Prerequisites

As indicated earlier, some prerequisites are general program prerequisites, and others are prerequisites to specific tasks within a program. Although we discussed the nature of prerequisites earlier, we did not indicate how they should be identified for a particular program. The identification of prerequisites is accomplished by examining the occupation that the program is designed to prepare people to enter.

The general characteristics which a person is assumed to possess when entering a program are identified by reviewing the general population of people that tend to enter and succeed in the occupation the program is designed to serve. This can be accomplished by constructing a table similar to Table 3-1.

TABLE 3—1

SAMPLE TABLE FOR LISTING
PROGRAM PREREQUISITES

Physical	Learning Ability	Basic Skills	Work-related Attitudes	Other
a. arms b. legs c. sight d. hearing e. speech f. mobility	a. learning speed b. memory c. reaction time d. etc.	a. reading b. writing c. arithmetic d. etc.	a. people b. objects c. safety	

Table 3-1 shows a listing of some items that might be checked as prerequisites for a particular program. The four basic areas of prerequisites are listed across the top. Under each of these is a column containing possible sample items that could be prerequisites for a program. For example, column 1 is labeled "physical." In this column are listed a number of different physical characteristics which might be assumed as prerequisites for a particular occupation. Some of these physical characteristics are essential in some occupations and not essential in others. If a physical characteristic is essential in an occupation, it can be considered to be a prerequisite for the program preparing people to enter that occupation. For example, if a person wants to become a bookkeeper, one would assume that the person should have arms, sight, hearing, and speech. However, it may not be essential for him to have good control of his legs or to have mobility. One could proceed through each of the other major columns of possible program prerequisites and identify additional characteristics that a person should possess, either before entering a program or after completing the program. Since most occupations require differing levels of a particular characteristic and generally do not call for a person either to have or not have a particular characteristic, it might be valuable to rate each of the possible prerequisite characteristics. A person could rate each characteristic for an occupation on a rating scale which goes from one to five. If a characteristic is rated "1," this would indicate that people in the occupation can succeed with minimal amounts of this characteristic. If a characteristic is rated "5," this would indicate that people in the occupation must have this characteristic well developed in order to succeed. For example, the physical disorder "color blindness" might be rated "1" for typists because distinguishing colors is not an important part of that job. However, it might be rated "5" for electronics technicians because they must be able to read color-coded resistors and other electronics parts. Such ratings are usually not as important with the physical characteristics such as arms or legs because a person either has these or does not have them; the rating scale would be important with characteristics such as reading ability, writing ability, arithmetic ability. Most occupations assume at least some level of competence in each of these. Some occupations require a higher level of competence than others. A sample table of welding program prerequisites and their ratings is presented in table 3-2.

TABLE 3−2

SAMPLE WELDING PROGRAM PREREQUISITES*

Physical	Learning Ability	Basic Skills	Work-related Attitudes

a. arms (5)
b. legs (5)
c. sight (5)
d. hearing (3)
e. speech (2)
f. mobility (5)
   etc.
	a. learning speed (2)
	b. memory (3)
	c. reaction time (4)
	   etc.
		a. reading (2)
		b. writing (2)
		c. arithmetic (2)
		   etc.
			a. people
			   1. co-
			      workers (3)
			   2. super-
			      visors (3)
			   3. others (1)
			b. objects
			   1. tools (4)
			   2. materi-
			      als (3)
			c. safety (5)
			   etc.

*Numbers in parentheses are ratings of amount desirable.

The advantage of specifying the program prerequisites in a form similar to tables 3-1 and 3-2 is that it provides the instructor with an opportunity and vehicle to communicate to counselors and others what he feels are important to success in an occupation besides mastery of the tasks. The table also forms a basis for discussion and the eventual acceptance of the prerequisites so people can identify what they are and can help students to develop them. There is nothing more frustrating for a student than to talk with an instructor who indicates that the student does not have sufficient prerequisites to enter the program, but the instructor is not able to specify what the prerequisites are.

If a student does not possess the necessary prerequisites to begin a program, a decision must be made concerning how and if the deficiency can be overcome. For example, lack of general basic skills prerequisites can sometimes be overcome through the use of preenrollment courses that would be taken before entering a program. Sometimes these skills can be developed while a person is progressing in the program. However, lack of an essential physical prerequisite may not be possible to overcome.

Although the general program prerequisites can be identified by the instructor, he usually must rely on specialists to determine the actual level of competence students should have on each of the prerequisites. A person may have to be able to hear in order to perform adequately in an occupation, but how well must he hear? A person may have to be able to do mathematical problems in order to be successful in an occupation, but what level mathematical skills are required? In order to determine the level of proficiency required, the instructor and an appropriate specialist should review the occupation or occupations which the program is designed to help people enter. The extent to which a person requires certain physical characteristics can be determined by observing people actually performing the tasks of the occupation. The basic reading and mathematical skills required can be determined by reviewing the manuals used and the tasks performed by people in the occupation. For example, the reading ability level required of auto mechanics can be determined by the literature which they are expected to read in order to perform their job, such as automobile manufacturers' manuals. The level of mathematics required can be determined by observing the types of mathematical problems mechanics actually have to be able to perform on the job, such as taking measurements and observing tolerances. It is usually not difficult to determine what the general program prerequisites have to be for an occupation. It is difficult to convert these generalities into ways of assessing whether or not the students actually have the competencies required in the prerequisites. This conversion usually requires some measurement or observation technique with which the typical instructor is not familiar, and, therefore, he must rely on appropriate specialists.

Even though program prerequisites are specified, the instructor must also specify the prerequisites required for undertaking each learning guide. Each time an instructor develops a learning guide, he is developing the guide for some theoretical student. This student has certain assumed general characteristics, specific skills, and specific knowledge. Usually stating the "given" section of a three-part objective for a guide specifies some of the more obvious prerequisites which the student must have in order to complete the guide. These prerequisite specifications generally take the form of the types of materials or objects which the students should have available in order to complete the guide. Although they are important, they are not sufficient to specify all of the prerequisites for a guide. An instructor can specify the additional prerequisites by completing a table similar to table 3-3. Learning guide prerequisites can generally be classified into three major categories; doing, knowing, and attitude prerequisites. These major categories form the column headings in table 3-3. In order to perform the task contained in a learning guide, the student is assumed to be able to do something, know something, and in some cases have a certain set of work-related attitudes which allow him to complete the task satisfactorily. We rarely find such attitudes specifically related to one task in a technical program where students are dealing primarily with objects (e.g., auto mechanics program). The attitudes which are assumed as prerequisites are the general attitudes assumed as prerequisites for the program. However, there may be unique work-related attitudes specific to learning guides in training programs designed to prepare people to enter occupations that deal primarily with people, such as a child development program.

Each learning guide has both doing and knowing prerequisites. The doing prerequisites are those skills which a student is assumed to be able

TABLE 3—3

SAMPLE TABLE FOR LISTING
LEARNING GUIDE PREREQUISITES

Doing	Knowing	Attitudes	Other

to perform and the knowing prerequisites are those knowledges which the student is assumed to have prior to undertaking the guide. The way in which the doing and knowing prerequisites are specified depends upon the nature of the task contained in the guide. If the task contained in the guide is a very simple task, one might specify the prerequisites as very small elements of doing and knowing. For example, if a student is being taught how to apply a high gloss finish to a rough board, one of the prerequisite doing elements which might be assumed is that the student be able to sand a board. One also might assume that the student knows about the grain structure of wood. Later, after the student has had experience with a wide variety of additional tasks similar in task size to the finishing task, it would not be unreasonable for an instructor to use finishing as the size prerequisite for a more complex task. For example, if the more complex task were to build a desk, one of the doing prerequisites would be that the student be able to "finish" and one of the knowing prerequisites would be that the student understand the different types of finishes.

Prerequisites are stated as different size elements depending upon the nature of the task that is included in the guide. If a program is totally individualized, it should be possible to specify the prerequisites for a learning guide in terms of the satisfactory completion of other learning guides. For example, if a learning guide was developed on how to sand, another on how to finish, and another on furniture construction, one could specify satisfactory completion of the learning guide on how to sand as a prerequisite for undertaking the learning guide on finishing. This technique works well and forms the foundation for the sequencing of instruction. Sequencing of instruction refers to the order in which learning experiences are provided to the student. It is based upon the logical order of task mastery in an occupation. Selected elementary tasks must be completed prior to undertaking more complex tasks which are dependent upon the mastery of the more elementary tasks. As was pointed out earlier, care must be taken to ensure that only those experiences that are truly prerequisite to satisfactory completion of a learning guide are listed. If unnecessary prerequisites are listed, they pose unnecessary restrictions upon the flexibility of the student. The student should be able to engage in instruction on any learning guide with a minimal amount of prerequisite task mastery. This allows students to engage in instruction on limited parts of the total program without being required to take substantial portions of the program. When a minimal number of prerequisites is combined with provisions for students to demonstrate prerequisite knowledge without actually taking part in instruction, a student is provided maximum flexibility. Sequencing is discussed further in chapter 5.

Table 3-4 is a sample listing of prerequisites for a learning guide pertaining to the task: diagnose a radio receiver. The listing indicates the competencies the instructor assumes a student will have when attempting the guide. It also indicates (in parentheses) the identification numbers of the guides which have been developed to assist a student with the development of these skills, knowledge, and work-related attitudes.

TABLE 3—4

LEARNING GUIDE PREREQUISITES

*Task: Diagnose a radio receiver**

Doing	Knowing	Attitudes	Other
1. Measure resistance (V) 2. Measure capacitance (VII) 3. Inspect and solder electrical connections (X) etc.	1. Identify resistors (V) 2. Identify capacitors (VII) 3. Identify the characteristics of a soldered connection (X) etc.	1. Demonstrate electrical safety (1) 2. Demonstrate proper care of tools and equipment (III) etc.	

*Roman numerals in parentheses refer to the learning guides which present the prerequisites.

Assessing Prerequisites

The assessment of whether or not a student has the necessary prerequisites to benefit from instruction generally requires the cooperation of a number of individuals. We will discuss the process of assessing a student's prerequisites by following a student through an educational institution. Some schools admit students to programs first and then assess the extent to which they possess the prerequisites. Others assess the extent to which students have the prerequisites first and then admit students. More and more schools are using the first approach because of federal and state laws pertaining to equal access to public education. Regardless of which approach is used, most of the schools follow the basic procedures outlined below and use the information obtained to assist students with their continued educational development. Few use the information as selection tools to close educational opportunities for applicants.

A student who applies to a program must generally apply to a personnel and guidance office that handles general admissions and the assessment of whether or not he possesses the general program prerequisites for the program to which he is applying. This assessment usually takes three forms. The first is the completion of an application form and the forwarding of previous educational records. The application form usually identifies the program to which the student is applying, provides general information on the student's prior background, and asks about any unusual physical characteristics. The student is then asked to take a series of entrance examinations which provides information on the learning abilities of the individual and the student's achievement level in basic skills areas.

The third assessment is an interview with someone from the personnel and guidance office in the school. The information previously assembled concerning a student is used as the base for the interview. The interviewer attempts to gather more information which will clarify and expand the information already gathered. He will also observe the student's general physical condition and assess the student's work-related attitudes in light of the occupation he wishes to enter. If the general program prerequisites and proficiency levels for each prerequisite have been adequately specified, the interviewer should be able to judge the acceptability of the individual into the occupations the program was designed to serve and the person's general ability to perform in the program. If the interviewer judges that the student does not possess the necessary prerequisites for the program, he must determine the personal commitment which the student has to entering that particular occupation. This can be accomplished by providing the student with information on the extent to which he meets the prerequisites of the course. If a student still would like to pursue the program even though he does not possess all of the prerequisites, the interviewer or some other member of the counseling staff must determine if the prerequisites which he does not possess are critical and whether the student could attain the prerequisites with some remedial work. If the student lacks critical prerequisites which cannot be developed through remedial work, the student should be informed and alternative occupational programs could be suggested. For example, if a student did not have the basic learning ability to enter an electronics program, he would not be encouraged to enter that program since it would be very likely that he could not succeed in the program.

If it were determined that the prerequisite that the student was lacking could be achieved with remedial work, the student could be referred to auxilliary services staff members in the school if they are available. They are people trained as specialists in diagnosing learning difficulties and designing appropriate remedial programs. The staff usually includes people such as reading diagnosticians and remediation specialists, arithmetic skills diagnosticians and remediation specialists, and work evaluators. If the student lacks basic skills in reading, he would be referred to the reading specialists; and if he lacks appropriate work-related attitudes or if he has physical handicaps, he would be referred to the work evaluator. Each specialist would try to determine the extent of the problem. If auxilliary services personnel are not available, the instructor should determine if he can assist the student with solving the problem. It is difficult to determine if an instructor should or should not attempt to assist the student because most instructors are not trained to help students with special learning problems. At times the instructor can help and at other times he can do more harm than good. If an instructor does not feel qualified to assist a student and does not know where to turn for assistance, he can turn to his department chairman or administrator.

Some students would be diagnosed as having a minor problem which would not impair their ability to learn in the program and would be referred back to personnel in charge of admissions and allowed to enroll in the programs without remediation; some students would be diagnosed as having a problem too severe to be solved within the school. If the problem could potentially be remedied, a remedial program would be designed to help the student develop the prerequisite skills. If the problem could not be remedied, the student would be referred back to the counseling group for counseling in terms of other possible occupational programs. The key to the whole process is to try and ensure that a student who attempts to engage in an instructional program has the prerequisite knowledge, skills, and work-related attitudes before attempting the program. If he does not, an attempt should be made to determine if the student can develop them or if the prerequisites which he is lacking can not be remedied within the school. If the prerequisites can be developed, the student should be allowed to enter remedial programs to help him meet the prerequisites either before or during the time he is enrolled in the occupational program.

The above discussion was in terms of the student's entering a program upon application. If, after a student is allowed to enroll in an instructional program, it is determined that he does not have sufficient general course prerequisites, the instructor should refer the student to appropriate specialists to have the student's problem diagnosed and a remedial program developed. After a student has been in the classroom for a reasonable period of time, most instructors can identify students who are having significant learning difficulties. Rather than have such students continue without adequate general program prerequisite skills, they should be informed about their lack of prerequisite skills. There are some skills which an instructor is capable of assisting students to develop and there are others for which the instructor must refer students to specialists.

The assessment of whether or not a student possesses the prerequisite learning guide skills can be conducted in a number of ways. One is to develop a prerequisite pretest for each guide that contains test items and performance items which determine if a student has the necessary knowledge and performance skills necessary to be able to complete the guide.

Each student would be expected to complete this prerequisite pretest prior to undertaking the guide. A prerequisite pretest should not be confused with the typical pretest used with learning guides. A typical pretest is used to determine if a student already has the necessary skills contained in the guide without completing the guide. If a student does not possess the necessary prerequisites, the student would be asked to take part in learning activities which would develop the prerequisites before undertaking the guide. The process of developing prerequisite pretests for each guide is very time consuming.

A second procedure can be used if the guides are carefully sequenced. If they are, the assessment of prerequisite learning guide skills takes place while a student satisfactorily completes other learning guides that pertain to prerequisites to the learning guide which he wishes to undertake. These prerequisite learning guides are identified using the sequencing procedures discussed in chapter 5. A person can demonstrate competency on these prerequisite learning guides by either satisfactorily completing the instruction and posttests for the guides or by satisfactorily completing the pretest, without taking part in the instruction. If the student can satisfactorily complete the pretest for a guide, he is certified as having mastered the content contained in the learning guide in the same way as if he completes the instruction and the posttest. Therefore, when the typical pretests and posttests are developed for each of the learning guides, the mechanism for determining whether students have the prerequisite knowledge and skills for other learning guides is also developed. The pre- and posttests used for certifying competency mastery become mechanisms for determining whether a student has sufficient prerequisite skills for another learning guide when the recommended instructional sequencing procedure is used.

One way to determine the adequacy of the pre- and posttests for the guide and the sequencing is to judge the extent to which students actually have the prerequisite knowledges, skills, and attitudes required to complete a learning guide after they have completed the prerequisite learning guides. If students can perform satisfactorily on the guide having completed the prerequisite guides, one can assume that the sequencing is adequate and that the evaluation instruments developed to certify task mastery for the prerequisite guides are also adequate.

Summary

Prerequisites are those things which an instructor assumes a student will bring with him to a learning situation. Whenever we develop objectives or learning materials we always develop them with a particular type of student in mind. Therefore, whether we realize it or not, we are establishing some prerequisites which we assume a student will possess when taking part in our course. Prerequisites can be classified as general course prerequisites and specific task prerequisites. General course prerequisites are those which are necessary for a person to perform most of the tasks contained in the course. Specific task prerequisites are those which are relatively unique to a particular task.

If a student does not possess the necessary prerequisites before undertaking a learning guide, chances are that he will not be able to benefit fully from the learning experience. Therefore, methods must be developed which assess whether a student possesses the prerequisites necessary to benefit from instruction. At times the instructor should assess if students possess sufficient prerequisites and at other times he or she must rely on specialists.

The assessment of prerequisites should not be confused with selectively admitting students. Students should not necessarily be turned away because they lack sufficient prerequisites. Every attempt should be made to assist the student with removing any deficiencies which he might have so he can benefit from instruction.

REFERENCES

1. U.S. Congress. Senate, Committee on Labor and Public Welfare. *Notes and Working Papers Concerning the Administration of Programs Authorized Under Vocational Education Act of 1963, Public Law 88-210, as Amended.* Prepared for the Subcommittee on Education of the Committee on Labor and Public Welfare, United States Senate, 90th Congress, 2nd Session, Washington, D.C.: U.S. Government Printing Office, March 1968.

Chapter 4   DEVELOPING VOCATIONAL INSTRUCTIONAL OBJECTIVES

After the vocational curriculum developer has considered methods for establishing program content in chapter 2 and for identifying student instructional prerequisites in chapter 3, the next major component of the "instructional" system deserving attention is developing appropriate vocational instructional objectives.

Since vocational instruction is keyed to occupations and *jobs,* it follows that the instructional objectives must also be derived from *jobs.* The major thrust of preparatory vocational instruction is that the students acquire sufficient skills and knowledge to be able to perform at an entry level in the job or job cluster for which the training is being provided. A job cluster is defined as a group of interrelated jobs usually with a high degree of similarity in their duties and entry requirements.

In order to determine the objectives a student should achieve to insure successful performance on the job, it is necessary to clearly define it.

Job Description

The definition of the job is assembled into a job description for the occupation in which training is to be provided. Job descriptions vary in format with different companies and employing institutions. Several samples are provided in Appendix 1.

The job description typically does not include the detailed analysis of the job that is necessary for the preparation of training materials. However, it does provide a basis for the preparation of the job analysis, which defines the actual tasks of the job.

The basic components usually included in a job description are (also see Fryklund 1970, pp. 33-37; Butler 1972, pp. 73, 74):

1. *Location and general working conditions.* This includes the location of the job within employing companies, the mental and physical effort involved, safety factors, health conditions, and other physical aspects.

2. *A general statement of job functions and relationship.* This explains the mission of the job within the structure of an organization and its relationship and accountability to other positions in the structure.

3. *General duties.* This is usually a broad statement of duties. For example, a description of the duties of an electrician repairman might be "to install, repair, test, and maintain electrical equipment and fixtures within the plant structure." There is considerable variation among companies as to how detailed or complete this section of the job description should be.

4. *Possible contingent responsibilities.* Contingent responsibilities might include the responsibility of the person in the job for the maintenance of the tools and equipment of the employer, responsibility for the safety of others, and the responsibility of providing certain goods and services to other departments or other positions.

5. *Job tasks.* A job task is a necessary part of doing a job. It is often a fairly complex procedure, but in the job description it is simply stated.

It is necessary and important that the vocational curriculum developer be cognizant of the job description components listed and, if necessary, be able to write all of them. However, major attention must be given the job tasks which become the basis for vocational instruction.

A job task is a complete element of work. A performed task usually generates a product or an observable change in the work environment. A job task statement, therefore, should begin with an action verb. The development of a list of job tasks should answer the question, "What is a person required to *do* in this position?" It is not necessary at this point to separate the *doing* components of the job and the *knowing* components of the job. What *is* required is a series of simple statements as to what is actually *done* on the job. Various writers (Butler 1972, pp. 78-79; Mager and Beach 1967; Smith 1971) have described rules for the enumeration of job tasks. The particular style for writing the job tasks is not critical. However, it is very helpful if there is consistency of style in describing job tasks within a vocational training institution. This allows persons within the institution to readily interpret the work of others and leads to more consistency in the development of instructional objectives. Since students may be working in more than one area of instruction, consistency also enhances their ability to use the learning materials effectively.

Some samples of job tasks derived from different occupations might be:

Truck Mechanic

>Replace water pump
>Change oil filter
>Determine cause of engine failure
>Replace fuel injection line
>Overhaul Mack engine
>Diagnose air line contamination
>Adjust injector valve
>Test thermostat control

Ornamental Horticulturist

>Mulch seed beds
>Lay sod
>Repair plastic pipe leaks
>Operate front end loader
>Maintain golf course greens
>Identify lawn diseases
>Establish turf demonstration plot
>Plant burlap-wrapped stock

Quality Control Technician

>Write descriptive paragraph without grammatical error
>Use Ohm's law in problem solving
>Design report layouts
>Operate lathe
>Apply *chi*-square test to problem
>Calibrate inspection systems
>Compute probability in problem situation
>Tap hole
>Conduct inspections
>Shape part on lathe

Educational Office Secretary

Complete State Department of Education fiscal reports
Maintain meeting schedule
Type daily bulletin and other reports
Perform receptionist duties
Operate office duplication equipment
Prepare requisition forms
Type dictated correspondence from transcriber
Handle telephone calls from mini-switchboard

Fashion Merchandiser

Create window displays
Sell sweaters
Wrap gifts
Price fashion merchandise
Receive merchandise
Mark merchandise
Ascertain correct size for customer
Write return slips

Chef

Practice personal hygiene
Identify beef cuts
Poach fish
Cut meat
Ice cake
Carve ice
Bake cookies
Cook soups

Apparel Alterations Specialist

Construct collars
Diagnose figure problem
Operate button hole equipment
Maintain single needle machine
Reline garments
Replace zippers
Alter coat length
Repair damaged garment
Create shoulder pads

Dental Assistant

Wash hands
Remove rubber dam
Fabricate wax patterns
Mix alginate
Remove excess cement
Schedule appointments
Make impressions

Child Development Assistant

Provides reinforcement to child for accomplishments
Gives directions
Provides motivation
Handles behavior problem
Encourages self-help

The job tasks which have been described focus on a variety of *action* verbs. There are differences of opinion among authors as to the necessity of beginning each task with a verb. Some would use "to formulate," "to assemble," etc. However, the limited research available suggests an advantage to the more definite "hard" verb beginning, rather than starting with the preposition "to."

Some action verbs have been found to be most useful when used with a particular type of content such as physical behaviors, art behaviors, and mathematical behaviors. Appendix 3 contains the National College Verb List (Claus 1968) which presents sample verbs that are commonly used with different types of content.

Where does a vocational instructor or administrator obtain a list of job tasks for a job if none has been developed? The basic data usually is drawn from two types of individuals—those currently employed in the job and those employed one level above the job who are very familiar with it and who supervise people employed in the job. Vocational educators should not rely on job requirements provided by personnel offices since they may be artificial in character, global, and not reflect actual job needs.

There are several ways to obtain the necessary task data from the persons working in the occupation. If the vocational instructor or administrator was previously a competent employee in that occupation, the instructor may expedite the process by preparing a preliminary list of job tasks from memory, personal records, literature, and other data. This preliminary list then should be carefully validated in a meeting or series of meetings with other skilled persons from that occupation. Validation as used here means asking these knowledgeable persons whether these listed tasks are actually being performed on the job. They may add to or delete from the task listing based on their occupational experience. A second successful method of obtaining a job task list is to enlist the services of a person skilled in industrial conference leading who will draw the job tasks from the advisory group of skilled employees in that occupation. Care must be taken to identify actual "need to know" categories. "Need to know" are those job requirements necessary for an entry position in that occupation. "Nice to know" characteristics are those which may enhance the trainee's overall knowledge or skill but which are not necessary for an entry position and may be acquired after beginning work. For example, a vocational program advisory committee member might specify the need for a course in calculus as a requirement for an occupation, but skillful questioning by the conference leader could reveal that knowledge of only one or two facets of calculus are actually necessary for entry into the position. Persons employed in a job are still the best single source of information about a job, but occasionally they may tend to overstate the requirements, perhaps to elevate the position in the minds of others. This usually can be avoided by having a committee of sufficient size (not less than five) to make the determinations.

Another method of obtaining job task listings should be mentioned, but often it is not available to the typical vocational educator. This method requires the person doing the job of task writing to "shadow" (or observe) a skilled employee in his work, writing a description of what is observed on an analysis sheet. Closed circuit television and television tapes currently make these methods more accurate and possible than in the past. However, vocational educators usually are not given sufficient time and course development funds to engage in these more sophisticated approaches to defining tasks. This procedure also requires special training for the observer if it is to be effective. A detailed description of these techniques for job study may be found in Gagné (1963).

Task Analysis

Identifying and listing of job tasks as a part of the job description can also be regarded as the first step of completing a task analysis. Each of the tasks must be taken from the task listing, or inventory, and studied to identify and isolate knowledges, skills, and attitudes with an intent to synthesize and build them into teachable elements. (See Davies 1971; Fryklund 1970; Gilbert 1962). This process is termed *task analysis*.

A job is not ordinarily a teachable element. For example, an industrial laboratory technician has a complex job which cannot be taught as one operation. An operation has been defined as "a unit of work in a job that involves the making, servicing, or repair of something" (Fryklund 1970). However, there are isolated examples where a job can be a teachable element. For example, a punch press operator may perform only one operation so the job can be the teachable element.

The task analysis must provide to the vocational curriculum developer an orderly method of breaking down, analyzing, and classifying not only the physical components of the task such as tools and aids but also the mental components including knowledge of processes, procedures, decisions, and abstractions (Davies 1971; Ammerman and Melching 1966).

Task analysis has been used most frequently and successfully by the military services to identify and organize "doing" tasks (Smith, Pucel 1970), but its application to related occupational training subjects (e.g. reading, science, mathematics) also has been documented (Gagné 1965). The basic instructional rationale of task analysis was tested by showing that task analysis can be used to identify and develop a hierarchical structure of terminal and component tasks in mathematics (see Gagné, Mayor, Garstens, and Paradise 1961; Gagné and Paradise 1962). The results of the experiment indicated that the level of final task performance for students was largely dependent upon mastery of lower level, prerequisite component tasks. In addition, it was also found that the instructional sequence was effective for both high and low ability students, although, as expected, lower ability students required more time to master the terminal tasks than the high ability students. (See Smith, Pucel 1970.)

Expert opinion is not unanimous regarding the terminology used in defining the "teachable element or unit" of a job. Butler (1972) sees an orderly job/duty/task/activity sequence as illustrated in figure 4-1. In this model, activities 1.1.1, 1.1.2, and 1.1.3 are learned first in that order, the sum of which would be equivalent to learning task 1.1. Then the learner proceeds with activities 1.2.1, etc., until all of the tasks of duty 1 are completed. According to Butler (1972),

> A duty is a major subdivision that has a distinct identity within the overall job. A task is a logical and necessary step in the performance of a duty—usually a relatively short and simple procedure. Actions or manipulations are short, simple operations that frequently are common to many different activities and involve using tools, devices, controls, and simple test equipment.

FIGURE 4–1
JOB-TASK SEQUENCE

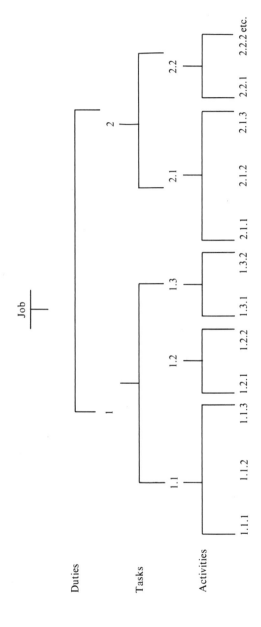

Duties

Tasks

Activities

Butler (1972) further specifies that the activity content of each task should be described in terms of the

1. cues, signals, and indications that call for the action or reaction
2. control, object, or tool to be used or manipulated
3. action or manipulation to be made
4. cues, signals, and indications (feedback) that the action taken is, or is not, correct and adequate

Mager and Beach (1967) recommend a task listing sheet (figure 4-2) that adds three qualitative dimensions: frequency of performance, importance, and learning difficulty. They indicate that knowing the frequency of performance required is useful in deciding how deeply to go into the subject, how much practice to provide, and how to sequence course material. They caution, however, that importance must be considered also since some tasks, performed frequently, may not represent critical skills, while others, performed rarely, are vital to job performance. Judging learning difficulty will, of course, be highly dependent on the experience and skill of the person making the evaluation.

TASK DETAILING SHEET

VOCATION: ARBORIST

Task: Pruning of a shade tree

No.	Steps in Performing the Task	Type of Performance	Learning Difficulty
1.	Note the location of the tree with respect to utility wires, buildings, and pertinent surroundings	Discrimination	Easy
2.	Inspect the tree for diseases and insect manifestations	Discrimination	Very Difficult
	etc.		

FIGURE 4—2

Mager and Beach (1967) also recognize the need to go beyond task listing into a process they refer to as "task detailing." They suggest that one "list each of the steps involved in performing each of the tasks in terms of what is *done,* rather than in terms of what must be known".

They provide the following "memory aids" for steps to be included in the task detailing:

Recognize when to perform the task.
Select appropriate tools and materials.
Locate the correct objects on which to work.
Perform the safety procedures associated with the task.
Check the work.

Mager and Beach (1967) also note that there are some steps which may be necessary in the performance of a task, but which are not *visible* while they are being performed. These are:

Identify the sequence of steps that must be followed to perform the task correctly.
Describe how . . . works.
Describe the theory of why . . . works.
Recognize dangers associated with performing the task.
Recognize the differences between a properly performed task and an improperly performed task.

Davies (1971) describes task analysis in terms of topic or job, duties, tasks, task elements, and acts as outlined in figure 4-3. He suggests thinking of the topic or job as a hierarchial organization of levels or components, each of which describe the job in successively greater detail. He describes the hierarchy in the following example: "In making a job analysis of a skill, the job could be that of an engine mechanic. His job is made up of a number of duties, including tuning the carburetor, adjusting the tappets, changing the oil, and cleaning the spark plugs. Each of these duties is made up of a number of separate tasks, all closely related to each other in sequence. For example, the duty of changing the engine oil includes the task of jacking-up the car, placing an oil container underneath the sump, taking out the sump drain plug, allowing the oil to drain away, etc. Finally, each task includes a number of task elements. Jacking-up the car, for instance, involves acquiring the right kind of jack, positioning it underneath the car to the required level. "In topic and job analyses," says Davies, "the task element is further broken down into 'acts'. An act consists of a basic movement that must be repeated if it is interrupted." Four acts occur most frequently—reaching for an object, grasping it, moving it, and positioning it.

Others who have defined systems of describing job tasks and then detailing those tasks include Evans, Glaser, and Homme (1962); Glaser (1963); Mechner (1965); Thomas, Davies, Openshaw, and Bird (1963); and Ammerman and Melching (1966).

As stated by Mager and Beach (1967), "There are probably as many techniques for performing a task analysis as there are people doing it." The objective of the process is to obtain sufficient definition of the job so

FIGURE 4—3

			Topic or Job			
Duty	Duty	Duty	Duty	Duty	Duty	Duty
	Task	Task	Task	Task	Task	
		Task Element	Task Element	Task Element		
			Acts			

effective instructional objectives and learning activities can be devised to teach the occupation to a willing learner. Perhaps the most important consideration in choosing a system is that the system be used reasonably consistently within a vocational instruction program, and that it be appropriate for the work circumstances of the vocational educator-user.

For example, a person charged with the responsibility of in-plant training for a new production facility where hundreds of workers are performing skill tasks would probably focus on a very detailed system because the detail included could save the company thousands of dollars each day. The process would probably go all the way through the skills analysis, including right- and left-hand choices, eye movement, etc. This process can be time-consuming and expensive. For example, Ammerman and Melching (1966) found that it took about 17-18 hours of instructional personnel time to decide what to teach for each hour of nonequipment military instruction.

In-service vocational educators seldom are awarded that amount of time and resources for curriculum development. The system described here, in the experience of the authors, is adequate for the objectives of individualized vocational instruction and is designed to be within the working-time-frame of a practicing vocational educator.

Task Analysis for Individualized Vocational Instruction

First, we recognize the necessity described by nearly all authors dealing with task analysis of starting with the basic job and breaking it down into successively more detailed components or levels.

Second, when task analysis is approached from the point of view of the vocational educator he should be trained to recognize the least detailed level at which effective individualized instruction can take place, so that unnecessary task detailing can be avoided.

Third, there is a need to provide for the job-related information and tasks which may not be visable but which are a necessary part of the instruction.

To accommodate the three requirements stated, we suggest the following occupational breakdown (with examples):

OCCUPATION

 Graphic Communications

OCCUPATIONAL SUBDIVISION

 Offset Press Operator

TASK

 Operate the Chief 20 Press

TASK DETAIL

Doing	*Knowing*	
	Related Technical	*Related General*
Prepare Chief 20 for operation	Paper characteristics	Safety procedures
	Ink characteristics	Ecology of paper industry
	Mixing principles	Necessity for punctuality
	Mathematics	

The first occupational subdivision is sufficiently large so that these job components almost represent occupations in themselves. A trainee completing one of these components might well be employable in that occupation, even though he did not receive the full range of training included in the other divisions. From these larger divisions the work is broken down into tasks which can be classified as *doing* tasks and *knowing* tasks. The knowing component can be further divided into related technical knowledge and related general knowledge.

Doing tasks are sometimes referred to as skill tasks, and the words can be used interchangeably if it is understood that some kinds of skills require considerable knowledge. Some examples of doing and knowing tasks are as follows:

Medical Assistant

Doing	*Knowing*
Wash hands	Medical laws of community
Inject medication	Anatomy & Physiology

Administer oral medication   Identify drug classifications
Organize physicians bag   Duties of medical assistants
Read urine culture   Tests of urine culture
Identify microorganisms   Use of Microscope
Transcribe shorthand note   Medical terminology
Mail statement   Monthly billing procedure

Cosmetology

Highlight hair   Current hair styles
Adjust chair cloth   Sanitation procedures
Loosen dandruff   Dermatology
Steam hair with towels   Angiology
Brush hair   Sterilization of implements
Apply astringent   Safety precautions

Fashion Merchandising

Sell men's shirts   Fabrics and materials
Create window display   Concepts of design
Make change   General retailing policies
Handle complaints   Psychology of customer relations
Price merchandise   Retail policy and federal
    regulations
Prevent shoplifting   Local laws

Heating and Air Conditioning

Repair oil furnace jet   Theory of AC motors
Install meter   Types and uses of meters
Diagnose failure   Theory of oil heat
Repair gas air conditioner   Types and theory of gas air
    conditioners
Test furnace for efficiency   Combustion testing

Graphic Communication

Prepare press for operation   Safety rules
Print on paper with black ink   Printing papers, weight, basic
    sizes, thickness, grain, price
Print flat color reproductions   Theory of flat color reproduction
Print line and halftone   Line and halftone reproduction
    reproductions   process
Print process color work   Theory of process color work
Troubleshoot press problems   Press operation concepts
Clean the offset press   Cleaning chemicals and materials

In the first part of this chapter we discussed the necessity and procedures for obtaining job tasks that were valid for the occupation for which instruction was being planned. Unless the curriculum planner is very knowledgeable about the occupation, it would be very appropriate for the vocational curriculum developer to return to the advisory committee *again* after the task detailing has been completed. The expertise and opinions of these knowledgeable people should be sought so that valuable time is not wasted in the development of performance and instructional objectives around task details that are irrelevant.

WRITING PERFORMANCE OBJECTIVES FOR OCCUPATIONAL TASKS

After completing and validating the task detailing, the next step toward individualizing vocational instruction is the preparation of performance objectives for the tasks of the occupation for which training is to be provided. A terminal performance objective for vocational instruction describes what an individual who is competent in the skills and knowledge of a particular task *can do.*

There is not total agreement among authors about the definition of *terminal performance objective* as we use it here. Butler (1972) has a similar description for what he refers to as "training objectives." Bloom (1956) focuses on "learning objectives," as does Davies (1971). Mager (1962) states ". . . the most important characteristic of a useful objective is that it *identifies the kind of performance* that will be accepted as evidence that the learner has achieved the objective," but he does not describe them as terminal performance objectives.

In order to clarify usage of *terminal performance objectives* it is necessary to refer to our previously described occupational breakdown:

OCCUPATION

    Graphic Communications

OCCUPATIONAL SUBDIVISION

    Offset Press Operator

TASK

    Operate the Chief 20 Press   *Write terminal performance objectives at the task level.*

TASK DETAIL

        Doing   *Knowing*

        Related Technical   *Related General* *Write intermediate (learning) objectives at the task detail level.*

The intermediate objectives at the task detail level will be discussed later in this chapter. They are introduced here as a means of understanding that each terminal performance objective (TPO), while a tool in the learning process, does not have to contain *all* of the details for instruction because it will be supported by intermediate performance objectives.

Each terminal performance objective (TPO) should have the following components:

(1) *The Givens.* A statement of the conditions that are given and that define the environment within which the student must perform. It is a part of the general philosophy of vocational-technical education that performance should be under realistic joblike situations so that there is a reasonable level of skill transfer from instruction to the job. Therefore the givens should describe a realistic job situation to the extent possible.

In general, tools and materials necessary to accomplish the objective should be specified in the "givens" and also any special aids such as manufacturer's manuals.

The environment within which the performance is to occur also is described if a particular job environment is generally involved whenever the task is performed. It may be necessary at times to specify particularly difficult physical demands of the job as a part of the "givens" so that the student is not surprised when he attempts the task on the job.

Finally, some reasonable limit must be set on the range of knowledge and skills that the student will be expected to demonstrate pertaining to this performance objective. This can be accomplished by limiting the performance expected to specific situations. For example, if a performance objective for truck mechanics reads, "Given a truck with an air brake malfunction . . ." instead of "Given a Ford L series truck with an air brake malfunction . . .", the knowledge and skill scope required might be prohibitive because of the great variety of trucks that have air brakes.

(2) *The Performance.* Performance can be described as the visible actions of the student while carrying on the learning activities. It is essential that both the student and the instructor know what performance or task the student is to learn how to perform. Much can be done to orient the thinking of the student and the instructor toward observable activities if the performance objectives are written with action verbs. Nonaction verbs like "know," "understand," and "appreciate" should be avoided. How can a student demonstrate that he *appreciates* the theory of the offset press process? The "better" action verbs for performance objectives are found in appendix 3 under the subheading "The

Functional, Forceful Four Hundred Fifty-Five." Many of the verbs listed under the subheadings "Study," "Arts," "Mathematical," and "Laboratory," have special reference for vocational education.

The terminology of the behavioral performance objectives should be that of the occupation in which training is being given, but the vocabulary should not be above the majority of reading materials available in that occupation. If the vocabulary is written at too high a level, it may exclude some persons from learning that occupation who might otherwise be qualified.

(3) *The Standard.*   A statement of the minimal acceptable level of performance and assessment criteria by which it will be known if the student performed at or above that level is a necessity. It is very important that the standards or level of performance stated be realistic for a beginning worker in that occupation. In some cases 100 percent accuracy will be necessary, while in others a lesser percentage is sufficient. For example, a student who is reassembling a carburetor after repairing it may be required to produce 100 percent accuracy—or the carburetor will not function. On a recall objective of naming the parts of the carburetor, a 90 percent score might be considered reasonable. Development of criterion tests to measure both the doing and knowing requirements of the task is discussed extensively in chapter 6.

Time factors are also important in most "standard" statements in vocational instruction terminal performance objectives. If a learner cannot perform the activity required in the performance objective within a time frame similar to most new entrants to that occupation he may not be employable or may not stay employed. A time standard is most often attached to the doing objectives, but it can be a factor in knowing objectives as well. This should not be confused with time required to learn the skill in a variable-time, fixed-competency model described in chapter 1. Rather, the factor here is "Can the learner do the job task in the time typically allocated a beginning worker in that occupation?" after he has learned it. In some occupations, particularly service-repair, time standards are contained in the manufacturer's service manuals. In many instances, however, the vocational curriculum builder will have to go back to the occupational sources or to the advisory committee for documentation of time standards. Chapter 6 deals, in some detail, with the criterion-referenced exam as an evaluation device in determining whether the standard has been met.

The following are examples of terminal performance objectives, selected from a variety of occupational instruction programs.

Chef.   Given a cut of beef, pork, lamb, or veal, and standard meatcutting and saute equipment; saute the cut of meat; to the standard identified on the instructors checklist.

Marine & Small Engine Mechanic.   Given an outboard motor with a defective fuel pump, specified tools, and service manuals; diagnose and repair the fuel pump by the process of systems isolation, install it on the engine, and test run the engine; within the time specified in the factory flat rate manual, and according to running quality factory specifications.

Video-Graphic Technician.   Given a specified variety of AV and TV productions; produce titling for these productions; according to standards of the posttest checklist specified by the instructor.

Office Machine Repairman.   Given a malfunctioning copy machine, necessary tools, and service manual; diagnose the malfunction and perform the necessary adjustments; within the time and at the quality level specified in the service manual.

Offset Press Operator.   Given an offset metal master which is developed with an image; produce 500 images on sheets of 11" x 17" stock; with a spoilage of less than 20 percent with results of salable quality (dense ink coverage with clean background and no offsetting according to checklist) in one hour.

INTERMEDIATE PERFORMANCE (LEARNING) OBJECTIVES

The terminal performance objectives we have been discussing have focused on the task level. These objectives, although stating succinctly the "givens," the "performance," and the "standard," are still most often too general to be used for the actual writing of the learning materials. For vocational curriculum writing, it is necessary to go to the next level and develop a series of increasingly specific subobjectives. These subobjectives have been labeled by various authors as micro-performance objectives, interim performance objectives, etc. It is our opinion that the term *intermediate* performance objectives is the most descriptive, so we have adopted it. Hence, we use terminal performance objectives (TPO) to describe the performance at the task level and intermediate performance objectives (IPO) to describe the subobjectives at the task detail or learning level. The task level used here with the TPO would compare approximately to the level described as task by Butler (1972) figure 4-1, p. 70; Mager and Beach (1967) figure 4-2, p. 71; and Davies (1971) figure 4-3, p. 73. We will use "activities," "steps in performing the task," and "task element" to refer to the task detail level used with IPOs.

The writing of the intermediate performance objectives must be considered especially carefully since these objectives will have a direct relationship to the development and selection of learning materials. While the TPOs could encompass both the doing and knowing elements of performance, experience indicates that there are advantages to separating doing and knowing objectives at the intermediate level.

To make these separations, the vocational instruction developer must have an understanding of different types of learning objectives. An examination of the literature and of a great number of learning objectives reveals that learning objectives can be classified broadly under three headings, sometimes referred to as *domains* (Davies 1971; Gerhard 1972; Bloom 1956).

1. Psychomotor
2. Cognitive
3. Affective

Psychomotor objectives.   Most of the intermediate performance objectives written for the *doing* element of the task will be psychomotor. These objectives describe the muscular and motor skills, including manipulation of materials and objects. They provide the base for the majority of vocational-technical training. Once the curriculum developer has mastered the technique of picking out the action-oriented, "hard" verb and has learned to use that verb as a descriptor for the performance of the learner, these "doing" IPOs are probably easier to write than those in the cognitive and affective domains. The examples on pp. 74-75 include such verbs as wash, inject, loosen, brush, transcribe, and print, all of which are descriptive of psychomotor activity. The "Arts Behaviors" verbs in the National College Verb List, Appendix 3, also illustrate good examples of psychomotor, or doing action verbs.

Cognitive Objectives.   The cognitive objective usually will be contained within the *knowing* component of intermediate performance objectives. Included in the cognitive objectives are the learner's recall and recognition of basic *knowledge,* including terminology and facts. At the next level the learner *comprehends* the knowledge to the extent that he can make use of it in limited situations. At the third general level the learner is able to *apply* the knowledge and to relate it to situations beyond those he has been taught (Krathwold, Bloom, Masia 1964).

Well-described intermediate objectives in the cognitive domain help to bring the vocational student's related instruction in concert with his psychomotor (doing) learning activity. Writers of individualized instructional materials need to consider the nature of the occupation in selecting levels of cognitive objectives. There has been a tendency on the part of some vocational educators to focus performance objective writing strictly on the psychomotor skills, ignoring the cognitive and affective domains. Their theory is that the student-learner will not be able to *do* the psychomotor activities unless he has the knowledge (cognitive) to support him. Therefore, the skills test also suffices as a knowledge test. This may be true, but only to a limited degree. It is the objective of most vocational instructors that their students will be able to function in a variety of closely related jobs, sometimes referred to as clusters, for which training is being given. If a student has learned to do certain tasks by rote on one machine but has no knowledge about the operation of that machine, the probability of the student's being able to operate similar machines of different makes or to be able to do different jobs using the same machine is much less than if learning had been supported by cognitive knowledge of the appropriate generalizations and principles underlying the operation of the machine and the process. The following are intermediate performance objectives based on knowing (cognitive) content drawn from the technical related details of the offset press operator occupation: (1) Given a problem in paper selection for a specified booklet, recall the six criteria used in selection of printing paper at 100 percent accuracy within ten minutes after receiving the problem; (2) Given ten inking problems common in the graphics industry, list the influences each of the four basic ink additives would have on pure printer's ink being used at 90 percent accuracy within thirty minutes after receiving the problem.

Some of the other action verbs that lend themselves well to cognitive performance objectives are:

choose	define	show	select	write	underline
state	list	contrast	name	compute	differentiate
determine	distinguish	compare	collect	isolate	categorize

Affective Objectives.   The affective domain of human behavior consists mainly of feelings and emotions. Affective learning objectives, therefore, are concerned primarily with the expression or communication of those feelings and emotions. A feeling or emotion that becomes internalized, that is, incorporated within an individual as a guiding principle, may be communicated consistently by that individual as an *attitude*. Job-related attitudes are often an important dimension for success in many occupations. For example, a student enrolled in a Child Development Assistant training program who has a generally hostile attitude toward small children would probably not be effective. Similarly, a student in a graphic communications training program might *know* (cognitive) all of the safety rules for the safe operation of the offset press. Yet if he does not internalize these rules of safety (affective) so that they guide his behavior while functioning on the machine and in the shop, it is questionable whether effective learning has taken place.

Writing effective objectives in measurable terms in the affective domain may cause the vocational instruction writer some problems in that they are probably the most difficult to define and to observe. Affective objectives are reflected in behaviors that you expect students to exhibit which are emotion related rather than knowledge related. One of the differences between affective objectives and cognitive objectives is that cognitive objectives can usually be measured with a written or oral test. Affective objective performance frequently can be measured only through observation of psychomotor activity.

Developing affective learning objectives involves essentially the following steps:

1. Identify and state the affective behaviors one wants the student to express or communicate;
2. Plan instructional activities designed to help the learner internalize and express the desired behaviors;
3. Observe the behaviors of the student and record them on a checklist.

Behavioral attitude measurement is covered in chapter 7.

An intermediate performance objective written in the *affective* domain to promote safety instruction in the offset machine shop could be: Given the conditions of an operating offset machine shop, *follow* all safety rules and *suggest* to other students *observed* breaking such rules that it is in the best interest of *all* students if safety rules are followed; at a 90 percent level on the instructor's monitoring checklist.

Other verbs that tend to lend effectiveness to writing affective performance objectives include:

accepts	persists	joins	asks	organizes	offers
chooses	rejects	consults	weighs	submits	shares
defends	evaluates	controls	advocates	promotes	subscribes

CONVERTING TASK DETAILS TO INTERMEDIATE PERFORMANCE OBJECTIVES

The vocational curriculum developer must be reasonable in converting task details to IPOs, or the process may become unworkable as an effective tool. If, in the attempt to fully individualize instruction, IPOs are written around every single task detail, the learning process may become much more complex than the occupational task itself, and the learning material will be rendered ineffective.

It is necessary to regroup the task details into combinations that represent logical, sequential instructional modules for the purpose of writing the intermediate performance objectives.

Figure 4-4 is a task analysis form which provides the necessary task detailing for the writing of intermediate performance objectives.

FIGURE 4−4

TASK ANALYSIS FORM

Frequency of Performance	Task Importance	Performance Difficulty
(low) (high)	(low) (high)	(low) (high)
1 2 ③	1 2 ③ ①	2 3

TASK: Lubrication of Nonsealed fitting type automobile

Acceptance Level of Performance: (Quality of work, time limits, etc.)	Lubricate 15 cars of various makes and models per the spec book in a maximum of thirty minutes each.

Conditions under which employee performs: (Tools, equipment, aids, manuals, etc.)	In garage location use work orders, check chart manuals, hand tools, gauges, and overhead lubrication equipment.

TASK DETAILS:

1. Write a work order and drive car into the lube bay.
2. Center car on hoist and set adapters per the check chart guide.
3. Open the hood and place fender protectors or fender covers in proper place.
4. Raise the car on the hoist, making sure that safety mechanism is engaged.
5. Check the lubrication guide book for proper model of car and also the number of lubrication fittings.
6. Wipe off all fittings with a rag and count them to be sure that you have wiped them all and have the same number that the specification book shows.
7. Check to be sure that the grease gun is set on low pressure and wipe tip of grease gun clean.
8. Lubricate all fittings—being careful not to blow out the rubber boot.

TASK ANALYSIS FORM—CONTINUED
AUTOMOBILE LUBRICATION—NON SEALED FITTING TYPE CAR

9. Check the tire pressure of all tires and also the spare for proper pressure.
10. Check the muffler and the tail pipe for possible leaks, rotting, or visible rusting.
11. Check the differential fluid level and replace cap—be sure it is tight.
12. Visibly check brake hoses, backing plate for signs of brake fluid leakage or seal damage.
13. Check the heat riser if car is so equipped for free play—if not free, use partease to loosen heat riser.
14. Check tires visibly for signs of wear, out of balance, or improper wheel alignment.
15. Check front end parts for tightness.
16. Lower car on the hoist to the floor.
17. Open the hood.
18. Remove the dip stick, and check the oil level.
19. Check radiator fluid level; also test for protection level of antifreeze.
20. Remove wing nut and check air cleaner for dirt.
21. Check windshield washer fluid level.
22. Check the battery electrolyte level and check for leakage as well as corrosion.
23. Test the radiator cap and radiator hose with a pressure tester.
24. Test P.C.V. valve with a tester if so equipped.
25. Test all lights and directional signals.
26. Check the wiper blades for wear.
27. Lubricate all door hardware.
28. Lubricate all trunk hardware.
29. Lubricate all hood hardware.
30. Start car in park and check automatic transmission fluid level.
31. Turn off car and remove fender covers and close hood properly, being sure it is properly locked.
32. Clean all windows, inside and out.
33. Vacuum the interior of the car.
34. Write all services that have been performed or sold on the work order.
35. Take car to the outside and park as well as remove keys.
36. Hang keys with the work order—being sure that it is properly extended.

The following are doing and knowing objectives for the learning of the task described. Numbers in parentheses refer to the task details being covered.

(1) Doing

Given an automobile requiring lubrication, write up lubrication work order according to instruction sheet within time specified.

(1) Knowing

Given an automobile requiring a work order, recall the procedures for writing a work order and write the required work order without ref-ence to the instruction sheet within the time specified and within check sheet error tolerance.

(1, 2, 3, 4) Doing

Given an automobile on which a work order for lubrication has been written and a garage with a lube bay, drive the car into the lube bay, center the car on the hoist, set adapters, open the hood, place fender covers, raise the car on the hoist, making sure that the safety catch is engaged, within the time specified and according to procedural stand-ards of the instructor's checklist.

(1, 2, 3, 4) Knowing

Given the conditions of an operating garage, recall rules for driving vehicles in the shop in safe manner as specified and procedures for engaging safety on hoist at a 100 percent level as evaluated by instruc-tor's monitoring checklist.

(5, 6, 7, 8) Doing

Given a car on a hoist on which a work order for lubrication has been written and a lubrication guide book, lubricate all fittings within the time specified in the guide book, and at the acceptance level of the in-structor's checklist.

(5, 6, 7, 8) Knowing

Given a car on a hoist needing lubrication and the lubrication guide book, demonstrate recall of knowledge by pointing out to instructor all fittings requiring lubrication, demonstrate knowledge of proper technique for wiping fittings clean, and for cleaning tip of grease gun, and indicate how it is known that the grease gun is set for low pres-sure, according to standards of instructor's checklist.

Other operation groupings of task details in figure 4-4 might include (9-16), (17-24), (25-33), and (34-36). These grouping decisions are some-what subjective, and there is room for an instructor who is experienced in his occupation to experiment with different combinations to deter-mine the "best" approach in a particular learning situation. The curricu-lum developer will need to rely on his own knowledge, expert assistance, and/or advisory committee to arrive at the appropriate combinations of task details for instructional modules.

Thus, these intermediate performance objectives (IPOs) become the direct learning objectives in an individualized instructional system. The direct learning objectives are those which, if mastered by the student-learner, will in summation be the mastery of the terminal performance objective. They are derived, not only by further breaking down the terminal performance objective, but also by determining what might be instructionally possible based on resources available. The organization of these direct learning objectives, the selection of learning tactics, the selection of learning resources, and the creation of an optimal learning environment to enable the student-learner to accomplish the learning objectives will be the topic of the next chapter.

Summary

In summary, the creation of instruction or learning objectives starts with obtaining or defining an appropriate job description for the job or job cluster in which training is to be given. Components of a job description usually include location and general working conditions, a statement of job functions and relationships, general duties, contingent responsibilities, and job tasks.

Tasks are an essential element of the job description because they are complete elements of work. Selection of the descriptive verb for the task is of great importance because of its later use in the development of terminal and instructional objectives. The task is usually too general to be suitable as a teachable element. Through task analysis the task is broken down into task details.

The writing of terminal performance objectives requires knowledge of the components of a TPO. These components are *the givens,* a statement of known conditions and environment, *the performance,* the observable behavior of the learner, and *the standard* which represents the minimum acceptable level of performance. Terminal performance objectives are written from task statements.

Intermediate performance objectives are the direct learning objectives and are generated by combining task details into sequential instructional components. Intermediate objectives may be written as doing or knowing objectives. Doing objectives are sometimes referred to as psychomotor objectives, meaning that they emphasize muscular and motor skills. A large portion of vocational instruction objectives are in the psychomotor domain. Knowing objectives are usually cognitive. Cognitive objectives are those objectives that deal with basic *knowledge, comprehension* of knowledge, and *application* of knowledge. Affective objectives focus on behaviors affected by attitudes and beliefs. Affective objectives are probably the most difficult to write on a performance basis, but should not be ignored for that reason.

REFERENCES

1. Ammerman, Harry L., and Melching, William J. "The Derivation, Analysis, and Classification of Instructional Objectives." Technical Report 66-4, Alexandria, Virgina: HumRRO, George Washington University, May 1966.

2. Bloom, Benjamin S. et al. *Taxonomy of Educational Objectives.* New York: David McKay Company, Inc., 1956, pp. 205-206.

3. Butler, F. Coit. *Instructional Systems Development for Vocational and Technical Training.* Englewood Cliffs, New Jersey: Educational Technology Publications, Inc., 1972, pp. 73-79; pp. 113-26.

4. Claus, Calvin K. "National College Verb List." From the text of a paper read at a meeting of the National Council on Measurement in Education, Chicago, Illinois, February 10, 1968.

5. Davies, Ivor K. *The Management of Learning.* London: McGraw-Hill Book Company (UK) Limited, 1971, pp. 35-43.

6. Evans, J.L.; Glaser, R.; and Homme, L.E. "The Ruleg System for the Construction of Programmed Verbal Learning Sequences." *Journal of Educational Research* 55 (1962): 513-18.

7. Fryklund, Verne C. *Occupational Analysis, Techniques and Procedures.* New York: The Bruce Publishing Company, 1970, pp. 33-37; pp. 87-117.

8. Gagné, Robert M. *The Conditions of Learning.* New York: Holt, Rinehart and Winston, Inc., 1965.

9. Gagné, R.M., ed. *Psychological Principles in System Development.* New York: Holt, Rinehart and Winston, Inc., 1963.

10. Gagné, Robert M., and Paradise, Noel E. "Abilities and Learning Sets in Knowledge Acquisition," *Psychological Monographs* 76 (1962): No. 7 (Whole No. 526).

11. Gagné, Robert M.; Mayor, John R.; Garstens, Helen L.; and Paradise, Noel E. "Factors in Acquiring Knowledge of a Mathematical Task." *Psychological Monographs* 75 (1961): No. 14 (Whole No. 518).

12. Gerhard, Muriel. *Effective Teaching Strategies With the Behavioral Outcomes Approach.* New York: Parker Publishing Company, Inc., 1971, pp. 174-80.

13. Gilbert, T.F. "Mathetics, The Technology of Education." *Journal of Mathetics* 1 (1962): 7-73.

14. Glaser, R. "Research and Development Issue in Programmed Instruction," in Filep, R.T., ed., *Perspectives In Programming,* New York, as cited in Davies, Ivor K., *The Management of Learning.* McGraw-Hill, London, Great Britain, 1971, pp. 39.

15. Krathwohl, D.R.; Bloom, B.S.; and Masia, B.B. *Taxonomy of Educational Objectives, Handbook II.* New York: David McKay Company Inc., 1964.

16. Mager, Robert F. *Preparing Instructional Objectives.* Palo Alto, California: Fearon Publishers, Inc., 1962, p. 13.

17. Mager, Robert F., and Beach, Kenneth M., Jr. *Developing Vocational Instruction.* Belmont, California: Fearon Publishers, Inc., 1967.

18. Mechner, F. "Analysis and Specification of Behavior For Training," in R. Glaser, ed., *Teaching Machines and Programmed Learning II: Data and Directions.* Washington, D.C.: National Education Association, 1965.

19. Smith, Brandon, and Pucel, David J. "Goal Structure and Change Definition in the Process of Curriculum Development," *The High School Journal* 53 No. 7 (April 1970).

20. Smith, Robert G., Jr. *The Engineering of Educational and Training Systems.* Lexington, Mass.: D.C. Heath and Company, Heath Lexington Books, 1971, pp. 36-37.

21. Thomas, C.A.; Openshaw, D.; and Bird, J. *Programmed Learning in Perspective.* New York: Educational Methods, Inc., 1963.

Chapter 5   INSTRUCTIONAL STRATEGIES

According to George Odiorne (1973), people engaged in an organizational undertaking will always find work to do. However, they often become so involved with the work activity, that they lose sight of whether the work is making any real contribution toward the objectives of the organization. In brief, they fall into an *activity trap*. They become so enmeshed in the activity of getting there, that they forget where they were going.

Similarly, it is easy for a vocational curriculum builder to become so absorbed in the possible instructional activities that he loses focus on the learning objectives which should remain the basis of all instructional strategy. The main function of instructional strategies must be to help the learner achieve and demonstrate proficiency in the learning objectives.

It is important that a *system* of instructional strategies be defined, whether the curriculum builder is preparing for one class-sized group of students, or for the students of an entire institution. The *system* is defined as an integrated combination of personnel, media, equipment, and methods which, if experienced by a learner, will enable that learner to demonstrate proficiency in the learning objectives. The focus of this chapter will be on a system of instructional strategies by which a learner can reach learning objectives, using individualized approaches to instructional strategy.

Selecting an Instructional System

The earliest types of education and training were highly individualized. Under the Socratic system, the scholar through skillful questioning would lead the student to self-discovery of truths. The content was variable, the time variable, and the eventual learning and proficiency were also variable.

Similarly, early vocational education consisted of parents teaching their children not only the household tasks but also the "cottage-industry" and agricultural tasks that provided the economic support of the family. As craftsmen began to be employed outside of their homes, they taught their skills to other apprentices as well as to their sons. Other education or training was available only to those who had economic means and those who sought those educational benefits diligently. Relatively little thought was given to an individual's obligation to seek further training, or to his "rights" to expect such training from society or the government.

As the population and volume of information grew and as occupations became more complex and technical, it became apparent that the master to apprentice relationship could not meet the need for trained persons in industry in the United States and other industrial and agricultural countries. The need for trained workers became sufficiently acute to stimulate the passage of the Smith-Hughes Act in 1917, providing federal financial assistance for vocational training. Funds from this act were designed to assist local school systems with the extra cost of implementing vocational programs because of smaller class size, more expensive supplies and equipment, and larger space requirements. Funds were also available to support related training for apprentices who were learning some of the skills on the job.

Payments from Smith-Hughes funds were almost universally made for salaries of instructors for *classes* of vocational education students. This provision, reinforced by the George-Barden Act of 1946, had a tendency to lock in group-centered instruction in vocational education. The basic educational concept was thought to be a fixed-content, fixed-time, fixed-proficiency model. As a practical matter, of course, fixed-proficiency was mythical because all of the individuals were different, and given the same content and the same time, proficiency was in fact most often variable. There was little in the funding or supervisory structure which encouraged development of specialized individualized programs or strategies of instruction for individual students.

The Vocational Acts of 1963 and 1968 recognized that this "class-oriented" approach was missing some segments of our population, namely the handicapped and disadvantaged. These acts specified that a fixed percentage of the vocational instruction funds be directed toward the (vocational) training of the handicapped and disadvantaged. This congressional direction did provide some impetus toward individualization of instruction because it became apparent that the class-centered instruction would not meet the needs of those individuals with special problems. The Manpower Development and Training Act with subsequent supporting legislation, later combined in the Comprehensive Employment and Training Act of 1974, also tended to focus attention on groups and *individuals* with special problems that were preventing their becoming wage earning citizens. The Job Corps was another part of this federal effort, directed primarily at the younger element of unemployed.

Unfortunately, many of the early efforts of these support programs were directed toward special "classes" for the handicapped and disadvantaged dropouts with learning still focused on groups rather than on the individual learner.

More recently, however, some Manpower Training officials have been reporting increasing success in employment results by placing their clients for training as "slot-ins" in vocational instruction programs. A *slot-in* is a trainee who is placed for training in an on-going vocational instruction program where the majority of students are "regular" in that they are not perceived to have any special learning problems. In the past, this would have spelled disaster for the "slot-in" because he could not possibly catch up to the content level of the rest of the class; there was no time for individual attention from the instructor. Therefore, the individual was doomed to become frustrated and a dropout. The fact that the slot-in or integrated system is becoming more successful is a strong indicator that the following circumstances are taking place:

1. Individualized learning materials are becoming available so that the trainee can start at his level of understanding rather than where the "class" is at the moment.
2. Trainees for whom the instructor has responsibility spend sufficient time in independent study so that the instructor has time to help learners with special problems.
3. Individual and group centered assistance is available to the special trainee to help with personal and related problems not connected with job skills but that have a bearing on continuity of employment.

The growth of high school or secondary level "shared-time vocational centers" is also having an impact on the development of individualized instructional materials. States such as Michigan, Minnesota, and Pennsylvania previously had a large number of very small secondary schools that could offer only a very limited secondary level vocational instructional program. With a greatly increased number of "shared-time centers," students from these small schools can now take advantage of expanded vocational instruction opportunities at the secondary school level. While the instruction time available is often not sufficient to provide job entry skills in all occupations taught, these secondary program graduates do arrive at the postsecondary vocational and technical institutes and community colleges with more skills and a greater range of skills than has been the case in the past. The postsecondary institutions are therefore under considerable pressure to make curricular adjustments so that their "new" students do not have to repeat content which they have previously mastered at the secondary center level. An individualized instruction system is clearly one of the more viable solutions.

In discussing the need for a system of strategies for individualized instruction, we have been tracing the "pressures" which have developed in the vocational technical sector of education. Similar pressures are underway in the field of general education. They have been well defined by Duane (1973) as follows:

1. Education and industry have joined forces to provide technology as well as teaching materials that will enable the teacher to organize his classroom on an individualized basis.
2. We have learned much more in recent years about the process of instruction itself. We have developed experience in producing programs of materials that teach a subject in relation to its basic structure and according to the best ways through which children learn. We know that children must be involved in their learning and not merely "told"; that pupil interest is a great factor in learning; that reinforcement and immediate feedback of answers aids learning rate; and that children learn best when allowed to learn at their own pace.
3. Our country has realized that local school districts cannot provide all of the financial support for a quality educational program and has significantly increased its financial support of schools. . . .
4. Teacher education institutions are preparing a "new breed" of teachers who are committed to making schools more challenging for children.
5. The current emphasis on community involvement in schools has led parents to question the value of group teaching and to demand that their children be provided instructional programs that individualize learning for all children.
6. There is a growing feeling among teachers themselves that they want to individualize instruction, but they do not have the time to prepare all the materials needed.

Thus it appears to be clear, as discussed in chapter 1 and reinforced here, that there are societal, humanistic, and practical pressures which are motivating a trend toward more individualization of instruction in all of education. To the degree possible, this chapter will focus on the special needs, problems, and applications of developing a system of strategies for individualized instruction in vocational and technical education.

Of the eight possible models of organizing an instructional program discussed in chapter 1, five were perceived to be feasible for an individualized vocational instruction program. These included:

Fixed-content, variable-time, fixed-proficiency
Fixed-content, variable-time, variable-proficiency
Variable-content, fixed-time, variable-proficiency
Variable-content, variable-time, fixed-proficiency
Variable-content, variable-time, variable-proficiency

We are inclined to favor the fixed-content, variable-time, fixed-proficiency model as the preferred mode for vocational instruction. Proficiency is used here to define the mastery of skills and related knowledge necessary for entry into an occupation.

A sound approach to the development of program content requires procedures as described in chapter 2. The vocational curriculum must be based on the actual tasks of the job, so the content to be learned cannot be randomly selected by the student. For example, individualized instruction in liberal education is sometimes seen as the student being free to learn what he *wants to learn,* ignoring that which does not interest him. If this were applied to vocational education, a student in Auto Mechanics might elect to learn a little about the history of the automobile, some simple design concepts, and an overview of the engine and brake functions. This might be a commendable career exploration approach, but it would not meet the objectives or performance requirements for most vocational education programs. In brief, if the vocational technical curriculum is appropriately designed (as described in chapter 4) and if the student's objective is job entry skills, that student cannot realistically be given a "pick and choose" option of the various task components of that auto mechanics program.

Another factor differentiating vocational and general education instructional designs is a need to account for speed of performance. In general education, if the student can learn enough knowledge and skills to be able to pass the criterion test, the instruction would be considered a success regardless of the length of time required for the student to complete the test. However, in vocational education, if a student cannot perform a particular task within the time limits standard for entering that occupation, then the performance is not adequate. We make a distinction here between learning time and task performance time.

The vocational educator's level of control probably will be a factor in the decision to employ a fixed or variable-time model in the instructional system. For example, in a secondary school vocational program the school's instructional organization may specify that the longest time available for a vocational course will be two hours per day for 180 days. The shortest time might be one hour per day for 180 days. Given this constraint, a vocational educator would have to modify the instructional strategy. If proficiency in the occupation could be obtained in a shorter period of time than the system specifies, the instructor has the "custodial" responsibility for occupying that student's time, so he would have to "enrich" the program to occupy the period of time between when the student mastered the required tasks and the end of the scheduled course. If the program requirements were such that most of the students would take longer than the allocated time to master the occupation, then two options would be open to enrollees in the program. First they might choose to take some part of each task in the program and to learn as much as possible (fixed-time, fixed-content, variable-proficiency). They would do this in the expectation that they would have to pursue a postsecondary program and gain more competence in each task in order to become employable. Second, they might consider the possibility of taking fewer tasks, but learning them at the mastery level (fixed-time, variable-content, fixed-proficiency). They might then be able to enter the occupation at a lower skill level—a detailer instead of a draftsman, for example.

On the other hand, if the institution is strongly supportive of introducing an instructional system which permits a variable time, and therefore program length, for the mastery of tasks, then the instructional system could be developed accordingly. We consider this to be a desirable format and reiterate our support for a fixed-content, variable-time, fixed-proficiency model for individualized vocational instruction.

We have introduced the topic of control level of the vocational curriculum developer and innovator because it may be a critical factor in the success of attempts to individualize vocational instruction. One system of strategies for individualized vocational instruction might be well conceived but be doomed to failure without support from top administration in the institution, or because of other factors beyond the instructor's control. We suggest that local opportunities and constraints be kept firmly in mind. The following group of questions applies to decisions to be made in choosing a system of strategies.

Question 1.   What will be the content-time-proficiency model? See p. 93 for the variables.) We have already taken a position in favor of the fixed-content, variable-time, fixed-proficiency model as being most applicable for vocational and technical instruction. We have also said that if time is fixed, it is nearly axiomatic that content, proficiency, or both will be variable since people simply do not learn at the same rate.

Question 2. If a time-variable model is selected, what controls, if any, will be applied to student's self-pacing? Self-pacing refers to a student's having freedom to develop skills and knowledge at his own rate. This allows the more rapid learners to move ahead in their learning pattern and decreases the possibility of their becoming bored with the pace of their slower counterparts. Complete student self-pacing assumes that all students will be sufficiently motivated at all times to pursue their learning at their own best rate and that all students at all times have appropriate and sufficient self-instructing learning materials. In a program of twenty cosmetology students each one could be in a different place in the curriculum at a given time. This situation has considerable implications to the instructor in the scheduling of "live-work" customer projects and other instructional activities. Self-pacing of learning by the student requires roles for instructors to which they may not be accustomed. The instructor must now be able to perform as a diagnostician, tutor, counselor, and manager of individual learning in order to assist the student in the accomplishment of the objectives he has selected.

The student also may have new concepts and roles to which he must become accustomed. If he is to succeed in the self-paced model, he must learn to substitute self-discipline for the previously imposed discipline of having to "keep up with the class." He is required to be actively involved, not only in the learning process but also in his own evaluation and program management.

The concept of "degree of student self-pacing" is also addressed in chapter 7, but it is posed as a question here because it will influence the instructional strategy being developed.

Question 3. To what extent will individual learning skills, styles, and preferences be accommodated? There is informal evidence that there are wide differences among pupils in

1. Preferred directive approaches, such as (a) prefer reading directions only, (b) prefer reading directions with oral support, and (c) prefer oral directions only;
2. Social learning style, for example, (a) prefer to work alone, (b) prefer to work with someone, or (c) prefer to work in a "family" group;
3. How motivated, as (a) am self-motivated, (b) am peer-motivated, or (c) am supervisor-motivated;

4. Preferred reinforcement style, as (a) need immediate feedback on success of learning, or (b) am sustained by daily knowledge of results of learning;

5. Decision-making style, which could be (a) just give me the facts—I will make my own, (b) want to check with a friend, or, (c) need to check with just about everybody.

Up to the consideration of this question we have not addressed in any depth the matter of student differences in learning skill, style, and ability. Rather, we have focused on a student's access to vocational instruction programs made possible by his ability to enter the program regardless of the level of learning of other students enrolled in the program and to make progress on the *fixed-content* of the program at his own best rate. Fixed-content would still be a requirement of an occupational training program, but there probably are a variety of ways to arrive at the competency required. A decision on the number of ways to provide for learning each intermediate performance objective is required in planning instructional strategy.

Question 4.   How will the content of the vocational instruction program be sequenced? In discussing the derivation of intermediate performance objectives from task details in chapter 4, we implied that sequencing could be based on the order in which the detailed tasks occurred on the job. However, this is only a part of the solution in that learning techniques as well as task organization become a part of the instructional strategy. The procedure we will recommend should provide satisfactory results, but will have to be time tested by each vocational educator against actual student progress in order to verify results.

Question 5.   What will be the strategy for providing evaluation, stimuli, and reinforcement to the student in support of his learning? A student who pursues individualized learning for a week without confirmation that he has learned anything may be on the way to losing interest in the instructional objective. How long a time *should* be permitted for a student without confirmation, knowledge of results, or KOR, as it is sometimes identified (Smith 1971)? Should KOR simply tell the student he is right or wrong? Should KOR provide the right answers? Should KOR provide the correct response plus the reasons *why* the response is right? These and other KOR questions become a part of strategy planning.

Question 6.   How will mastery of the terminal performance objectives be defined and evaluated? Will there be an assessment of the *doing* skills as well as the knowing components of the objective? Will the student be permitted to use the pretest (see chapter 2) to "test out" of the instruction, and if successful, not be required to go further to obtain credit for that objective?

Question 7.   What will be the overall plan for organizing the individualized work for the student? Learning packages? Units? Other?

There is probably more than one "right" answer to some of these questions. For example, the decision about content-time-proficiency may well influence all of the other decisions. The point is that *all* of these questions and their relationships should be considered in arriving at the design specifications for the instructional system—or, the strategies of the system.

Specifying an Instructional System

Having clarified the variables that must be addressed in the specification of an instruction system, we will proceed with the specifications for *one* such system. We do wish to make clear however, that this system's specifications would not fit all vocational instruction situations; each vocational educator and administrator should look at his local structure in view of the questions asked previously. A sample system's specifications with rationale follows.

1) Content-Time-Proficiency.   *The instructional programs will be fixed-content, variable-time, fixed-proficiency.* We have previously discussed the rationale for a fixed-content model which specifies the required skills and knowledges of the occupation in which the learners will seek employment. The fixed-proficiency is the entry level skill and knowledge requirement for those going into that occupation. The *given* institution for which this specification is planned is a postsecondary technical institute with provision for shared-time secondary school students to begin training at the secondary school level and to continue the training full time at the postsecondary level, if required. Thus there are no serious fixed-time administrative constraints.

2) Student Self-Pacing.   *Students may accelerate their program learning time to whatever degree they deem practicable within personal health and stamina limitations. Standard (average) learning times for each instructional program and its components will be developed for regular, handicapped, and disadvantaged students. Learning times will be estimated first by instructors and then modified based upon experiences of students. Student progress will be monitored, and regular students performing at less than 75 percent of standard expected time will receive counseling about their progress.* These statements on student self-pacing do not allow the student total control over his learning rate. Complete student self-pacing assumes that all students will be sufficiently motivated to pursue their learning at their own best rate and that all of the learning materials will be equally self-motivating. *This assumption may not be* *true.* Because of personal problems or other reasons, a student's attention may be straying regularly from the learning materials he is using. It cannot be assumed that when the student and learning materials are brought together, learning will take place. Thus a system of monitoring student progress, aimed at guidance and encouragement, should be provided to help motivate the student when learning has slowed or stopped. Attendance also can become a factor in self-pacing. A student might "choose" to attend only one day a week as his preferred pace. However, it may not be fiscally feasible to keep that training position or "slot" open for one student for one-day-a-week attendance. Further, if there were no other skill reinforcement taking place, that level of attendance might not be sufficient to retain skill from week to week, and the learning materials would have to be adjusted to provide review. Of course, if there seemed to be a general lag in learning in one or more programs, the materials should be scrutinized closely for their validity and motivational value. Students may not be attending because the program is inadequate. Another factor requiring the monitoring of a student's self-pacing is the reliance that others may have placed on completion of the program by the student in the standard time. "Others" might include parents, veteran's administration, vocational rehabilitation agencies, etc. who could be understandably disturbed if the student falls substantially behind the standard time for program completion and they are not informed before the end of the standard program completion time. Monitoring student progress is discussed in detail in chapter 6, but it is mentioned here as a design consideration when planning overall instructional strategy.

3) Accommodation of Individual Learning Skills, Styles, and Preferences.   *One option for learning each intermediate task will be developed until all tasks are individualized. Thereafter, up to five additional options will be added to each intermediate task objective as time and resources permit. Extra options will consider: preferred directive approaches, preferred social learning style, differences in motivational stimuli, preferred reinforcement styles, and preferred decision-making styles.*

Experience indicates that if practical limits are not set during the development stage of individualized vocational and technical instruction, it is possible to take *one* intermediate performance objective and nearly go into infinity with the possible combinations of individual learning styles, skills, and preferences. Concurrently, the instructional-materials-support library required for that one intermediate objective could become nearly unmanageable. This might be desirable in demonstration situations, but it is simply not practical for a working vocational educator and curriculum developer trying to individualize an entire occupational training program. Since an occupational training program cannot really function at all as an individualized program until all of its objectives have the support of individualized materials, it is critical that at least *one* option for each intermediate objective be developed initially. Thereafter, the instruction can be perpetually enriched, based on experience and the development of new materials. The total of five learning options mentioned above does not have support of a research base and is not intended to be forever limiting. It is just being set in this example as a possible "second level" of learning options so that some balance can be kept throughout the vocational instruction program.

4) Sequencing of Content. *Sequencing of instruction, or the order in which learning experiences are presented to the student, will be based upon the logical order of task mastery in the occupation. Selected elementary tasks must be completed prior to undertaking more complex tasks which are dependent upon the mastery of the more elementary tasks. Only those experiences that are truly prerequisite to satisfactory completion of a learning guide will be identified.*

The need for sequencing, chaining, or ordering of instruction grows out of the fact that in order to acquire certain skills it may be necessary that other skills be learned first. However, if unnecessary prerequisities are listed, they may pose unnecessary restrictions upon the flexibility of the student. The student should be able to engage in instruction on any learning guide with a minimal amount of prerequisite task mastery. This allows students to engage in instruction on limited parts of the total program without being required to take substantial portions of the program. When a minimal number of prerequisites is combined with provisions for students to demonstrate prerequisite knowledge without actually taking part in instruction, a student is provided maximum flexibility.

The information provided by filling out the table of prerequisites for each guide described in chapter 3 is useful in the sequencing of instruction because it provides documentation on the prerequisites for every learning guide associated with the program. Sequencing also provides the instructor with information on learning guides that cluster together and form a larger instructional unit. When sequencing is planned correctly, it is possible to inform a student interested in mastering a task that he must first demonstrate mastery of prerequisite guides related to prerequisite tasks. For example, it would appear to make sense for a student to be taught how to use a screwdriver before he is asked to use a screwdriver to repair the machine; therefore, the learning guide related to how to use a screwdriver would be sequenced prior to the learning guide on how to repair the machine and the student would be expected to demonstrate mastery of using a screwdriver before undertaking the repair of the machine.

The sequencing of tasks and clusters can be presented graphically in a sequencing flow chart such as the one presented in figure 5-1. Figure 5-

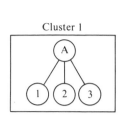

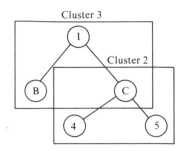

FIGURE 5—1

SAMPLE SEQUENCING FLOW CHART

l shows an instructional program with nine learning guides. These learning guides form three clusters. Learning guides 1, 2, and 3 are shown as prerequisites to learning guide A, and therefore are all contained in cluster 1. If a student wishes to develop competence in the task contained in learning guide A, he would be required to demonstrate mastery of all the tasks contained in learning guides 1, 2, 3, and A. Learning guides 4 and 5 are prerequisites to C and are contained in cluster 2. Learning guides B and C are prerequisites to learning guide I. Learning guides B, C, and I are contained in cluster 3. If the chart is made large enough and the name of the task contained in each learning guide is used as a guide label on the diagram, it is possible to examine the logic of the curriculum for the program by looking at the chart. Such a diagram is useful to the instructor in planning the program and to others who review the program to determine its logic. It also is useful to students as they select tasks and learning guides to study as they progress through the course.

The instructor should be careful to use sequencing only when it is absolutely necessary. One of the aims of individualized instruction is to allow a student to develop competency in a large number of unrelated tasks. If a student is required to know how to use a screwdriver to repair a machine but is not required to know how to use a saw, the student should not be asked to complete the learning guide on how to use a saw as a prerequisite to the learning guide on how to repair the device. Unnecessary prerequisites only restrict the flexibility which students have in designing individualized programs of instruction.

The vocational curriculum planner also must make decisions as to whether to include prerequisite skills in the required learning materials or to make reference to them as requirements for the beginnings of a new learning package. For example, the dicing of vegetables is a basic skill in institutional cooking that is necessary for preparation of many vegetable and meat dishes. Hence, "Dicing of Vegetables" could be included in the instructional content of the task to "Prepare Beef Stew," or it could be identified as a separate task for instruction purposes and be listed as a prerequisite for starting to learn "Prepare Beef Stew."

It is important in an individualized vocational instruction program that the clusters be kept as independent of each other as possible. If all clusters are required to be essentially sequential, curriculum planning is affected in two ways. First, the open access objective is severely limited because it is then difficult for a new student to enter "midstream." Second, it has an impact on the volume of instructional materials to be developed because in the early stages of instruction, nearly all students must be in the same location in the program, and all will need copies of both printed and other instructional materials for the same task at the same time.

5) Stimuli and Reinforcement to Support Learning. *The maximum standard time that a student will work on one unit of learning objectives without positive success confirmation will be ten hours. Active feedback to the learner will be provided in the following forms. Performance feedback will be provided using a performance checklist (psychomotor). Knowledge feedback will be provided using response to multiple-choice tests (cognitive). Attitude feedback will be provided using attitude checklists (affective).* There is little empirical or research evidence to support the ten hour time limit suggested above. This is the authors' best judgment *for given programs in a given institution,* based upon their experience.

Vocational curriculum readers also will experience difficulty in finding hard data on which to base the average length of time intermediate learning components should be designed to require. Expert opinion will vary (Bryan, Rigney, and Van Horn 1957; Goldbeck and Campbell 1962; Hake and Eriksen 1955; Hirsch 1952; Krumboltz and Bonawitz 1962; Rosenstock, Moore, and Smith 1965). Local students and conditions are so different from experimental models that locally observed experience will tend to have more validity than transferred experimental evidence. The ten hours specified above, for example, could represent less than two days for a postsecondary vocational student attending six hours per day. For a secondary school student attending two hours per day, it could be a learning period of a week or more. Reinforcement needs may vary among individual students, as suggested earlier, and they may vary markedly among groups of students enrolled in different program areas. Until more experimental data is collected that relates specifically to vocational instruction, the curriculum developer will have to rely on perceived judgment of the student clientele being served and seek immediate assessment of the effects of the reinforcement time decisions as the students start to work with the materials.

6) Evaluation of Proficiency of Students in Pretesting and Posttesting on the Terminal Performance Objective. *A criterion exam will be developed for each terminal objective that will encompass both the doing and knowing components of the objective. This criterion exam will serve as a pretest for the objective, which if passed at the specified level, will be recorded in the student's record as MTO (Mastery by Test-Out). If the student does not pass the pretest or elects to complete the specified learning activities for the task, he may elect to take a later test as evidence of mastery of the terminal performance objective. If passed, his record will show an M (Mastery) on that performance objective.*

Criterion exams are an essential part of any plan for individualized instruction. The development and administration of criterion exams is discussed in detail in chapter 6.

7) The Master Plan for Organizing the Work for the Student. *The basic learning component of the individualized system shall be the individualized learning package (ILP). The two major components of the learning package will be the Learning Guide and the Learning Materials.* The learning guide will include the following:

A. A *preface page* which will contain
   1. a statement of the task to be learned;
   2. a statement summarizing the broad purpose of the task which provides motivation for the learner by indicating how the task relates to other objectives in the package;
   3. an identification of the task for cataloging and retrieval;
   4. a listing of prerequisites for the task which must be mastered before the task can be undertaken.
B. A *learning contract* page which will include
   1. student data, including name and identification;
   2. length of contract in instructional hours;
   3. terminal performance objective of contract;
   4. listing of intermediate performance objectives;
   5. statement of agreement between learner and instructor, including completion time frame;
   6. signatures of student and instructor;
   7. identification of the task for filing and retrieval.
C. *Intermediate Performance Objective pages*—as many as required—which contain
   1. a statement of the intermediate performance objective;
   2. a listing and description of the *learning steps;*
   3. an identification of the *learning resources available;*
   4. an identification of the task, TPO, and IPO for cataloging and retrieval.

D. A *criterion exam* which
1. evaluates doing components of proficiency through instructor's checklist;
2. evaluates knowing components of proficiency through utilization of multiple-choice questions;
3. evaluates attitudinal components of proficiency through instructor observation checklists;
4. may be available as a pretest so that the learner may test-out of the task instruction, if already competent.

Each of the above four components of the learning guide is illustrated in Appendix 4.

The learning materials in the learning package may include any or all of the following:

1. *Print Materials* in all forms.
2. *Moving Visual and Audio-Visual Media* including film, television, and videotape.
3. *Static Visual Media* such as slide transparencies and photographs.
4. *Audio Media* such as tape recordings, radio, disc recordings.
5. *Situational Information* such as in drama, role playing, educational games, and case studies.
6. *Computers* including computer-assisted instruction and computer-managed instruction.
7. *Human Resources* including teachers, peers, and resource persons from various occupations.
8. *Models, simulators.*

Thus we have proceeded through the specification of an individualized instructional system addressing these critical topics:

1. A content-time-proficiency model,
2. Level of student self-pacing,
3. Accommodation of individual learning skills, styles, and preferences,
4. Sequencing of content,
5. Stimuli and reinforcement to support learning,
6. Procedures for evaluation of student performance,
7. A master plan for organization of the learning for the student.

The next significant step in becoming operational with an individualized instruction system is to construct the two components of the learning package—the learning guide and the learning materials.

Constructing the
Learning Guide

Appendix 4 contains a working model of an instructional learning guide to which frequent references will be made in this section. The task, "Set Up and Operate the Chief 20 Press," is one of 240 tasks identified in a curriculum structure judged as necessary for an instructional program in "graphic communications." The decision to include graphic communications as a part of the occupational curriculum in this institution was made on the basis of occupational data and student interest information as described in chapter 2. The tasks to be included in the instruction were specified by an instructional advisory committee made up of persons from the industry, and the task detailing was accomplished according to procedures supplied in chapter 4.

This learning guide begins on its first page by naming the task and providing a statement of its purpose. The purpose statement serves a motivational function in that it describes how this particular learning guide complements the other 239 required for mastery of all tasks required for entry into the occupation. The first page also contains a numerical identification of the learning guide so it can be identified for student record purposes and for classification purposes for storage and retrieval in the learning resource center (LRC). The LRC can be defined most accurately by saying that it functions as a technical branch library for specified program areas. It usually will have spaces for learners to utilize learning materials and storage and checkout accommodations. The LRC is discussed in chapter 7 as a part of the management structure of an individualized instruction system. The prerequisites for the learning guide are listed in the right-hand box of the identification numerals. This means that the student will have to check his own progress record to see if he has completed all of the prerequisites for this guide before proceeding further. In this instance the prerequisites are Task 304, "Metal Master Negatives," 904, "Shop Safety," 902, "History of Graphics," and 727, "Paper and Inks."

Page 2 of the learning guide, the "learning contract," usually remains blank, and supplementary copies of the page are provided in the learning package so that the contracts can be written between learner and instructor and still retain the learning guide for the use by other learners. Time is one of the factors in the agreement. This time represents learning time, rather than the industry time standard for operation of the Chief 20. The instructor, initially from his experience and later from the experience of students, develops a standard estimated time for completion of the learning guide.

The time factor inclusion has several values. First, it helps the student develop a sense of the importance of time in production graphics work. This is an affective performance objective in that a successful worker in the graphics industry must have an attitude favorable to the effective use of time on machines. The time factor also assists the instructor in the management of the learning experiences of the students for whom he is responsible. If he knows how many students are "ready" for instruction on the Chief 20 and the standard time for instruction, he can make tentative scheduling commitments for the machine, with allowances for overages and acceleration. Standard time estimates also provide information to the learner in the form of a low pressure comparison of how well he is achieving compared to others who are receiving similar training. If the student is consistently taking longer than the standard time for each program task being completed, he may have to plan for a longer than standard time for total completion of the program. Conversely, a student that is consistently ahead of standard time may expect to complete early and enter wage-earning employment in the labor market ahead of his original expectancy.

The "student data" section of the contract page identifies the student's name and social security number. The social security number is a convenient numerical code that is useful if the data is to be stored and analyzed with a computer.

The reader may wish to note that the "basics" of a terminal performance objective have been included: the "givens" (metal master, clean machine, paper); the "performance" (print 500 sheets of 11″ x 17″ stock on the Chief 20 offset machine); and the "standard" (80 percent of 500 sheets to be of salable quality, and the project completed within one hour).

The opportunity to test-out of the package is not described on the contract sheet. This information is included in another learning package that is designed to teach the student the learning system in which he is functioning. Some students enrolled in postsecondary vocational and technical programs may have acquired sufficient skills while in secondary school or through other experiences to pass the criterion exam and would not be required to complete this learning contract. Adults who are in the vocational program may have had sufficient on-the-job experience to be able to run some machines and may also test-out of any performance objective in which they are already qualified.

Number 2a on the learning contract page identifies the intermediate performance objectives around which the learning materials are planned. IPOs, as described in chapter 4, are derived from combining task details from the task analysis into logical, sequential steps. The first intermediate performance objective (doing, psychomotor) is "Given an offset metal master which has been developed with an image and a clean Chief 20 offset machine, prepare the Chief 20 machine for operation." The task details from which this IPO was written are:

1. Lower the pile Board
2. Load the feeder
3, Raise the pile board
4. Set the tail guides
5. Set the sheet separators
6. Adjust feeder suckers
7. Adjust blast adjustors
8. Place the pile height governor in position
9. Adjust sheet caliper
10. Adjust speed wheels
11. Adjust sheet forwarding wheels
12. Place guide ball holders
13. Adjust collars of holddown bands
14. Set side guides
15. Set front guides
16. Set ink form rollers
17. Set distribution rollers
18. Set ink ductor roller
19. Check auxiliary vibrator
20. Adjust ink fountain control
21. Adjust washup device
22. Adjust vibrator stroke adjustment
23. Set lower form dampener roller
24. Set upper form dampener roller
25. Set water ductor roller
26. Prepare new blanket
27. Install blanket on cylinder
28. Pack the blanket
29. Adjust blanket tension
30. Adjust plate for register
31. Install plate on cylinder
32. Set plate to blanket pressure
33. Parallel the impression and blanket cylinders
34. Adjust for stock thickness
35. Set sheet counter
36. Adjust delivery pile
37. Set delivery joggers
38. Set delivery strippers

Intermediate Performance Objectives 2 and 3 were prepared from similar combinations of task details taken from the analysis of the task, "Set Up and Operate the Chief 20 Press."

Knowing (cognitive) objectives 2 and 3 are derived from the prerequisites, as are the knowing (affective) objectives 4 and 5.

Page 236 restates Intermediate Performance Objective 1 and identifies the learning steps and learning resources by which the learning is to be accomplished. How the vocational curriculum developer attempts to approach the development of learning steps and learning resources will depend on his position and objectives. If development time is not a problem and if no other instructional resources are available, he should immediately begin a more detailed analysis of the task details, and, perhaps more scientific observation of the performance of a skilled worker on the machine. Thus he should begin to assemble this type of description:

Task Detail

1. Lowers the pile board

Subdetail

    a. Lift the feeder pile throw-off pawl handle, and

    b. Turn the feeder pile handle counterclockwise until the
       feeder platform is all the way down against its stops.

After subdetailing all of the intermediate tasks, the vocational curriculum developer must then come to grips with how these hand (psychomotor) processes can be conveyed to the individual learner. Here again the specific circumstances of the learning situation must be considered. If the curriculum developer is committed to a totally "self-instruct" package, all materials must be totally descriptive of the process. However, if the developer is also a vocation instructor, he may want to develop materials which assume that the instructor remains active in the learning process.

Two immediate questions that must be faced at this point are: (1) What shall be the "directive" approach, that is, by what stimuli shall the learner be directed or led through the learning steps and learning resources? (2) What shall be the social learning style, i.e., do the directors assume that the learner will work alone? with someone? with several other learners?

The "directives" or learning steps as provided in the sample learning guide, p. 234, may be in print form (as illustrated); or audio (such as a cassette tape), or audio-visual (video cassette). Usually, in the first development of an individualized program, much of the directive material will be in print form simply because of the economics of time and money. This might not be the case if there was a special problem such as a program provided for persons who were disadvantaged by being nonreaders. Audio directives might then be a requirement for the learning guide.

Ideally, there might be several social learning styles from which the learner might choose. However, in the development of this "first" learning guide a decision must be made as to whether the directives or learning steps will require the learner to proceed alone or in the company of one or more other learners. Several factors, if known, might influence the decision. First, if the learners' preferences are known, their preferred learning style could be considered. Second, in some occupations, such as carpentry, the occupation lends itself to working in teams. Third, the availability of space and equipment compared to a given number of learners might influence the decision. In the learning guide illustrated, the directives are almost entirely designed for a student to work alone.

After deciding on the method to be used in providing the directives to the learner, consideration must be given by the vocational curriculum developer to learning resources—hardware and software—to be developed and/or selected. Hardware is a term used to describe the equipment, such as a film projector, being used. Software means the content of the educational material being presented and its organization.

Instructional Technology— Hardware and Software

Any discussion of instructional media, equipment, procedures, and devices introduces some problems of definition. "Educational technology," according to Michael Eraut of the University of Sussex, is the broadest of the family of terms, encompassing the use of machines in education, a technology of instruction, management of instruction, and curriculum development (Eraut 1971). Dragoljub Najman sees educational technology as "providing general support to the teachers" whereas instructional technology "carries a definite part of the curriculum to the student at regular intervals; it is the use of machines, that is media and services, to transfer knowledge" (Najman 1971).

For purposes of this book, we adopt the second of two definitions of instructional technology provided by the *Commission on Instructional Technology,* which stated

> Instructional technology goes beyond any particular medium or device. In this sense instructional technology is more than the sum of its parts. It is a systematic way of designing, carrying out, and evaluating the total process of learning and teaching in terms of specific objectives, based on research in human learning and communication and employing a combination of human and non-human resources to bring about effective instruction (Najman 1973).

Thus, in an individualized instructional system we do not see the technology—the hardware and the software—as being something apart from the curriculum mainstream. We see it as an integral part of both the educational process and educational content. While this chapter will focus more on mechanistic ways of delivering instructional content to willing learners, we wish to continue emphasis on the need for interaction of those mechanics with the learner and the instructor in the learning process.

The introduction of educationally designed hardware and software into the instructional system does not make the job of the instructor easier, but it may bring changes. Instructors increasingly may be required to become program developers, diagnosticians, and managers of the learning process. The change from a traditional system to a technology-oriented system often does not become a fact overnight. Students, as well as instructors, need time to learn to work in the new system. If individualized instruction, as well as additional technology is being introduced, the instructor may be required to teach for a time partially in the traditional style and partially in an individualized learning style with media support. This interim period will very likely involve *more* work than was needed under the traditional system.

When curriculum change is planned, instructors are too often left out of the planning process and do not receive adequate training in the new system or in the new media. This may result in some resistance to the effective utilization of the newer instructional technology. As Beckworth (1971) said, "The reason so little instructional technology is used in education today is that its visible faults always end up being compared with the teacher's visible virtues." If the instructor does not perceive new materials or hardware to be of more value than the trouble to use them, the new technology is not apt to become a part of the regular instructional process.

The 1960s will be remembered by educators and media manufacturers as a boom and bust period for educational hardware. Hardware technology, often transplanted from other fields, raced ahead of professional capabilities to develop viable, effective programs of education to utilize the new media. Fanned by massive inputs of federal funds, the *visions* of media persons, new publishers, new hardware manufacturers, and new technologists turned into disastrous mirages. The three "Rs" of recrimination, retrenchment, and reorganization came later after the multi-million dollar mistake, and along with it a new caution.

In looking at the broad field of instructional technology, it is fair to say that there is almost unlimited hardware capability today which can be exploited by vocational curriculum planners *if* the benefit perceived by the decision makers is great enough, the numbers of benefited students large enough, and the cost reasonable enough.

The underlying problem is one of software. In this book the substance of the intermediate learning objectives, programmed or organized to enter the mind and motor systems of the learner and affect his behavior in a specified manner, are the content software.

The development of quality software has proceeded very slowly. After being "burned" on overinvestment in hardware production, publishers and other business firms have proceeded very cautiously in their attempts to move into the needed area of software development. This is understandable because if the software is not extremely high-priced, a substantial sales volume is necessary for a write-off of the costs of software development. This has tended to affect the development of individualized instructional materials for vocational and technical instruction adversely since many of the programs are limited in numbers on a nationwide basis. For example, an individualized instruction software program in English might have a potential market in thousands of high schools across the country and could absorb a high development cost. On the other hand, an individualized instruction program for the training of prosthetics technicians might also have a high cost but may have a potential sales market of only five instructional programs across the country.

Due to the high cost of program software development, it also has been difficult for educational institutions, public and private, to generate extensive development programs. Nevertheless, this is where a considerable amount of the current effort in software development is being undertaken. James DuMolin (1970) has called this a "cottage industry" approach in which school systems, or even separate schools within a system, try to meet their own needs. Molin sees this method as a "major" deterrent to achieving quality in software development. The difficulties are that people in these local situations often do not have sufficient time, money; or expertise to produce high quality software. The advantage of the approach is that the software developed frequently receives immediate testing and exposure in a real-life educational situation.

There seems to be little doubt that effective use of instructional hardware is going to be highly dependent on software development in the future. There appears to be a real need for a concerted research effort on the ways and means for development on a larger scale than is currently available. The cruciality of need in vocational and technical software may be even greater than in the general education sector since the attractive large markets are generally missing.

Given agreement on the need for individualized instruction and an apparent need for special software and hardware to support this method of instruction the question of *which* software and *which* hardware becomes very real.

The Centre for Educational Research and Innovation (1970) defined eight forms of media as being particularly useful in the individualization of learning.

These are, as listed earlier, print in all forms, moving visual and audiovisual media, static visual media, sound media, situational information, information from physical objects, computers, and human resources.

PRINT MATERIALS

Textbooks may have lost some of their primacy as the *sole* data source in many educational programs, but they still remain a major educational force, particularly as references. The most recent revolution in textbook technology was the post World War II trend toward inexpensive paperback books. This trend was advantageous to individualized instruction because it facilitated production of small books, covering only a single unit. Some such books produced by manufacturers of technical machines and equipment resemble a series of individual instruction sheets bound in sequence. These manufacturer's manuals are often well illustrated and produced by excellent technical writers employed or contracted by the manufacturer. They can be of real assistance to the development of viable individualized instructional learning guides by vocational educators with limited time and resources. The developer of the learning guide on "Set Up and Operate the Chief 20 Press" in Appendix 4 was fortunate to locate the *ATF Chief 20 Instruction Manual,* published by American Type Founders (1966). The manual is divided into four chapters: (1) Description and Functions, (2) Preparing the Press, (3) Operation of the Press, (4) Lubrication and Maintenance. An instructor can save a great deal of development time by utilizing such excellent printed material.

For this learning guide, the developer was also able to identify a practical textbook, *Lessons in Printing* (Bureau of Education 1972). This textbook was produced and published by the International Typographers Union for the purposes of training apprentices in their organization.

All print materials identified as resources through which the learning steps can be accomplished should be evaluated rigorously, utilizing the following criteria:

Content	Does it closely follow the requirements of the intermediate tasks? What percent of the total intermediate tasks can be covered with this resource? Are there serious omissions, outdated information, or overemphasis on minor aspects?
Level	Is the vocabulary written at a difficulty level similar to other print materials in that field? Is the style readable?
Format	Are there sufficient and clear illustrations? Is the binding, type, and paper appropriate for the intended usage?
Authorship	Is the author a recognized authority? Has the publisher developed a sound reputation through previous publications?
Treatment	Is there unbiased presentation on matters regarding labor, government, minorities, and controversial issues?

Sometimes the printed material obtained is not sufficiently inclusive to cover all of the tasks to be learned and must be supplemented with additional print material authored by the vocational instructor and curriculum developer. This additional material is usually referred to as "information sheets" (Rose 1966; Fryklund 1970). These information sheets usually have several basic components:

1. *A title.* The title is usually taken directly from the intermediate learning objective or from the task analysis.
2. *Introduction.* A brief summary of the content and how it will be used makes up the introduction.
3. *The body.* The body represents the content, simply presented.
4. *References.* Typically, the information sheet has been greatly condensed. Therefore, references should be provided so that the student can explore the topic in more depth, if needed.

It is important that the information sheets deal with material not covered elsewhere and that they be organized and presented in an effective manner.

Job sheets are confused sometimes with information sheets. A job sheet is more inclusive than an information sheet in that it usually includes a list of general directions on how to do each task (Rose 1966; Fryklund 1970). The job sheet, as we describe it, would include the information sheet plus the learning guide in a generalized way. The information sheet is more pertinent to the system being described in this book, and we mention the job sheet only to help the reader avoid confusion in his other readings.

VISUAL MEDIA

Gropper and Glasgow (1971) have provided a useful classification of visual inputs into the learning process. They identify these inputs as being *realistic, reproduced,* and *fabricated.* Examples of this classification system are (1) realistic—a wrench, (2) reproduced—a photograph of a wrench, (3) fabricated—a line drawing of a wrench.

Vocational and technical education has a long history of emphasizing the *real* tools of the trade with instruction by the master craftsman who is highly competent with these tools. The tools and equipment used in the vocational education shops and laboratories will often be the same as the equipment found in industry, hospitals, and businesses. In the example of the Chief 20 press, the instruction planner should not overlook the possibility of the individualized instruction being provided by the expert Chief 20 instructor-operator *demonstrating* the operation of the machine to the student. Demonstration is usually thought of as being a group instruction technique. However, if the instructor is able to save time by having the students learn cognitive information from learning packages, he may be able to use that time for individual help and demonstration for some of the psychomotor skills. A major advantage of the individualized demonstration method is that the student can usually try the process himself immediately and receive corrective feedback from the instructor. The demonstration, like all teaching, requires careful planning. If the instructor has to leave the process to get a tool or piece of equipment or fumbles through the demonstration, it will be a very poor learning experience. It is also highly essential that *every* safety practive be followed strictly by the instructor-demonstrator.

There are two major disadvantages to the use of demonstration in individualized instruction. The first disadvantage is that it is difficult to be consistently effective in giving the demonstration. There may be more than one "correct" way to handle the machine, and if a student sees more than one demonstration, he may become confused. Furthermore, under the individualized system students will be "ready" for the demonstration at different times, and if the number of machines under the instructor's responsibility is large, he may become inundated with multiple demonstrations. If students are ready for demonstrations and they cannot be given, it is wasteful of the student's time as well as that of the instructor. This problem will tend to lead the instructor toward considering a *reproduced* visual input.

Reproduced visual input is a direct image of the "real thing." It may take a number of formats, including moving visual and audio-visual media (film, television, videotape) and static visual media (slide transparencies, photographs). These are usually supported by print or sound media (tape recordings, radio, recording discs, recording belts).

For the practicing vocational educator who is also developing individualized curriculum, and who is seeking learning resources to support that curriculum, time and financial considerations may dictate a move toward a reproduced visual input that is most available and at lowest cost. Such a move may not be as bad as it might intially seem, in that studies show students do learn from nearly all forms of visual media, and the advantages of one type of media over another are usually not clear-cut (Davies 1971). Butler (1972) advises, "The best procedure is usually to select the least elaborate and least costly medium that apparently will enable the learner to acquire the desired capability." Some studies have found that crude but simple visuals were more effective in terms of learning than a polished color version of the same film costing ten times as much (Davies 1971).

If the curriculum developer has the resources to generate visuals of all types (i.e., photographs, slides, 8mm and 16mm motion film, videographic cassettes, etc.), examination of the task details and intermediate learning objectives may provide some clues to the selection of the most appropriate media. Some of these clues are:

1. *Color*—In the development of learning guides for electronics, nursing assistant, or cosmetology, color might be very important and should be identified as essential in the resource specifications. However, research by Kanner (1968) indicated that the lack of color could be overcome with appropriate verbal cues.

2. *Motion*—If the psychomotor process being taught requires a particular style or critical approach to the skill activity, a motion visual might be the most feasible way to teach the process. Wendt and Butts (1962) have documented the general effectiveness of using 8mm film loops, shown repeatedly, for instructing in physical skills. The commentary in the motion film is very important, as demonstrated by Laner (1955) and Vernon (1952). The Vernon study concluded that it may be more effective to show still pictures and diagrams with a good commentary than to show film with an inferior one.

3. *Location of Learning*—Location of learning refers to the shop, laboratory, classroom, learning resource center, etc. where the learning is expected to take place. If the learning process requires that the visual media be utilized beside a lathe in a machine shop, the conditions may dictate that a certain type of hardware be used, thus limiting the selection of media.

4. *Flexibility*—A person who is developing individualized vocational instruction around specified intermediate learning objectives may experience difficulty in finding prepared materials that are exactly "on target" in providing the learning resources necessary to meet those objectives. Thus, one criteria to be used in the selection is, "Does the visual material (with accompanying sound) lend itself to being modified by the instructor to meet objectives of *that* instruction program? In addition, our experience indicates that if it is possible for the instructor to inject more of himself into the materials he will tend to consider their usage more favorably.

5. *Concepts and Principles*—Research has demonstrated that, for the most part, films and television are the optimal media for teaching concepts and principles, as well as for reaching affective objectives (Davies 1971).

As defined previously, reproduced visual input transposes the real situation into some form of direct image for instructional purposes. One might think that this process would be the best possible usage of media for instruction since it deals with a total image of the "real thing." Research in general, however, tends to support the advantages of *fabricated visual media* over reproduced images as having the most instruction advantages.

Fabricated visuals are those visuals which are not reproduced as a direct image of actual equipment or product being taught, but are simulations of the originals. They can be line drawings, sketches, charts, graphs, computer and electrocardiogram readouts, diagrams, etc. Studies have indicated that animation can materially aid learning by directing learner attention to relevant cues (Lumsdaine, Sulzer, Kopstein 1961). Dwyer (1967) compared oral presentations involving simple line drawings, detailed shaded drawings, realistic photographs, and oral presentations containing no visual aids at all. He found that simple line drawings were optimal for understanding the location, structure, and position of parts and for facilitating transfer of the learning to the ability to identify and locate parts on a three-dimensional model. Similarly, the use of an animated "implosion" technique which showed component parts of a unit "jumping" into their place in proper sequence was shown to be particularly effective for teaching assembly-disassembly skills (Sheffield, Margolius, and Hoehn 1961). The main advantage of the fabricated visual over the direct visual image seems to be the ability to separate out the irrelevant detail which appears on photographs and other direct images, and which may tend to confuse and distract the learner. "Keep it simple," seems to be the best advice. Lumsdaine (1958) found that preparation of elaborate fabricated visuals which increased the cost by tenfold did not increase the instructional effectiveness.

Reproduced and fabricated visual media are somewhat "hardware independent" in that both can be utilized with much of the same equipment. For example, drawings which become animated with motion picture equipment can be shown on the same type of film and equipment as motion pictures of the realistic equipment. Therefore, we will introduce a limited discussion of visual and sound hardware, with some guidelines for evaluating its effectiveness.

Film Projectors. 16mm, 8mm, and Super 8mm are the most common film formats used in education. Because of its large image area, size, expense, and operational complexity, the 16mm film has found more utilization with broader topics and larger student audiences. Operating skills required for the 16mm projector have been reduced by automatic threading devices. Because of the software (film content) available on 16mm film, which is not found on other media, most vocational education programs will want to have one or more of these machines available. For individualized instruction there is much more single topic software available on the 8mm and Super 8mm film than on 16mm film. Single topic software refers to film content directed to a specific learning objective, such as "Aligning a Car Wheel." Where an institution is producing single topic films for its individualized instructional program, it should focus on developing the films around each intermediate performance objective. The Super 8mm has smaller and differently positioned sprocket holes along one side, thus providing a larger image area than the 8mm films. These films, combined with improved projectors which now utilize rear screen projection and permit stopping the action and holding for more intensive study, appear to be growing in usage in vocational individualized instruction programs. They can also be readily used on audio-visual carts located in the shop or laboratory, with ear phones if required. They are not restricted to study carrell applications. Study carrells are individual student desks built up on three sides for sight and sound screening, in which individual students may work with all types of learning materials. They are often placed in libraries or learning resource centers. However, it is practical to have a few carrels placed in the shop or laboratory. This enables a student who is working on a learning project in the shop to stop and review his related knowledge individually if progress on the project has become blocked because he has forgotten a vital prerequisite.

Most of the 8mm and Super 8mm films designed for individualized instruction today are being produced in cassett containers. Since they can be inserted, rewound, and removed from the hardware with minimum opportunity for damage to the film, cassettes facilitate individual student ability to operate the necessary equipment without instructor or instructor aide assistance. Manufacturers of the 8mm and Super 8mm films have devised effective means to combine sound with the film which greatly enhances the instructional capabilities.

The advantages of all types of films for education are those described previously for instructional needs where color and motion are a requirement. The disadvantages are three-fold; these are cost, availability, and lack of flexibility. Production and development of 8mm films is expensive; this has tended to discourage that production where an institution is producing materials primarily for its own usage. Similarly, commercial firms have tended to concentrate their efforts in those program areas where volume sales might exist, omitting many less populous but important vocational instruction programs. The films lack flexibility to the extent that it is not possible for the typical vocational instructor to make changes in either the visual or sound mechanism. Thus, material irrelevant to the individual instructor's learning objectives cannot be omitted, and special oral sound changes which might make the material more effective locally cannot be inserted.

Videotape Players. In our opinion, closed circuit television, as originally conceived, was classroom oriented and did not have a great deal of applicability to individualized vocational instruction. However, some systems have been developed where an instructor (or student) can call in to a central library where the video tapes are stored and request that a certain tape be placed on the machine and transmitted via the closed circuit to the individual television receiver. This has an advantage over the more typical closed circuit system but still has some severe disadvantages. The time delay factor in getting the tape set up, the necessity for staff to be available continuously for that purpose, and the susceptibility of the tapes to damage are difficulties working against that system.

The advent of the colored video cassette tape has been a real breakthrough in the use of television in individualized instruction. These video tapes have the advantage of the combination of action, sound, and color along with simplification of both production and use of the tapes by students. As video cassette players become more available in the consumer market, the potential for individualized vocational training in the home also will increase tremendously.

Criteria for the evaluation of film and videotape instructional materials could include:

Content	Does it follow the requirements of the intermediate tasks? What percent of the total intermediate tasks can be covered with this resource? Are there omissions or outdated information?
Level	Is the material appropriate for the age level of the viewers? Is there sufficient action? Is the pacing and sequencing appropriate?
Presentation	Is the material more effective for instruction than demonstrating, reading, discussing, or experimenting?
Authorship	Are the producer and editor qualified?
Technical Quality	Are images sharp? Is the color natural? Is sound intelligible and realistic? Is continuity natural and understandable? Are there conflicts of music and speech? Are there difficulties in following image and/or sound? Is there synchronization of image and sound?

Overhead Projectors, Slide Projectors, Opaque Projectors, Filmstrip Projectors, and Other Static Visual Media. The software for this type of equipment is usually combined with sound media such as tape recordings or disc recordings. The overhead projector is designed to project transparent images onto a screen or suitable wall surface. The slide projector and filmstrip projector will transmit either pictures or fabricated designs as recorded by a camera onto a screen or wall. The opaque projector will "mirror" a direct image such as a picture in a magazine or an instructor's diagram onto a screen or wall. The overhead and opaque projectors, by design, are intended for group work. They take materials of natural size and "blow them up" on a screen so that an entire group can see them at one time. The *material* developed for presentation on these machines to a group has value later in individualized instruction for review by a learner who did not understand the group presentation or who was absent on that day, but the machines would not be required for that review.

Filmstrips or 2x2 slides developed from 35mm film also can be enlarged and projected for group instruction. Since slides and film strips are too small to be used directly by individual learners, projection equipment must be available for their use in carrels and/or shops and laboratories.

The advantages of all static visual media are twofold: low cost and relative simplicity. Neither the purchase nor the development of instructional materials and equipment for this type of instructional technology is as expensive as the motion visual media described earlier. Most instructors can learn easily the technical skill required for taking 35mm slides with the newer automatic light adjustment cameras, and commercial development and mounting of slides is available to nearly everyone. In many applications of the learning process, slides and filmstrips have been found to be as effective as motion film and television (Hoban 1960). When using 35mm slides, it is relatively easy to combine some "local" slides with commercially prepared materials to add authenticity. Instructor-prepared audio-cassette tapes also can be added if the prepared material is not appropriate for the instructor's intermediate learning objectives. One manufacturer has capitalized on the simplicity of the 35mm slide by developing a "sound-on-slide" projector. This projector permits the recording of an instructional message on a magnetic field "around" each slide. The "sound-slides" advance with the press of a button in the same manner as the conventional slide projector, except that as each slide is projected, the instructional message is broadcast either through a small speaker or earphones. By depressing a separate button, the learner can obtain a "replay" of the instructional message for that slide as often as he considers it necessary. It is also quite simple to "back up" to previous slides, if the learner so requires. The slides can be purchased with a "canned" prerecorded instructional message, or the instructor can record his own message. The instructor or a school audio-visual specialist can also take the picture and then record the instructional message. If a message is not deemed to be effective or if a picture is not effective, both can be replaced inexpensively.

The disadvantages of the static visual media are also twofold. First, still visuals are inadequate where the style of the psychomotor action required demands that either a demonstration or a motion visual be utilized. Second, the "advantage" of low cost and simplicity has resulted in the development of a large volume of materials of unproven quality both commercially and in local institutions. Hence, the materials selection or development process may be even more important than for other media because the media are being *used* more. Criteria for the evaluation of static visual media and their related audio materials could include:

Content	Does it focus on the requirements of the intermediate tasks?
Level	Is the spoken vocabulary commensurate with the level of learners for the occupation?
Format	Is the key idea dominant? Is the pictorial material technically correct?
Technical Quality	Are the sounds, voices, and instruments adequately differentiated and clearly understandable? Is sufficient action implicit in the content and is the continuity understandable? Is the synchronization of sound and image complete, if required?

SIMULATION EQUIPMENT

Simulation equipment for instruction represents the construction of special instructional equipment, the operation of which will be almost like "the real thing." One of the first and still well-known simulators was the Link Instrument Trainer for the training of aircraft pilots. In this trainer unit, the pilot-learner had the same instrumentation as the real aircraft, and flying conditions were duplicated so effectively that the flying sensation was quite real. Newer, more sophisticated simulators for the upgrading of commercial airline pilots are now in regular usage. This is the only way the pilots can "practice" landing with two engines not working or in a violent windstorm, without undue hazard to life and a multi-million dollar airplane.

Vocational education has moved more slowly into the simulator concept of instruction since vocational educators have long held that experience on the "real thing," the tools and machines of the occupation itself, was superior to any simulation that could be derived. This stalwart view of vocational education is still strong, but there are certain types of instructional situations where the first phases of instruction can be provided more effectively, more safely, and more economically in simulated learning situations. The use of an instructional truck driving simulator for the early part of the training of a truck driver is probably one of the best illustrations of this rationale encouraging the use of a simulator for the following reasons:

1. The instructional equipment (truck and tractor) is inherently dangerous in the hands of the trainee until he has developed the knowledge and skill to adjust quickly to emergency situations.
2. The instructional equipment (truck and trailer) is too expensive ($50,000 plus high fuel cost) to be used for the entire training process.
3. The instructional equipment (truck and trailer) has a mechanism (16 position shift) that is so complex it must be learned separately before a totally integrated driving performance is required.
4. A particular learning situation does not occur frequently enough in normal operation to acquire a sufficient degree of skill (e.g., air brake failure in truck driving).

Sometimes simulation is used for only one of the above reasons, but the rationale is still compelling. For example, computer simulators became popular early because of the high cost of the first and second generation models. More recently mini-computers are bringing the cost down, so hands on experience can be obtained on actual computers at lower cost.

Circuitry in television sets and other electronic instruments is often concealed, so simulated circuits are often used for instruction.

Similarly, it is difficult to assemble equipment showing all of the functions of hydraulics within a reasonable space, so simulators which combine all of the functions into one piece of instructional equipment are frequently used.

When it appears that a proposed vocational instruction program may meet one of the four conditions described previously, a careful analysis should be made of the program being planned.

1. What part of the instruction involves critical skills that are difficult to teach on standard instructional equipment?
2. What is the potential difference in costs between real equipment and a simulator?
3. Can simulation be programmed as a part of the total instruction?

4. Can the degree of positive transfer from the simulation training be measured?
5. What is the possibility of improper skills being learned and practiced?

EDUCATIONAL COMPUTER TECHNOLOGY

Computers are often regarded as the glamour line of educational technology. Vocational educators have been interested in three instructional aspects of computers. First is the electronic data processing (EDP) career. This can range from keypunch operator through console operator, programmer to systems analyst. Second, they have been concerned about training of persons in electronics for the construction and repair of the computers as machines. Finally, the most extensive use of computers in vocational instruction is for related training. Related training refers to learning experiences that are not the immediate job experiences, but are supportive of these experiences. Computers touch almost *all* occupations today in some way, and it is important that most students of vocational education have an opportunity in their training program for experience with them.

Computers may also be used in the management of instruction, sometimes referred to as CMI. Some of the functions performed by the computer in CMI can include scoring and recording student test scores, keeping track of progress of students on individualized learning materials, and creating a prognosis of individual student progress based on data about the student and his progress in the instructional program. Cost of instruction data also can be built into this system, providing management data about the cost-effectiveness of various methodologies of instruction.

When utilizing computers for career training, the curriculum development process is not unlike that used with other occupational training. The job description, task analysis, and development of objectives sequence should be followed in arriving at a valid instructional program for "hands on" training. The same format is essentially true when the students are being trained in the construction and repair of computers as machines.

It is in the selection of computer experiences as related training for learning guides that more vivid differences appear. Much of this type of training falls under the category usually referred to as computer-assisted instruction (CAI), which is an outgrowth or extension of programmed instruction. There are six commonly identified instructional modes for using the computer to assist instruction: drill, tutorial, simulation and gaming, retrieval and reorganization of information, problem solving with computation and display tools, and artistic design and composition.

The early attempts to assist vocational instruction with computers were largely confined to problem solving for technical mathematics and physics and to simulated business games for distributive education. Program software was developed earlier in these occupations because there was potential volume of usage in general education at the secondary school level, and in colleges. Software for more specialized vocational instruction has been slower in development, but progress is being made, and most of the following applications are available to vocational educators who keep up with their occupational field.

Accounting.   It has become increasingly necessary for the accountant to be conversant and knowledgeable about data processing functions. Software has been developed in the areas of accounts receivable, accounts payable, general ledger, cost accounting, financial statement analysis, payroll, taxes, and inventory control.

Agri-Business.   The student should be familiar with computer-related applications of inventory control, credit verification, accounts receivable, grain marketing, soil testing, animal feed formulation, fertilizer formulation, and ordering. The student should also obtain skill in using the computer to calculate transportation costs, D.H.I.A. (herd testing), and A-I (artificial insemination).

Architectural and Mechanical Drafting.   Students learn how to use the computer for the following calculations and projections: structural calculations, specifications writing programs, mechanical and electrical system programs, construction cost estimating, strength of materials, engineering parts explosion (bill of materials processing), construction scheduling (PERT). Computer-aided instruction in mathematics is also a need for many students in this program.

Audio-Visual and Media Technology.   Applications required by students in this program include inventory control of equipment, software, print and nonprint materials, stock control, purchasing, and repair inventory.

Building Energy Systems and Fluid Power.   The student will need to learn to use programs in heating and cooling load calculations, electrical feeder load calculations, and temperature controls. Other instructional applications include power plant operation simulation, simulated power distribution games, and water treatment control.

Building Trades and Technology.   A working knowledge of the use of computers in inventory control, production scheduling, payroll and time reporting, cost accounting and job cost accounting is required. Other applications required by some students include parts cross reference listings, credit verification, warranty and maintenance records, cooling and heating estimating, and refrigeration pipe and line sizing.

Chemical and Plastics Technology.   Students in these programs will require training in computer applications such as raw material inventory control, costing of jobs associated with various machine and chemical processes, analyzing machine and chemical functions, cross referencing for machine parts, and design of parts and equipment. Packaged programs are available for determining chemical and atomic rates of reaction.

Civil Technology. Instructional requirements include computer applications in surveying, right-of-way selection, traffic problems, soil analysis, and strength of materials.

Dental Laboratory Technician and Dental Assistant. The primary computer application to be learned is an on-line patient record keeping system. Other applications include computerized billing system, supply inventory control, credit check, and preventive maintenance.

Design Technology. Computer applications required by students include strength of materials, machine design, numerical control programs, and structural calculation. Application software is available that will design gears, design structural members, and provide the points for numerical controlled machine processes.

Electromedical and Biomedical Technology. Utilization of computers to simulate varying patient conditions on biomedical equipment is a necessity for this training.

Electronics and Electro-Mechanical Technology. Computer-assisted instruction is utilized to provide exercises and drill and practice experience in mathematics commands and logic interpretations. Knowledge of machine or assembly language for a computer is required for students in computer technology courses. Programming knowledge is necessary to perform computer diagnostics and simulation techniques for fault finding.

Food Services. The student should receive training in computer applications for inventory control, sales control, accounts receivable, accounts payable, formula production scheduling, personnel management, portion control, cost accounting, production scheduling, and menu planning.

Graphic Communications. Students should acquire skill and knowledge in computerized typesetting. They should also learn to use existing programs and to develop new programs to format, edit, convert, hyphenate, and justify data. Other applications include the use of a TEXT processor, mathematics drill and practice, photo composition, cost estimating simulation, production control simulation, marketing simulation, inventory control, and creative reaction data gathering.

Health Occupations. This broad occupational grouping includes occupations such as medical secretary, central services technician, medical assistant, institutional housekeeper, and medical record technician. Applications required include accounting functions, patient billing, insurance processing, inventory control, patient or customer information file, work order cost accounting, and preventive maintenance.

Home Furnishings and Fashion Merchandising.   Computer applications required for training include business decision making and competitive strategy simulation, inventory control, on line order entry, credit verification, credit and collections, store operations analysis, demographics for store location, and processing of market research data.

Industrial Technology.   The knowledge of computer applications required of new employees in this occupation includes planning of floor layouts, inventory control, labor reporting, testing and evaluation programs, job order processing, time standards, line balancing systems, and drill and practice in engineering mathematics.

Law Enforcement Occupations.   Computer applications used regularly in these occupations include on-line systems for criminal information, traffic records, and stolen property.

Machine Shop.   A special programming language is utilized by the student as input to the computer that generates the control paper tapes to operate numerically controlled machine tools in metal fabrication, cutting, and forming shops. The programs perform all the geometric calculations in three dimensions to program the motion of the cutting path of the machine tool. Other applications required by the student include statistical programs in regressions and curve fitting, cost estimating programs, and inventory control.

Office Occupations, Model Office, Secretarial.   A very high percentage of these graduates will obtain positions that will require them to generate input for the data processing operation as well as to analyze computer-generated output. Typical applications required include accounts receivable, accounts payable, general ledger, financial statements, inventory control, payroll, personnel reporting, sales reporting, purchasing functions, credit card application processing, customer records, on-line order entry, computerized billing, and records management.

Optical Technology.   Applications are available for computerized control of making lens and frames. Training is also required in use of the computer for calculating lens angles—refraction and curvatures.

Practical Nursing, Hospital Station Secretary, Medical Record Secretary.   The student must learn how to input a problem oriented medical record into the computer, develop a patient index on the computer, develop and retrieve statistical data relating to patients, diseases, operations, and physicians. Other required applications include inventory control, billing of patients for supplies and drugs used in the hospital, and records of medications.

Sales, Marketing, Merchandising and Purchasing.   This "family" of occupations has turned to the computer for services in inventory control, accounts receivable, accounts payable, budgeting control, financial statements, customer accounts, credit card applications, and credit verification. Point-of-sale terminal systems are becoming increasingly common. In the point-of-sale system, the salesperson "ringing up" a sale on the electronic cash register also performs the following additional functions: updates the store inventory for the items purchased, updates the store's gross sales record for the day as well as the cash or credit sales total, credits the individual customer's account if it is a credit sale, and provides basic data for the daily profit and loss statement. Less common, but operational, are systems wired directly into banks, where the customer's end-of-the-month account is automatically deducted from the customer's checking account at the bank and paid directly to the store.

Transportation.   The primary application in the automotive and truck repair industry is inventory control for auto and truck parts. Parts countermen are expected to utilize the computer and computer printouts to locate parts, identify suppliers, and enter transactions from purchases and sales records. The automotive repair industry has standardized part names with group numbers and part numbers. The industry also has a standardized inventory system with specific format and output listings. Larger automotive mechanic and body mechanic vocational training programs have found it expedient to keep the training institution's parts inventory on the computer and to utilize this system for training parts countermen. Other applications include accounting, credit verification, diagnostic simulation, fleet maintenance simulation, truck (traffic) simulation scheduling, auto body repair estimating, maintenance record keeping, and tool inventory.

Use of the computer for individualized instruction is natural because it is one of the "things" of educational technology that inherently lends itself to individualized learning. Most of the applications described for related training in vocational programs do not require a computer to be on site. They can be accomplished through access to a remote terminal. The most common types of terminals are remote job entry (batch input), teletype, and cathode ray tube. The batch input is usually handled through a card reader which records images obtained from punches made in standardized data processing cards. Another form of batch input is from a scanner which reads messages placed on cards with magnetic pencils or typewriter imprints. These batch-mode devices provide for computer input only, and the computer's reply has to come from a printer which may be located at the site of the computer, but may also be remote from the computer location.

The most commonly used terminal, which is both an input and output device, is the teletype machine. This terminal continues to be the most commonly used terminal in education because of its relatively low cost and because it produces a printed record of the input-output messages on paper, a "hardcopy."

Coming into increasingly greater usage in education is the cathode ray tube (CRT). The CRT has a screen which resembles a television screen and displays the instructions being typed on the teletype to the computer. Thus the message can be verified visually by the operator before the "send" switch is depressed, sending the entire message into the computer. The reply also appears on the CRT screen, and from some CRT machines it can be converted into hardcopy.

Different industries have focused on different systems of remote job entry. The airline companies, for example, use CRTs very heavily in maintaining customer reservation arrangements. It is necessary that in planning the use of a remote terminal in a vocational instruction program, the standards and general practices of the program-related industry be considered. Advisory committees from the occupation often have valuable information on computerization practices of their industry. Quite commonly an industry will be using more than one type of terminal device, and instruction must be planned accordingly. Thus while the computer is only one of the instructional technology modes available to the vocational curriculum planner, it is an important one, fast-growing and wide-spread in potential use. It is clearly one of the resources to be considered when planning learning steps for an intermediate performance objective.

The last of the eight forms of media defined as being particularly significant in the individualization of instruction is human resources (teachers and peers). In their evaluation of instructional technology Keppel and Cornog (1971) stated, ". . . machine and software combined cannot succeed unless those that use them are convinced they work and should be used." If the developer of the individualized instructional program is a teacher, he must be convinced of the need for the program, and that the program can succeed. If the program is being developed by a person or persons other than the teacher of the program, it is equally important that they and the teacher be convinced of the merits of what is being done. The availability of the teacher of the program *and* other teachers and adults can be built into the learning guide. The occasional "see your instructor" instruction programmed into the learning guide assures the student that the teacher has not abandoned him to an impersonal learning structure and also that the teacher has given very personal attention to the planning of the guide. The reference may also be to another instructor who may be in a position to be of special assistance on a particular skill or topic.

Similarly, the learner's peers should not be neglected as potential learning resources. Many parents and teachers have agonized over having children and students place more credence on the words of their peers than on the "superior" wisdom of adults. Individualized instruction presents some unique opportunities to capitalize on the tendency to relate to peers. The practice of teaming or placing together a "lead" and slow student on an instructional auto repair job, for example, gives the slow student great opportunity to learn from a nonthreatening peer. At the same time, the "lead" student reinforces his knowledge by having to explain his actions as he proceeds.

Summary of Media Resources

It is clear that a host of educational resources are available to support the learning steps of the intermediate performance objectives—so many that the curriculum developer may become quite anxious in trying to make the right selection. It is also true that the learning objectives for each guide probably can be reached in several different ways. We have discussed criteria that can be applied in selecting resources from several different types of media. There are a few criteria that seem to prevail regardless of the media being considered. They can also serve as a basis for making a determination or selection between two possibly unlike resources being considered for a learning step. These common criteria are:

Content	Does it follow closely the requirements of the intermediate tasks? What percent of the total intermediate tasks can be covered with this resource? Are their serious omissions, outdated information, or overemphasis on minor aspects?
Level	Is the vocabulary, written or oral, at a level suitable for persons who ordinarily enter that occupation?
Presentation	Is the material effectively presented? Will it be interesting and meaningful to students?
Technical Quality	Are print and/or visual images sharp? Is the color natural? Is the sound intelligible and realistic? Are sound and image synchronized, if required?

In the learning guide on pp. 234, the curriculum developer focused strongly on two publications already available—the ATF Chief 20 manufacturer's instruction manual for the machine and a union-produced text-book, *Lessons in Printing*. The developer (an instructor) found it necessary to supplement this with some narrative of his own origination and a sound-on-slide presentation in which he collaborated with the audio-visual department of his school.

The manufacturer's instruction manual was closely aligned to the instructor's requirements for the intermediate tasks. The manual was specifically designed and written to self-instruct persons who were going to be using the machine. A boldface directive on the title page says, "Give this Instruction Book to the Press Operator. Do not file it away in the office." Vocabulary was written at a level expected of press operators. This is also true of *Lessons in Printing*. These materials are not "written down" to anyone. All of the technical terms and verbs of the trade are there, but there is an absence of nonconsequential educational jargon which might confuse the learner. The materials are effectively presented, are interesting, and will be meaningful to a student who wants to enter the graphic communications occupations; the technical quality is also good.

Perhaps we have constructed this situation to be "too easy" in that the vocational instructor and/or curriculum developer was able to find a majority of the instructional materials needed to meet the intermediate performance objective. Yet this was not a minor task on the part of the instructor. To obtain a perspective of the scope of individualized vocational instruction curriculum development, consider our earlier statement that this task. "Set up and operate the Chief 20 Press" was one of 240 tasks in a graphic communications program. This task had three intermediate tasks. The one intermediate task with which we have been dealing has 38 subtasks, and it is far from being the most complex of typical tasks of a vocational training program.

Next we will consider the combining of the learning guide and resources we have discussed into a "learning package."

The Learning Package

The learning package or learning packet is usually differentiated from the learning guide as being more inclusive. The learning guide defines the objectives, steps, procedures, and resources required to master the content of that guide. If we take the learning guide, the audio-visual software and print material associated with it, an instrument for evaluating mastery, and combine it into an envelope or box, with a special library resource number for the entire lot, it becomes a package or packet. If the required audio-visual hardware is small enough, it may also become part of the package, but it is not a requirement for the use of the term.

Decisions about the degree to which packages should be standardized within an institution have considerable significance for both instructional and physical plant organization. If, for example, it is determined that sound-on-slide trays for learning guides will be included in the basic packages, then appropriate sized boxes to accommodate the trays have to be purchased. Compatible sized shelving will also have to be provided. The cost of replicating all of the slides and the sound media will have to be considered. The decision may well be instructional. If all students are to start from a given point in a stated program and all are expected to proceed at essentially the same rate of learning, then nearly all of the instructional components will have to be provided to each member of the class concurrently. If, on the other hand, there is continuous student entry into the program or if students are proceeding at greatly varied learning rates, as is true of most individualized programs, copies of a given learning package within a program might be replicated in quantities as small as one-fourth of the total number of students enrolled. It is also possible that a given sound-on-slide tray or other software aids may need to be present only a fraction of the total time a student is expected to spend on a learning guide. In those cases, it would be prudent to have a lesser number of these trays in the learning resource center for checkout to those who are ready to use them. The learning resource center or instructional materials center is discussed in more detail in chapter 7.

Summary

In summary, specification of an instructional system involves decisions about relationships between content, time, and proficiency; standards of achievement; timing of success confirmation; student responses expected; learning guidelines and procedures. A working learning guide is a necessity for individualized vocational instruction. The terminal performance objective (TPO) is broken into intermediate performance objectives drawn directly from job tasks. Learning steps and resources are drawn from a host of available materials, including print materials, moving visual and audio-visual media, static visual media, magnetic tape, sound media, situational information, information from physical objects, computers, and human resources. Computers have had some usage in vocational education in career training and in computer technical training, but their application is needed in nearly all occupational programs.

Software for vocational-technical instruction has been slow in development, but it is now making excellent progress.

REFERENCES

1. American Type Founders. "ATF Chief 20 Instruction Manual." Elizabeth, New Jersey: American Type Founders, 1966.

2. Beckworth, Hugh. "Innovations in Industry Likely to Affect Instructional Technology During the Next Ten Years." as cited in Sidney G. Tickton, ed., *To Improve Learning, Volume II.* New York and London: R. R. Bowker Company, 1971.

3. Bryan, Glen L; Rigney, Joseph W; and Van Horn, Charles. *An Evaluation of Three Types of Information for Supplementing Knowledge of Results in a Training Technique.* Los Angeles, Calif.: University of Southern California, Electronics Personnel Research, Technical Report No. 19, 1957.

4. Bureau of Education, *Lessons In Printing (I & II),* Colorado Springs, Colorado: International Typographers Union, 1972.

5. Butler, F. Coit. *Instructional Systems Development for Vocational and Technical Training.* Englewood Cliffs, New Jersey: Educational Technology Publications, Inc., 1972, p. 136.

6. Commission on Instructional Technology. "To Improve Learning," A Report to the President and the Congress of the United States, March 1970, Chapter II, p. 19; as cited by Armsey, James W. and Dahl, Norman C. in "An Inquiry Into the Uses of Instructional Technology," A Ford Foundation Report. New York: The Ford Foundation, 1973.

7. Davies, Ivor K. *The Management of Learning.* London: McGraw-Hill Book Company (UK) Limited, 1971, pp. 113-14.

8. Duane, James E. *Individualized Instruction, Programs and Materials.* Englewood Cliffs, New Jersey: Educational Technology Publications, 1973.

9. Dwyer, F. M. "Exploratory Studies in the Effectiveness of Visual Illustrations," *A-V Communication Review* 18 (1970): 235-49, as cited in Davies, Ivor K. *The Management of Learning.* London: McGraw-Hill Book Company (UK) Limited, 1971, p. 115.

10. "Educational Technology, The Design and Implementation of Learning Systems." Report based on the results of a workshop organized by CERI in conjunction with the British, Dutch, German, and Swedish Authorities at Leiden, Netherlands, April 1970, OECD, 1970, p. 25, as cited by Armsey, James W. and Dahl, Norman C. in "An Inquiry Into the Uses of Instructional Technology," A Ford Foundation Report. New York: The Ford Foundation, 1973.

11. Eraut, Michael. "Educational Technology and the Training of Teachers." A final report to the Department of Education and Science from the Centre for Educational Technology, University of Sudan, Brighton, March 1971, p. 5.

12. Fryklund, Verne C. *Occupational Analysis, Techniques and Procedures.* New York: The Bruce Publishing Company, 1970, p. 202.

13. Goldbeck, Robert A, and Campbell, Vincent N. "The Effects of Response Mode and Response Difficulty on Programmed Learning." *Journal of Educational Psychology* 58 (1962): NO-18.

14. Gropper, George L., and Glasgow, Zita. *Criteria for the Selection and Use of Visuals in Instruction, A Handbook.* Englewood Cliffs, New Jersey: Educational Technology Publications, 1971.

15. Hake, Harold W., and Ericksen, Charles W. "Role of Response Variables in Recognition and Identification of Complex Visual Forms." *Journal of Experimental Psychology* 52 (1956): 235-43.

16. Hirsch, Richard S. *The Effects of Knowledge of Test Results on Learning of Meaningful Material,* Port Washington, New York: Special Devices Center, Human Engineering Report 269-7-30, 1952.

17. Kanner, J. H. "The Instructional Effectiveness of Color Television," Stanford, California: Stanford University, ERIC Clearinghouse of Educational Media and Technology, 1968.

18. Krumboltz, John D, and Bonawitz, Barbara. "The Effect of Receiving the Confirming Response in Context in Programmed Material." *Journal of Educational Research* 53 (1962): 89-92.

19. Laner, S. "Some Factors Influencing the Effectiveness of an Instructional Film." *British Journal of Psychology* 46 (1955): 280-92, as cited in Davies, Ivor K. *The Management of Learning.* London: McGraw-Hill Book Company (UK) Limited, 1971, p. 118.

20. Lumsdaine, A.A., and Gladstone, A. "Overt Practice and Audiovisual Embellishments." In M.A. and A.A. Lumsdaine, eds., *Learning from Films.* New Haven, Connecticut: Yale University Press, 1958, pp. 58-71.

21. Lumsdaine, A.A.; Sulzer, R.L.; and Kopstein, F.F. "The Effect of Animation Cues and Repetition of Examples on Learning From an Instructional Film." In A.A. Lumsdaine, ed., "Student Response in Programmed Instruction: A Symposium." Washington, D.C., National Academy of Sciences, National Research Council Publication No. 943.

22. Najman, Dragoljub. (Director of UNESCO's Division of Educational Studies and Teacher Education) Interview, December 7, 1971. Cited by Armsey, James W., and Dahl, Norman C. in "An Inquiry Into the Uses of Instructional Technology." A Ford Foundation Report. New York: The Ford Foundation, 1973.

23. Odiorne, George. "The Activity Trap." *Northliner.* St. Paul, Minn.: Webb Publishing Co., February 1973.

24. Rose, Homer C. *The Instructor and His Job.* Chicago, Illinois: American Technical Society, pp. 144-48.

25. Rosenstock, Edward H; Moore, William J; and Smith, Wendell. "Effects of Several Schedules of Knowledge of Results on Mathematics Achievement." *Psychological Report* 17 (1965): 535-41.

26. Smith, Robert G., Jr. *The Engineering of Educational and Training Systems*. Lexington, Mass.: D.C. Heath and Company, Heath Lexington Books, 1971.

27. Vernon, M.D. "The Use and Value of Graphical Methods of Presenting Quantitative Data," *Occupational Psychology* 46 (1952): 11-17.

28. Wendt, P.R., and Butts, G.K. "Audio-Visual Materials," *Review of Educational Research* 32 (1962): 145-55.

Chapter 6   MONITORING STUDENT PROGRESS

         The role of educational evaluation in an individualized vocational instructional program is to provide feedback to the instructor which allows for student competency certification and the diagnosis of learning deficiencies. Competency certification refers to the process of verifying that a student has mastered a task. Diagnosis refers to the process of identifying where students need to increase their proficiency to master a task. Both of these processes are very important to the instructor. The process of certification allows him to determine when a student has mastered a task and the process of diagnosis helps him determine why the student has not mastered a task. Some students come to the learning situation with tasks already mastered or partially mastered. If the instructor wishes to take prior learning into account he uses a process called pretesting. Instruments used in pretesting are administered before a student takes part in the learning activities relative to a task to determine the state of a student's knowledge and skill relating to the task. If it is found that the student possesses all of the necessary knowledge and skill, he is certified as having mastered the task without being required to take part in the instructional activities. If he has not developed all of the necessary knowledge and skill, he is encouraged to take part in those learning activities designed to develop them. If a student does undertake instruction, posttests should be available for the student to demonstrate that he has mastered the task. Posttests are administered after a student has completed the learning activities. Sometimes the pretest and posttest for a guide are the same, but ideally they would be tests which measure the same thing with different items.

Figure 6-1 diagrams the process of competency certification. A student who wishes to undertake instruction on a task would first be required to complete the pretest relating to that task so that the instructor could diagnose what specific help the student needed. If the student was capable of achieving satisfactorily on all of the assessment instruments relating to the task, the student would be certified as having mastered the task and would be allowed to move on to another without taking instruction on that task. If a student did not demonstrate mastery of the task, the student would undertake instruction on the task, and at the point the student felt that he would like to attempt to demonstrate mastery of a task, he could take the posttests. If the student demonstrated that he could perform satisfactorily on all the assessment instruments, he would be certified as having mastered the task and would be allowed to move on to another task. If the student did not demonstrate that he could satisfactorily complete all the assessment instruments, then his performance on the assessment instruments would be reviewed to diagnose what particular intermediate performance objectives the student had not attained, and the student would be asked to do further work in those areas. When the student again felt ready to demonstrate mastery of the task, he would be allowed to repeat the posttest, and if he satisfactorily completed each of the

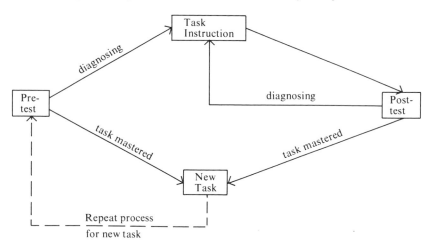

FIGURE 6–1

STRUCTURE OF THE CERTIFICATION OF TASK MASTERY

instruments he would be allowed to move on. If he did not, he would be asked to repeat work on those objectives which he had not mastered. This process would continue until the task was mastered.

The process described above seems simple enough and it is, if the instructor is aware of some of the basic concepts and techniques of evaluation. The remainder of this chapter will deal with these concepts and techniques. The first concept is: what is evaluation and how does it differ from the typical measurements made in an occupation? This is followed by a discussion of techniques for documenting that the instruments developed will provide the information needed to make judgments about a student's mastery of a task. The discussion then turns to defining "mastery level" and finally to how to construct the assessment instruments.

Evaluation is defined as the measurement of student progress in a complex situation. It is characterized by the identification of the basic aspects of the complex situation and the assessment of each of them with more than one measure. The assessment of student progress toward a task objective is a complex situation. It typically requires measures of three aspects: doing or performance, knowing or technical information, and attitude. Each of these aspects are then evaluated by using more than one measure. Using more than one measure refers to the development of more than one instrument which each result in separate scores. Another way of looking at multiple measures is to develop one instrument with more than one item measuring each specific objective in a learning package. In either case, students are asked to apply what they have learned to a number of different performance activities to measure their ability to do, a number of different situations which imply their ability to know or understand the technical information, and a number of different situations which imply possession of desired attitudes. The need for multiple assessments is obvious if one examines the process of measurement. All measurement, regardless of how precise, has some error associated with it. This error is usually due to instrument or human error. Such error is minimized by taking a number of different measurements and averaging the results. For example, when machinists want an accurate assessment of the diameter of a steel cylinder, they measure the diameter a number of times with a micrometer and average the readings to obtain an average reading. The average reading is correct more often than any of the separate readings. When determining the blood count of a person's blood, medical laboratory personnel conduct a blood count on a number of different samples of blood to obtain a more accurate assessment. If multiple assessments are used as a basis for accurate assessment in such exact situations as micrometer reading and blood counting, the need for multiple assessments in education should be apparent.

Educational assessment is much less precise than the physical measurements which vocational instructors use in their subject matter areas. A person that works in the area of commercial foods knows that a "cup" is a unit of measure which is accurate and means the same thing from one time to another. A machinist realizes that one thousandth of an inch means the same one time as it does another. Therefore, if one bowl has two cups of flour and another has one, we can say one bowl has one cup more than the other. Similarly, if one piece of steel measures five thousandths of an inch and another eight thousandths, we can say that one is three thousandths of an inch larger than the other.

Such precise statements are difficult when trying to compare one student's evaluation instrument scores with those of another student or with some standard test score. Measuring student performance is subject to error. Later we will discuss how we can minimize this error but it can not be eliminated. Error can arise from each of four major sources: (1) student error, (2) instrument error, (3) scorer error, and (4) guessing error.

Student error refers to mistakes made by students who know the content being assessed but who for some reason make a mistake. For example, a student may not read a test item carefully and, therefore, puts down the wrong answer. Another student might put the answer in the wrong place because of skipping a previous item. Another student might miss a word in reading a question. This type of error is not a guessing error, it results from human error. Student error is difficult to control. A teacher can try to minimize it by trying to motivate students to be careful and to do their best, but student-initiated mistakes can be corrected only by the students. Most vocational instructors do not have a counterpart of student error when they measure things in their fields. A piece of steel does not make a mistake nor does a part of a car. But students are not things, they are people and people make mistakes which show up as error in student assessment.

Instrument error is the result of items being written in such a way that the careful student might misinterpret an item and put down the wrong answer. Instrument error is usually due to inability on the part of the instructor to communicate with the student through the evaluation instrument items. Students read the items and do not understand them or they get the impression that they should do something other than what the instructor intended. One primary source of this type of error is the difference between the vocabulary of the students and the instructor. In order to become a vocational instructor, a person must have developed a high level of competence in the area to be taught. When one has developed a high level of competence in a field, he or she uses terms which have become meaningful over a long period of time. The natural tendency of instructors is to use these same terms when they are developing their evaluation instruments since they are very meaningful in the field. However, most beginning students do not understand many of the terms used in an occupation because they have not had enough experience. When such items appear in an instrument used with beginning students, many students do not understand what the instructor wants and instrument error develops. If the item makes no sense to the student, the student will typically guess. If the item makes sense to the student but the student does not get the same understanding that the instructor thought he or she would, the student will probably select a different answer than the one the instructor defined as correct. The answer may be correct as the student understood the item, but not as the instructor understood it. Instrument error can be controlled largely by the instructor as the test is developed or refined and improved.

Another major type of error in educational assessment is scorer error. A student might not make any mistake due to carelessness and the instrument may be constructed with no error, but error can still contaminate an educational assessment in the form of scorer error. Scorer error, which is made during the correcting process, generally occurs when the person who designed the instrument did not adequately indicate how to judge if the student responded with the correct answer. Since the scorer (usually the instructor) does not know exactly what the correct answer should be, a great deal of judgment must be used in scoring a student's instrument. The problem is not that the instructor has exercised judgment, but that such judgment rarely can be applied uniformly to all students. The instructor might think that he or she is very objective, and therefore the judgments are free of personal bias. But experience of educators has shown that many outside influences influence how a person judges another person's performance. If the student being judged is very similar to the instructor doing the scoring, the instructor tends to judge higher; if the overall general impression of the answer due to grammar and neatness is good, the instructor doing the scoring will tend to judge higher; etc. These factors do not relate to how well the student has mastered the content, but they relate to other factors which the person doing the scoring cannot separate from his judgments.

The final type of error is guessing error. Guessing error refers to error caused by people not knowing the answer to a question and guessing the answer. Guessing causes a student's score on an instrument to vary from one time to another even though his or her knowledge does not vary. If a student takes a test today and happens to guess at some of the items and guesses correctly, his score would tend to be higher than would actually be reasonable based upon his knowledge. The score would be equal to the amount of knowledge known by the student, reflected by those items he got correct because he knew the answer, plus the scores on those items that he got correct because he guessed correctly. If the student took the same test the next day and no learning took place between the time he took the first test and the time he took the second test, his score would be equal to the score he got on those items that he knew plus the score that he got on those items that he guessed. If during the second administration he guessed incorrectly more often than correctly, the score would be lower than the previous score. Therefore, during both test administrations the part that the student actually knew would result in the same score, but total scores would vary based on the difference in how well he guessed the first time and how well he guessed the second time.

As you can see, there are many sources of error that can affect a test score. However, if the instructor always tries to use multiple assessments he can reduce error to a minimum.

Besides needing multiple measures to reduce error, it is also desirable to measure more than one dimension or aspect of performance. For example, it is usually desirable to measure both the knowing and doing components of a task. However, many instructors argue that if we measure a person's ability to "do," we have already measured whether a person "knows." This probably would be true if we would measure every possible "doing" activity that one would perform on the job relative to a particular task. However, since it is usually not possible to measure a person's ability to perform a task in all situations and under all conditions that the task is likely to be performed on the job, this argument is not sound. Assume we taught a student how to use a soldering iron to solder wires to terminals in an electronics course. We could assess his ability to solder a particular size wire to a particular size terminal. However, this would not tell us if the student could solder a different size wire to a different size terminal. It would not be feasible to test the student's ability to solder all combinations of wire sizes and terminal sizes. We might assess the student's ability to "do" by having him solder a wire to a terminal. We could then assess the student's ability to generalize the process to other situations by testing the "knowing" or generalizations associated with how to solder wires to terminals. If the student can perform the task in one situation and "knows" the rules, principles, or generalizations for performing the task in other situations, one can be more assured that the student can perform the task in other situations. This method calls for assessments of "doing" and "knowing" which complement each other and provide more information concerning whether a student has mastered a task than either a knowing or doing assessment alone. Most vocational instructors would like to have their students be able to apply what they have learned to situations which are new to the students. They do not want to prepare people to be "parts pushers" or robots who can do what they are trained to do but who do not have the background to be able to adapt to new and ever-changing work situations. Few vocational educators would want to train a person to replace component A when red light B goes on without the person's realizing why. A person trained in this way would not be able to generalize to new situations where the machine is the same but the parts are labeled differently. Such a situation could develop if an instructor specified an objective such as "the student will replace component A when red light B goes on," and only measured if the student could do it. It would be very important that the student know why, in order for him to be able to apply what was learned to similar but new situations.

Instructional Feedback

The information gained from educational evaluation should be fed back to students and to the instructor. Feedback refers to providing information about performance back to people who can modify future performance. The information is needed by the student so the student can plan what to do next and, therefore, modify future performance. It is needed by the instructor so the instructor can determine the effectiveness of the instruction and where a student may need assistance so he can modify his future performance or the student's future performance.

The timing of feedback is important. Information should be provided as quickly as possible so the student and the instructor can remember the specifics of the performance situation and can modify the performance before it is repeated incorrectly many times and becomes routine. Typically, the longer the time between the performance and feedback, the less impact the feedback will have on modifying future performance.

Evaluation that can accomplish these goals requires the development of assessment instruments which are keyed to specific learning objectives so that one can diagnose where a student has not succeeded in mastering a task. With course materials organized as learning packages with terminal performance objectives (TPOs) and intermediate performance objectives (IPOs), this can be accomplished by directly relating assessment instrument items to specific TPOs or IPOs. When instruments are constructed against objectives, it is possible to diagnose specifically which objective has or has not been mastered by examining the items pertaining to each objective. For example, if the objective is for a student to master the preparation of fruit pies, the performance items should be related to the process of making a fruit pie and the knowing items should be related to the knowledge that would allow for wise judgments concerning the processes involved in making fruit pies. A person who masters both the processes and the knowledge should be able to adapt to new and novel situations concerning the preparation of fruit pies. When the "doing" items are keyed to specific intermediate performance objectives, it is possible to examine those items to determine what a student can or cannot do relative to making fruit pies. When the knowing items are keyed to specific intermediate performance objectives, one can determine which of the processes the student understands and which he does not understand.

When the information becomes available, it should be reviewed to determine if the student has mastered the task. If the task has been mastered, the student should move on to another task. If the student has not mastered the task, the instructor should diagnose which specific intermediate performance objectives the student has not mastered and how the student might approach developing sufficient proficiency to master those competencies. If the instructor finds out that a number of students are having difficulty mastering a particular task, the instructor should thoroughly review the learning package for that task. The objectives, learning activities, learning resources and/or evaluation instruments might need revision. The objective is to assist all students who attempt a learning package to complete it. The package can be judged as not being effective if large numbers of people fail to master the task upon completing the package.

Establishing the Mastery Level Score

Assessment instruments designed to measure "doing" and "knowing" proficiency provide the instructor with information for making a judgment concerning a student's progress, but they do not provide a basis for judging which scores on the instruments indicate mastery. Mastery was defined earlier as the attainment of a task proficiency level which indicates that a student can perform satisfactorily at entry level jobs in an occupation. In order to judge mastery, a minimal score must be defined for each of the instruments developed to measure the specific aspects of a task defined as important. If the student attains a mastery level score on each instrument, the task has been mastered.

The process of establishing a mastery level score is similar to the process of calibrating a measuring instrument. In all fields we have instruments that require calibrating. If we make a new ruler in a machine shop, we must in some way compare the new ruler with an old ruler or some other measuring device which will allow us to calibrate the new ruler and put the markings on it that will allow us to measure in inches. If we buy a new syringe for giving injections that is not marked or calibrated, we must have some way of calibrating that syringe so that we know how much fluid we are injecting. If we buy a new voltmeter, we must calibrate that new voltmeter by comparing the readings obtained from it with the readings obtained from some other instrument that we know is accurately measuring volts. The same problem exists when we construct assessment instruments. We would like the instruments to be able to help us separate those people who have mastered a task from those who have not mastered it. However, the test instrument will only produce a series of numbers which in and of themselves are not meaningful. The problem facing the instructor is to take those numbers and calibrate them against something that is known, so that the numbers become meaningful and a mastery level score can be obtained. The solution to the problem is simple if the student is expected to perform everything totally correctly or to get a 100 percent score. If this is the case, the student either gets everything correct or is judged to have not mastered the task. The problem becomes quite complex if the student is not required to get everything correct in order to be judged as having mastered the task. The question becomes: what score must a person obtain in order to be judged as having mastered the task?

One way of arriving at this mastery level score is to calibrate the scores against people who are satisfactorily performing in the occupation. People who are satisfactorily performing in the occupation are selected, and they are administered the assessment instrument. The scores they obtain on the instrument are then used to calibrate the instruments. The other method is to use expert judgment. Expert judgment is used as the base against which the test instrument scores are compared to calibrate the instrument. Experts are asked to judge the performance of students and then the students actually take the instrument. The scores on the instrument are then compared with the expert judgment and a mastery level score is assigned.

Both of these procedures have inherent problems. The first procedure is difficult because it requires the identification of people who are performing satisfactorily in the occupation, and it requires that these people be available for assessment. The second procedure relies heavily on the judgment of a group of specialists. The judgments are only as good as the quality of the experts and their knowledge of the particular task.

The following is an example of how a mastery level score can be determined using people who are performing satisfactorily in the occupation. Let us assume that we must establish some way of certifying mastery of the task: perform a vertical weld on mild steel. When reviewing the task, we determine that a student must be able to do certain things and know certain things. Therefore, we feel the need to assess both doing and knowing. We then construct instruments which measure the knowing and doing aspects of the task. Assuming the instruments are well constructed, the next concern would be to determine how to judge the results or scores obtained from the instruments. If we use the procedure of assessing workers on the job, we would identify a group of welders who are judged as being able to perform a vertical weld on mild steel satisfactorily and who are judged to have a sufficient amount of knowledge of how to perform a vertical weld on mild steel. Assume that we are able to identify thirty welders who are judged by their employers as having at least entry level job skills related to performing a vertical weld on mild steel. We would administer our doing and knowing assessment instruments to the welders and determine their scores.

The scores on each instrument would then be placed in separate frequency distributions. A frequency distribution summarizes the number of people who attained a certain score on an instrument. Let us assume that our thirty welders achieved the scores on the knowing assessment instrument indicated in the frequency distribution presented in table 6-1. One welder attained a score of 90, five attained a score of 82, none attained a score of 78, etc.

TABLE 6−1

FREQUENCY DISTRIBUTION FOR THE KNOWING ASSESSMENT

Score	Frequency	
90	1	
89	0	
88	0	
87	3	
86	2	
85	2	
84	3	
83	4	
82	5	
81	3	
80	2	[natural break
79	2	
78	0	"mastery level"]
77	0	
76	1	
75	2	
	$N = 30$	

The mastery level score would be determined by reviewing the frequency distribution and looking for natural breaks in the scores near the low end of the distribution. A natural break is a point in the distribution that seems to separate one group of scores from another group. A natural break appears near the bottom of the sample distribution between the scores of 79 and 76. One group of people had scores of 79 and above and another group had scores of 76 and below, separated by a break in the scores. Therefore, it would be logical to set the mastery level score at 78. If there is no natural break in the distribution, the mastery level score is established at the lowest score achieved by the group. This procedure produces a mastery level score above which most people performing satisfactorily in the occupation would fall. The lowest score is not always selected because at times there are members of a group who perform far below the majority of the members. Since these people are viewed as not typical of the group, the mastery level score is established above their scores just following the bulk of the scores of the group.

When we use this method, we must assume that those people to whom we administered the instruments do really represent a typical group in the occupation. If the thirty welders that were selected were people who were far above the typical welders in their ability to "do" and their ability to "know" how to make a vertical weld, the mastery level scores established would not be appropriate for welders in general. The same would be true if the group that we selected was a group of very poor welders. If we can assume that the group of welders selected represents the range of successful welders, the mastery level score established by this method will be quite accurate.

The other method of establishing mastery level scores used by instructors is the method of expert judgment. It relies primarily upon the judgment of the instructor or other knowledgeable people in the field as to what score a person should be able to obtain on an instrument in order to be judged as being capable of performing at entry level jobs in the occupation. People review the instrument and judge which score would be necessary in order to be reasonably sure that a person has mastered the task. This score is later adjusted based upon information gathered on students as they actually progress through the program. It is adjusted by answering the question, "Does the mastery level score that was originally set actually separate those students who have mastered the task from those who did not?" In order to answer this question, the instructor must obtain some judgment of the proficiency of the students on the task and also assessment instrument scores. After these two pieces of information have been gathered over a sufficient number of students, the mastery level score can be checked for reasonableness by observing how many of the students who were judged as having mastered the task actually achieved scores above the mastery level and how many students who were judged as not having mastered the task achieved scores below the mastery level.

Using this procedure with our welding example, we would do the following. The instructor would construct the doing and knowing assessment instruments and select a mastery level score based on his judgment or upon the judgment of his advisory committee or another group of knowledgeable people in the field. A separate mastery score would be assigned for each type of instrument. The instructor or the other individuals who make the judgment would select the score they feel would reflect a sufficient level of proficiency to perform satisfactorily at entry level jobs in the occupation. Let us assume that the mastery level score for the "knowing" assessment instrument was established at 81 or above and the mastery level score for the "doing" assessment instrument was set at 56 or above. The instructor would then begin to use the instruments and these mastery level scores as students progress through the course. The two pieces of information necessary to judge the adequacy of these mastery level scores (judgments of student performance and the assessment instrument scores) would be obtained as follows. When a student wished to be certified as having mastered a task, the instructor would administer the appropriate assessment instrument. During the time the student was taking the assessment instrument or prior to the time the instructor saw the score the student attained, the instructor would make a judgment concerning the student's proficiency in terms of whether the student had developed a sufficient amount of proficiency to perform at entry level jobs in the occupation. It is important that the instructor make this judgment prior to seeing the assessment instrument scores. The objective of checking the scores against the ratings is to see how satisfactory the mastery level score is. If the instructor views the assessment instrument scores before making the judgments, knowledge of the assessment instrument scores might affect the judgments.

The judgments and the scores of individuals would be placed in a table similar to that presented in table 6-2. In some cases students will achieve scores above the mastery level score and other students will achieve scores below the mastery level score. If a student does not attain the mastery level score the first time and re-takes the instrument later, the score from only the first attempt is recorded. If we only included those scores that people attained after they mastered the task by getting scores above the mastery level score, it would not be possible to judge the reasonableness of the mastery level score. All students would attain scores above that mastery level score.

Table 6-2 presents a summary of a group of students' first attempts at completing the certification assessments for the task. Each assessment instrument score is accompanied by a prior rating of the student's proficiency level based on a judgment of the instructor or someone else skilled in the task being assessed. As one can see by examining table 6-2, Paul was rated as having unsatisfactory performance, but he obtained a score on the assessment instrument of 87, which was relatively high. Warren was judged as having satisfactory performance, but he obtained a score of

TABLE 6—2

EXAMPLE SUMMARY OF INSTRUCTOR'S JUDGMENTS
AND INSTRUMENT SCORES

Student	Knowing		
Name	Rating	Assessment	
John	S	90	
Sam	S	90	
Pete	S	89	
Mary	S	88	
Paul	U	87	
Ken	S	85	
Sally	S	85	
Jim	S	84	Original
Bill	S	82	Mastery Level
Steve	S	81	
Jerry	U	79	
Howard	S	79	
Dave	S	79	New
Bob	S	78	Mastery Level
Ray	U	74	
Jack	U	74	
Lyle	U	72	
Don	U	71	
Warren	S	70	
Stan	U	70	

S = satisfactory
U = unsatisfactory

70 on the instrument, which was relatively low. There does, however, appear to be a meaningful separation of those judged to be satisfactory from those judged to be unsatisfactory between a score of 78 and 74. This does not agree with the originally established mastery level score of 81 or above. Therefore, the mastery level score would be adjusted to "78 or above" for the future. This procedure would be repeated periodically to check on the reasonableness of the mastery level score.

This technique relies heavily upon the judgment of the instructor or some other knowledgeable people in the field. The extent to which their judgments are accurate will determine the extent to which the mastery level score established through the procedure will be accurate. The above procedure is repeated whenever it appears that the mastery level score is no longer appropriate. If the mastery level score appears to be too low or too high, as the instructor continues to teach in the program, the mastery level score can be readjusted using this same procedure.

The methods of determining the adequacy of the established mastery level scores discussed relate to each guide in a program. It is also possible to obtain an overall indication of the adequacy of the mastery levels set for an entire program. What if all of the mastery level scores are set consistently too high or too low? Follow-up studies of students who leave the program can provide answers to this question. If students completing your program have not developed enough skill to perform adequately on the job, the mastery level scores could be set too low. It is more difficult to determine if the scores are set too high unless they are set extremely high. If the scores are set much too high, the students will be overtrained for an occupation, and many students will leave that occupation for a more challenging occupation. In both cases continued placement in occupations related to the training program will be low.

Characteristics of Assessment Instruments

Regardless of which type of assessment instrument an instructor wishes to construct, he or she must be concerned that it has certain characteristics in order to obtain an accurate and consistent measurement of what is to be assessed. You should become thoroughly familiar with these characteristics since they will be referred to continually during the later discussion on constructing assessment instruments.

The most important characteristic of any instrument is validity. Validity refers to whether an instrument measures what you want it to measure. Instruments are constructed to assess a student's competence in a particular area. Therefore, an instrument should be constructed in such a way that it will measure whether the student has the competence. For example, an instrument designed to assess whether a student can disassemble and assemble a two-barrel carburetor should provide information which will allow one to judge whether the student can disassemble and assemble the carburetor. Validity is referred to as the most important characteristic because if an instrument possesses validity, it also possesses each of the other characteristics of a good instrument. However, if an instrument does not possess each of the characteristics discussed below it will not be valid.

Reliability refers to the accuracy or consistency of an instrument. Instructors would like to see their instruments measure the content they wish to have measured accurately so the results they obtain from the same instrument will be consistent from one time to another. For example, if John and Joe have developed *exactly* the same amount of knowledge relating to types of steel and cutting speeds, they should both obtain the same score on a test to measure that knowledge. If they do not obtain the same score, the test has error associated with it and is not accurate. That is why the test does not produce consistent results. An instrument that measures a particular body of content but does not measure it accurately will not produce consistent results and is really not measuring what you would like it to measure. Therefore, reliability is one of the characteristics of a test that contributes to its validity. It is possible to have a reliable test that measures accurately and consistently without the test being valid. But it is not possible to have a valid test that is not accurate and does not produce consistent results. For example, a highly reliable test developed for machine shop would be of little value to someone teaching practical nursing. It would be reliable because it will produce highly consistent results but it would not be valid because it does not measure what you want it to measure. A test of how to disassemble and assemble carburetors would not be very valuable in assessing whether a person can disassemble and assemble carburetors if it is not accurate. In this case the test is measuring the correct content, but it is not measuring what you want it to measure because it is not accurate. Therefore, reliability should always be a concern of the instructor. The reliability of a test is greatly affected by error in assessment, which we discussed earlier. We referred to student error, instrument error, scorer error, and guessing error. All of these contribute to a lack of reliability because they do not allow the instructor to obtain an accurate or consistent assessment of a student's proficiency.

Assessment instruments should also be comprehensive. A comprehensive instrument is one that reflects all of the content to be assessed by the instrument. A comprehensive instrument need not include all possible items that could be written, but the items that are included should reflect all of the content to be assessed. This is usually accomplished by including a sampling of items covering each intermediate performance objective contained in a guide. For example, if we wish to assess a person's competence on a task contained in a learning guide with one terminal performance objective and ten intermediate performance objectives, we would want an instrument designed to assess proficiency on all of the objectives included in the learning guide. If it did, it would be a comprehensive assessment of the learning guide. If, however, the assessment instrument only included items which reflected five out of the ten intermediate performance objectives, the instrument would not comprehensively assess the learning guide. If the objective of a guide was: set up and type a business letter, an assessment instrument designed to assess how to set the margins on a typewriter would not comprehensively assess the content included in the guide. Whether or not the student can adequately set the margins would be one part of setting up and typing a business letter, but it certainly would not reflect all of the objectives included in the guide. The comprehensiveness of an assessment instrument must be conscientiously developed as the instructor develops the instrument. It is very easy to construct only items on those intermediate performance objectives which lend themselves most easily to assessment. Some things are very difficult to assess. If an instrument is not comprehensive it cannot be valid. If it does not reflect all of the content included in a guide, yet it is developed as an instrument to certify competency on the task for which the guide was constructed, it does not measure what you want it to measure and it is not valid.

Assessment instruments should discriminate between those who have mastered a task and those who have not mastered the task. Throughout earlier sections of this chapter we have discussed the concept of mastery of a task. Discrimination refers to whether an instrument is capable of separating those who have mastered a task from those who have not. Instruments can be constructed in such a way that the items contained in them really do not get at the basic factors which differentiate those who mastered the task from those who did not. Items can deal with relatively insignificant facts or pieces of information which some of the students will be able to respond to correctly and others will not, but which are not truly related to whether a person can perform the task or not. Therefore, different students will get different scores, but the scores will not reflect the extent to which they have actually mastered the task. Items that are critical to whether a person has mastered the task or has not mastered the task are the ones that should be included in an instrument. It is difficult to tell when an instrument is truly capable of differentiating those who mastered the task from those who didn't without gathering information. It is possible to make a determination as to whether a test can discriminate if one uses the method of expert judgment described earlier during the discussion of establishing a mastery level score. If the test truly discriminates, those people who are judged to have mastered the task should consistently receive higher scores on the assessment instrument than those people who are judged as not having mastered the task. Another method of determining if an instrument discriminates is to conduct an item analysis. Those interested in knowing how to conduct an item analysis should consult a text on test analysis. If an instrument does not discriminate, it really does not do what you want it to do and therefore, it is not valid.

Another characteristic of a well-constructed instrument is that it be objective. An objective instrument is one that can be scored consistently and fairly. Different individuals scoring an objective instrument will arrive at the same score for the same person. Earlier we discussed the fact that one possible source of error in evaluation is scoring error. If an instrument is truly objective, the scoring error is eliminated. If error is possible during the scoring of an instrument, the instrument is called a subjective instrument. A subjective instrument is one which calls for scorer judgment during the scoring process. Because different scorers will exercise judgment in different ways, the scores which different people assign to the same individual using the same instrument tend to be different. Throughout our discussions concerning instrument development we will stress the need for developing objective instruments. When subjective instruments are used and teacher judgment is involved in scoring, it is possible for personal teacher biases toward a student to creep into the scoring process. Since the objective of evaluation is to assess a person's proficiency on a task, an instrument that is not objective does not allow us to measure what we want to measure. Therefore, an instrument which lacks objectivity also lacks validity.

From the discussion above it is apparent that the primary characteristic of any instrument should be validity. Each of the other characteristics discussed are really only possible causes of invalidity. A review of each instrument that you construct in light of these characteristics will allow you to assume that the instrument is valid.

Identifying What Is to Be Assessed

Instrument development is generally a three-stage procedure. The first stage is to specify the objectives to be assessed, the second is to create items which assess those objectives, and the third is to judge whether the items are actually capable of assessing the objectives. How to specify objectives has already been discussed in chapter 4. The following is a discussion of how items should be developed to assess these objectives.

The first step in developing assessment instruments to evaluate whether a person has mastered a task is to identify those knowledges, skills, and attitudes that a person must possess in order to be able to perform the task adequately. This is done by reviewing the terminal performance objective and the intermediate performance objectives of the learning guide developed as an aide to teaching the task. If the objectives were properly constructed, there should be a list of those things thought to be essential. These objectives form the base for constructing the learning guide evaluation blueprint. The learning guide evaluation blueprint is a chart that allows the instructor to record how each of the intermediate performance objectives are being evaluated. Table 6-3 is an example of such a blueprint for the task: change and adjust points in an automobile engine. The terminal performance objective is listed along with each of the intermediate performance objectives. To the right of the objectives are spaces to record the identifying numbers of the items that are designed to measure whether a person has mastered each of the intermediate performance objectives. There are also spaces to insert comments on the evaluation of each objective.

Most objectives in the technical fields are evaluated with both knowing and doing assessment instruments. The doing assessment is designed to assess those things that you can observe a person doing. The knowing assessment is designed to assess those things that a person must know in order to perform competently. You cannot observe those things while a person is doing. They allow people to generalize their knowledge of "how to" to those situations where the application of a particular task is appropriate. Since many learning guides are aimed at the mastery of a technical specialty task, they do not reflect a sizeable attitude component. That is not to say that attitude is not important, but it is typically not evaluated in each guide designed to assist a person with mastering a highly technical task. Attitudes toward tools, others, customers should be evaluated at some point in the program, but they need not be assessed as part of each guide. Therefore, the example guide does not include an attitude assessment, but it does refer to the guide where the assessment of the attitudes related to this guide was conducted. Later we will describe another learning guide evaluation blueprint for a field which deals primarily with interpersonal communications. The attitude assessment will be a major part of the evaluation of that guide.

The items designed to assess the ability of a person to "do" are typically assembled into performance evaluation instruments. The items designed to assess a person's understanding or knowledge are typically assembled into tests of understanding. Throughout the following discussion the terms performance evaluation and tests shall be used to refer to the two types of assessment instruments.

Usually there is only one test per guide; however, there may be more than one performance evaluation instrument per guide. If the guide includes two major performance components within the same terminal performance objective, it might be meaningful to construct more than one performance evaluation. In the case of the task: change and adjust points in an automobile engine, presented in table 6-3, there are two major performances required the way the objectives for that guide are written. The first major performance is to change points. The second major performance is to adjust points. Therefore, it may be meaningful to construct one performance evaluation instrument that would allow for the evaluation of whether or not a student can properly remove old points and install new points and another to assess whether the student can adjust points. Of course, another way to handle this situation would be to con-

TABLE 6–3

Sample Learning Guide Evaluation Blueprint

Course: Automotive

TERMINAL PERFORMANCE OBJECTIVE

Given: An operating automobile engine, the correct type new points, a set of points installation tools, and a dwell meter

Performance: Change and adjust points in an automobile engine

Standard: So the automobile engine will run and the dwell angle will be within plus or minus one degree of the dwell angle recommended by the manual.

Intermediate Performance Objectives	Evaluation			Remarks
	Doing Assessment	Knowing Assessment	Attitude Assessment	
1. Recall principles and terms associated with automobile points		1, 2, 3, 4, 5, 6, 7		Attitudes toward tools and materials are evaluated in learning guide number 6
2. Remove automobile points	I-1, I-2, I-3	8, 9, 10, 11		
3. Inspect automobile points	I-4, I-5	12, 13, 14, 15		
4. Install automobile points	I-6, I-7, I-8, I-9, I-10	16, 17, 18, 19		
5. Adjust automobile points	II-1, II-2, II-3, II-4, II-5, II-6, II-7	20, 21, 22, 23, 24, 25		

151

struct two learning guides, one aimed at the removal and installation of points and the other aimed at adjusting points. This decision would be the option of the instructor. It depends on how much material an instructor wishes to include within each guide.

The sample learning guide evaluation blueprint indicates that there are five intermediate performance objectives that the student should satisfy in order to master the terminal performance objective. The spaces provided to the right of the intermediate performance objectives, under the heading "Evaluation," allow the instructor to indicate the instruments and items that are designed to assess whether a person has mastered each intermediate performance objective. This learning guide evaluation blueprint indicates that a total of three instruments were developed to assess whether a person has mastered this task, two performance instruments and one test. One performance instrument assesses whether a student can remove and install new points while the other assesses whether the student can adjust the new points. The first instrument (Roman numeral I) has ten items and the second (Roman numeral II) has seven items. The third instrument is a twenty-five item test designed to assess the extent of the understanding students have of the process of changing and adjusting automobile points. The attitude component is not assessed with any items specific to this learning guide, but the remarks section indicates that the attitudes toward tools and materials which would be relevant to this guide are evaluated in the attitude assessment instrument developed for another learning guide, learning guide 6.

The learning guide evaluation blueprint provides a number of valuable pieces of information which are useful not only in developing instruments, but also in interpreting the information obtained from the instruments. The blueprint indicates how the guide is being evaluated. It indicates the types of instruments that are being used and which items relate to each intermediate performance objective. Earlier, we discussed the fact that assessment instruments should be comprehensive. It is possible to determine whether the instruments that were developed to assess mastery of a particular learning guide are comprehensive by scanning the blueprint for that guide. If items were developed to assess all of the intermediate performance objectives, the learning guide is most likely comprehensively evaluated. Since the items can be documented as having come directly from the content of the guide, it is possible to indicate that the instruments are really measuring what the guide was designed to communicate, and therefore, it has met one of the major considerations for judging the validity of the evaluation.

The blueprint also facilitates diagnosing where students are having difficulties. For example, if the student is not able to perform the performance items I-1 and I-2, the instructor is able to determine that the student cannot remove points correctly. This allows the instructor to diagnose the specific problem which the student is having and allows him to communicate with the student so that the student can correct the problem. The same is also true with the knowing assessment. If the student misses items 12, 13, and 14 contained in the test, this would indicate that the student did not understand the general principles involved in inspecting automobile points. The blueprint also indicates that the attitudes or feelings of the students towards the type of tasks and objects included in this guide were assessed as a part of learning guide 6.

Table 6-4 presents another sample learning guide evaluation blueprint for a task contained in a medical secretary program. One can see that the types of intermediate performance objectives are different than those presented in table 6-3. Table 6-3 presents a task that is primarily a technical skill task. Because it does relate to a technical skill task, it primarily involves an interaction between the person performing the task and things or objects such as tools. Table 6-4 presents a task which re-. quires the interaction of people. The task is for a receptionist to: demonstrate appropriate behavior during the reception of patients. The task has four intermediate objectives. The third intermediate objective, perform the correct job function, requires the person to perform a job function. The terminal performance objective of the guide is designed to help students develop appropriate behaviors during the reception of patients. It is likely that mastery of each of the job functions that might be performed during the process would be large enough to require separate learning guides for each function. If each had a separate learning guide, it would already possess instruments designed to evaluate whether or not a student has mastered a particular function. Therefore, there would be no point in developing new instruments to assess the ability of students to meet intermediate performance objective three. The blueprint refers to the guides which were developed to assist students with mastering the functions (25, 26, 27). When evaluating whether a student has mastered the terminal performance objective presented in table 6-4, the instructor could either assume that the student already had mastered the job functions or could go to the referenced learning guides and use the evaluation instruments designed for those guides. This highlights the need for the sequencing of learning tasks and therefore, the sequencing of learning guides so that one need not teach everything in one learning guide, but learning guides can be used in a cumulative way so that knowledge gained in one learning guide can be assumed in another.

The example in table 6-4 is different from the example of table 6-3 in that the first and the fourth intermediate performance objectives also require the assessment of attitude. The blueprint indicates that the first five items in the attitude assessment were aimed at assessing the student's

TABLE 6-4

SAMPLE LEARNING GUIDE EVALUATION BLUEPRINT

Course: Medical Secretary

TERMINAL PERFORMANCE OBJECTIVE

Given: A patient ready for receiving into a hospital

Performance: Demonstrate appropriate behavior as a receptionist during the reception of the patient

Standard: With 80 percent accuracy as judged by performance on the guide assessment instruments

Intermediate Performance Objectives	Evaluation			Remarks
	Doing Assessment	Knowing Assessment	Attitude Assessment	
1. Identify the patient's emotional state	1, 2, 3, 4	1, 2, 3, 4	1, 2, 3, 4, 5	
2. Identify the job function the patient requires of you		5, 6, 7, 8, 9		
3. Perform the correct job function	assessed in learning guide numbers 25, 26, 27	assessed in learning guide numbers 25, 26, 27		
4. Perform the job function consistent with the patient's emotional state	5, 6, 7, 8 9, 10, 11, 12	10, 11, 12 13	6, 7, 8	

154

feelings during the process of identifying the patient's emotional state. These items probably would deal with how a student feels about people in various emotional states. Attitude items 6, 7, and 8 are related to performing a job function with people in the various emotional states.

We have now seen that the evaluation necessary for the certification of mastery of a task contained in a learning guide usually requires assessment of doing (performance evaluation instruments), knowing (tests), and attitudes (attitude assessment instruments), and how the blueprint can be used to facilitate making sure that the guide is thoroughly evaluated. The next question is, "How are the various items actually constructed?"

Major Types of Evaluation Instruments

There are two major item construction procedures that are used in the development of instruments to assess competence development relative to a task. The first procedure is used in the development of written tests of understanding. The second procedure is used in the development of instruments for the assessment of performance and attitude. The development of tests for assessing understanding will be discussed first since most people have had more experience with this type of instrument than with instruments designed for the assessment of performance and attitude. Later discussions of performance and attitude assessment will build upon the information presented on constructing a test.

CONSTRUCTING WRITTEN TESTS

As indicated earlier, the function of a test is to determine if a person knows those things which allow him or her to perform competently. Usually the things assessed with a written test instrument are not directly observable. They are the generalizations or principles which provide a basis from which a person can perform competently in the occupation.

Test instruments may include each of two basic types of test items: recognition type items and recall type items. Recognition type items are those items which call for the student to recognize the correct answer from among a number of alternative answers provided. Recognition type items include true-false items, multiple-choice items, and matching items. In each case the student is called upon to recognize which of the possible answers presented is the correct answer. In a true-false item the student is asked to recognize whether the statement is true or false. In a multiple-choice item the student is asked to select the answer which best answers the question from among a number of choices or alternative answers. A matching item requires the student to match items in one column with possible alternative answers in the other column. Each of these items will be discussed in detail later.

Recall type items are those which require the student to recall an answer from all of the information which the student possesses. No choices or alternative answers are presented to the student. A situation is presented which requires the student to make a response that must be selected and assembled from all of the information the student possesses. Completion items, listing items, and essay items are classified as recall type items. The completion item requires the student to correctly fill in a blank or blanks in an incomplete sentence. The student must recall the correct words or phrases from all of the knowledge which the student possesses. A listing type item requires the student to list a specific number of things of a certain type. The essay item requires the student to write an essay or description as an answer to a question.

At first glance it would appear that recall type items would provide the best evaluation of a student's ability to understand since they require the student to respond from all of the information possessed, rather than to select from a number of alternatives presented. This first impression leads many vocational instructors to adopt recall type test items when constructing tests. This first impression is incorrect, however. Although the student is required to select the correct answer from a much larger pool of answers when recall items are used, the chances for scorer error in correcting these items offsets this advantage.

Since the number of possible alternative answers to completion items, listing items, and essay items is so great, they are very difficult to score, and usually more than one answer is correct. Therefore, the experience of the person doing the scoring and the flexibility of that person will dictate which answers will be judged correct. Since different instructors have different experiences and different levels of flexibility, they tend to score the same person's test differently, and the test becomes subjective. Although the recognition type items are more susceptible to guessing because the student has to select among a number of alternative answers available, they have the advantage of being objective type items which allow for consistent scoring and, therefore, the elimination of scorer error. The chances of guessing can be calculated for the objective type test items and can be accounted for in the development of an instrument. However, it is usually not possible or feasible to determine the amount of scorer error that occurs while using recall items.

In light of the above problems with recall items, it is not recommended that they be used to assess knowing when trying to assess whether a person has achieved the mastery level. They are valuable during the teaching process when the instructor would like to get some feedback on how well the class is doing or on how well a particular student is performing. However, they are not precise enough to be recommended as part of the assessment used to certify that a person has mastered a task. Another problem with the recall test items is that they cannot be scored by someone who is not thoroughly familiar with the content of the field. It is not possible to allow teaching aides or other people not familiar with the field to score these items. It is also not possible to use computerized scoring techniques with them. The recall items require judgment to score which leads toward subjectivity and consequently a lack of validity of a test.

Levels of Test Items.   When writing test items it is important to remember that the function of a test is to determine whether a student understands what you have taught. It is not the function of a test to trick the student or to pose questions in such a way that the student has to expend considerable effort trying to determine what you are asking. Therefore, the vocabulary level and the sentence structure of the items should be clear and written at the appropriate level for the students that you have. All questions should be clearly understandable to the students.

Many instructors are concerned about the value of written tests. They feel that performance on a test seems to have little relationship to how well a person can actually perform on a job. This feeling is correct if the written tests are developed to measure certain levels of understanding, but is not correct if they are developed to measure other levels of understanding. The *Taxonomy of Educational Objectives* (Bloom et al. 1956) describes six different levels of educational objectives which have implications for the way in which test items are constructed. The first three of the six levels appear to be useful in trying to describe why some tests appear to be able to measure a person's understanding related to performance and others do not. We have adapted them to our example in the following discussion.

The usefulness of a test is related to how it is written and the objective of the test. A test can have an objective of measuring a person's knowledge, comprehension of the knowledge, or ability to apply the knowledge. A test developed to assess a person's knowledge is designed to measure a person's ability to repeat facts. It does not attempt to assess whether a person understands the facts, or can apply the facts, but only that a person can repeat the facts. The following is an example of an item written to measure a person's knowledge.

What is the formula for Ohm's Law?   (*answer:* $E = IR$)

If people can answer this question, we know that they can repeat the formula for Ohm's Law. We do not know whether they understand the formula or whether they can apply the formula.

Items written at the comprehension level are designed to determine if a student can use the knowledge in specified or taught situations or can translate the knowledge into their own words. Items written at the comprehension level allow the instructor to determine that the student understands the material but do not allow the instructor to determine if the student can use the material in a situation other than one that the instructor specifically taught. For example, if we assume that the instructor taught the student to calculate the resistance in a circuit using Ohm's Law if amperage and voltage are given, the following item would be a comprehension level item.

Using Ohm's Law, calculate the resistance in a circuit that draws three amperes of current at 120 volts.   (*answer:* $\frac{120}{3} = 40$ ohms)

If the student can arrive at the correct answer to this question, we know that the student can do what he was taught. We still do not know whether the student can apply Ohm's Law in a setting where a unique problem is encountered and he is not told that Ohm's Law is the principle that should be used in obtaining a solution. However, we do know that the student has more of a command of Ohm's Law than just knowing the formula. Another example of a comprehensive level item related to the Ohm's Law formula would be:

Describe the relationships between voltage, amperage, and resistance as presented in the Ohm's Law formula in your own words. (*answer:* voltage is equal to the current in amperes times the resistance in ohms.)

In this example the key to whether or not the item is a comprehension level item as contrasted with a knowledge item is whether the student is asked to present the relationship in his own words. If the student repeats back the relationship in the exact words that were taught, then the item is a knowledge level item. If the student can internalize the information taught and repeat the information back in his own words, then the student has comprehended.

The third level at which test items can be written that appears to be meaningful to vocational instructors is the application level. Items designed to measure understanding at the application level are designed to determine if students can apply knowledge in new, untaught situations. In other words, given a situation where the knowledge should be applied, it will be applied even though the student never saw that particular situation before. Most vocational instructors would like their students to eventually be able to apply knowledge of the field whenever appropriate and not only in those specific instances or cases that were discussed in class. This type of testing usually requires the presentation of a real life problem which the student is asked to solve or react to. Assuming that the information concerning Ohm's Law was taught as indicated above, the following item would be an application level item.

What size fuse would be needed in order to operate a hairdryer which has 80 ohms resistance on a 120-volt circuit?

(*answer:* $\dfrac{120}{80} = 1.5$ amperes)

The key differences between an item written at the comprehension level and an item written at the application level are whether or not the student is requested to use the information learned in a new situation that was untaught and if the principle to be applied in arriving at the solution is unspecified in the question. The comprehension example items ask the student to take the information that was taught and either to restate the information in new words or to apply the information in a setting similar to the one in which the information was taught. The application level item asks the student to react to a new situation that the student has never seen before, to determine what information is appropriate to arrive at the correct answer, and to apply that information to arrive at the correct answer.

As you can see, instructors can obtain more and more information about the ability of students to utilize the information they are taught if they design their test items to measure at the comprehension and application levels instead of at the knowledge level. One of the reasons that many vocational instructors are suspicious of written tests is that many of the written tests that they have seen or developed themselves are written to measure primarily the knowledge level. Such items would assess the ability of students to repeat or recognize definitions, require people to write down memorized lists, or require people to write out formulas. These kinds of items really do not get at whether a person can utilize the information in an occupation. Since instructors wish their students to perform in an occupation and these items do not relate to whether a person can actually use the information, tests constructed with items developed at the knowledge level really do not fill the need. However, if items are written at the comprehension and application levels (particularly the application level) they can assess whether a person can use the information in an occupation and, therefore, should be related to whether a person can perform in the occupation. The point is, you can only evaluate the effectiveness of a test if you are sure which level you wish the items to be assessing. If you wish to assess a person's comprehension or ability to apply knowledge, you should not use knowledge level items.

There are times when items written at the knowledge level are appropriate. During the teaching of any material, instructors will first introduce basic definitions, formulas, and principles which they then build on and show students how to apply. During the initial introduction of the material, it may be very appropriate to test a person's knowledge of basic facts. One should have the basic formula for Ohm's Law thoroughly in mind before attempting to apply the formula. Therefore, knowledge level items are typically used when first introducing information. Most instructors then move on to applying facts to a series of highly prescribed examples that they used during teaching. These examples are used to show students the basic applications of the information. Students are then tested with comprehension level items to determine if they can apply the knowledge in those situations which they were taught. Later students are asked to apply and integrate many types of knowledge that they learned earlier to new situations which they have never seen before. In most occupations, when students have arrived at the level of understanding which allows them to apply the knowledge to situations which they have never seen before, they are ready to enter the occupation. At this stage, application level items would be appropriate.

Constructing Test Items.   Earlier the advantages and disadvantages of the different types of written test items were discussed. The following is a discussion of how each of the items should be constructed along with some hints that are useful when trying to improve the quality of the items. Although all of the types of items are unique, there are some general rules which one should observe when constructing any of the types of items. You should review them briefly before reading the sections on constructing each type of item and then return to read them in more detail after you have read the other sections on the types of items.

1. The directions for how to complete a type of item should indicate (a) what to do, (b) how to do it, (c) where to place the response, and (d) one example.
2. The example for each type of test item should not be numbered but should be indicated with an "X." (This makes the examples easily distinguished from the other items and does not confuse the numbering of the tests.)
3. The responses to the items on a test should not form a pattern which can be detected by a student (e.g., all true items should not be followed by all false items).
4. Highlight any unusually crucial words in an item that students should be sure to take into account when selecting the correct choice by underlining them. (For example, if you would like

the student to select the choice which is not correct from a number of choices that are correct, the word *not* should be underlined. This practice calls crucial words to the students' attention so they read the items correctly.)

True-False Items: True-false items can be divided into regular true-false items and modified true-false items. A regular true-false item presents the students with a statement which must be judged as a true statement or a false statement. For example,

True-false 1.   A magnet will attract glass.
                 Answer   1.   F

Since this statement is false, the student should indicate that the statement is false. The student could do this in a variety of ways depending upon the directions which are given. A sample set of directions might be:

The following statements are either true or false. If the statement is true place a "T" in the blank space with the same number as the item number on your answer sheet. If the statement is false, place an "F" in the blank. The first item is answered as an example.

The same test item presented above could also be written as a modified true-false item. A modified true-false item requires the student to indicate if the statement is true or false and if it is false, the student is asked to indicate why. For example, the student could be presented the above item and told if it is false, write the word that makes the statement false in the blank space provided on the answer sheet. If this statement was added to the directions given above, the answer would appear as follows:

Answer Sheet 1.   F   glass

There are a large number of possible modifications that can be used. Any of them are acceptable as long as the directions are clear so the student is aware of exactly what to do.

At times a person wishes to write a number of regular true-false items all pertaining to the same principle. For example:

T   F   1. A magnet will attract iron.
T   F   2. A magnet will attract glass.
T   F   3. A magnet will attract aluminum.
T   F   4. A magnet will attract steel.

In such a case it is possible to combine all of these regular true-false items into a cluster true-false set to conserve space on the test and item writing time. A cluster true-false set is composed of a "root statement" followed by a number of incomplete statements that will complete the root statement resulting in either a true or false statement. For example, the above regular true-false items could be combined into a cluster true-false set as follows:

> A magnet will attract:
> Ⓣ F   X. iron.
> T   F   1. glass.
> T   F   2. aluminum.
> T   F   3. steel.

Each possible completion of the root statement is considered to be an item because it calls for a student response. All of the items that relate to the same root statement are called a set. The directions for a cluster true-false set might be written as follows:

> Incomplete sentences are presented below followed by a number of phrases which will complete the sentence and make it true or false. If a phrase completes a true statement, circle the "T" before the phrase. Circle the "F" if the phrase completes a false statement. The first item is answered as an example.

The example in such a cluster true-false set would be the first item of the first set in the test. The above sample set shows the example indicated by an "X." Cluster true-false items are written using the same general guidelines used when writing any true-false item. However, they are generally written only if there are at least three items in the set. If there are only two possible items, they can be written as regular true-false items.

The following are a number of hints which are helpful when writing any type of true-false items.

1. Make approximately half of the items true and half of the items false.

2. Make sure the true statements are not consistently longer than the false statements. (There is a tendency for true statements to be longer than false statements because true statements generally must include more description of a specific situation in which the statement is true. Few things are true in all situations.)

3. Avoid using absolute terms such as "always" and "never." (Few things are always true or never true. Therefore, statements including these terms are usually false.)

The major advantage of true-false items is that they are easy to construct and score. The major disadvantage is that a student has a 50 percent chance of guessing them correctly, and therefore a true-false test must be quite long in order to provide a reliable assessment of a person's understanding.

Multiple-Choice Items: Multiple-choice items are characterized by a statement (root statement) followed by at least four other statements (choices), one of which is in a direct way related to the first statement. The student is asked to select the choice that is correctly related to the first statement as the correct answer. One possible relationship between the first root statement and the following choices may be that one of the choices completes the root statement. For example,

Vocational education is designed to serve the needs of
  A. minorities.
  B. unemployed.
  C. youth.
  D. all of these.

The relationship between the root statement and the choices might be that the root statement asks a question and the choices are possible answers to that question. For example,

What group is vocational education designed to serve?
  A. minorities.
  B. unemployed.
  C. youth.
  D. all of these.

The relationship between the root statement and the choices might be that the root statement presents a problem and the choices present possible solutions to the problem. For example,

What ampere fuse would be required in a 120-volt circuit operating a 60-ohm iron?
  A. .2 ampere.
  B. 1 ampere.
  C. 2 amperes.
  D. 3 amperes.

There are many possible relationships between the root statement of a multiple-choice item and the choices; we have discussed but a few. The directions given the student must be comprehensive enough to cover all of them. Many people use the following directions for multiple-choice items.

Directions: Each of the questions or incomplete statements listed below is followed by several words, phrases, or a series of numbers. Choose the one which best answers the question or completes the statement correctly. Place the letter associated with that choice (A, B, C, or D) in the numbered blank space on your answer sheet. The first item is answered as an example.

The following hints are usually helpful when writing multiple-choice items.

1. The root statement should contain a problem which requires the student to *apply* knowledge rather than to just repeat facts.

2. Each item should have at *least* four possible choices. (This reduces the chances of guessing the correct answer. The chance of guessing the answer to an item can be calculated by dividing 100 percent by the number of possible choices—$4)\overline{100} = 25$ percent. If three choices are used, the chance of guessing increases to 33⅓ percent.

3. Make sure all of the possible choices would be reasonable to someone who does not know the content. (An obviously wrong choice is the same as no choice at all and the chances of guessing the correct answer increase.)

4. Choices should be called for at the end of the root statement rather than at the beginning or in the middle. (See the discussion of completion items.)

5. If choices are a series of numbers they should be placed in ascending or descending order (e.g., 10, 15, 20, 25 or 25, 20, 15, 10). The purpose of an item is to determine if a student understands which is the correct answer and not whether he can sort out a series of numbers.

6. List each choice on a separate line. (It is much easier for a student to see and review the separate choices if they are placed on separate lines going down the page than if they are placed across the page. See the sample items presented earlier.)

7. Use capital letters to indicate each choice. (Capital letters are easier to distinguish from the rest of the printing on a page.)

8. Punctuate items just as you would punctuate a sentence. (If the choices are complete sentences, they should begin with a capital letter and end with a period. If they are not complete sentences they should not begin with capitals or end with periods. If the root statement is a question it should be followed by a question mark, etc.)

The multiple choice item is the most widely used type of item. It has the advantages of being an objective type of item with no scoring error as well as having a relatively low guessing error. It is also flexible in that it can be written in a variety of forms as seen earlier.

Matching Items: Matching items are combined into a set of items that all relate to some common topic. They require a number of choices to be made from a pool or group of choices. A matching set can be viewed as a method of simplifying the writing of a series of separate multiple-choice items relating to the same topic. For example, we could write the following test items relating to characteristics of a good test as multiple-choice items.

1. A test which measures what you want it to measure is
   A. objective.
   B. valid.
   C. reliable.
   D. comprehensive

2. A test which measures accurately and consistently is
   A. objective.
   B. valid.
   C. reliable.
   D. comprehensive.

3. A test which can be scored consistently by different people so they will all arrive at the same score for the same student is
   A. objective.
   B. valid.
   C. reliable.
   D. comprehensive.

All of these items deal with a common topic, characteristics of a good test. Therefore, they could be combined into the following matching set.

Directions: Match the definitions of characteristics of a good test in the left-hand column with the correct term in the right-hand column and place the answer in the corresponding blank before each definition. The first term is answered as an example.

Definitions   *Terms*

___D___ X. A test which samples all of the   A. objective.
content you wish to assess is   B. valid.

_____ 1. A test which measures what you   C. reliable.
want it to measure is   D. comprehensive.

_____ 2. A test which measures accurately   E. subjective.
and consistently is   F. discriminatory.

_____ 3. A test which can be scored con-   G. random.
sistently by different people
so they will all arrive at the
same score for the same student is

This matching set allows us to assess the same things as we did with the multiple-choice items, but allows us to do it more efficiently.

The relationships between the things to be matched can be stated in as many ways as the relationships between the root statements and the choices in multiple-choice items. Therefore, each separate matching set included in a test usually requires separate directions which point out the relationships among the things to be matched and the choices.

The following are a number of hints that are useful when writing matching items and matching sets which go beyond those discussed relative to multiple-choice items.

1. Matching sets usually include at least three but not more than ten items to be matched. (If there are only two items it is more efficient to write two multiple-choice items. If there are more than ten, the items should be broken down into two sets.)

2. Include at least three more choices than there are things to match. (The last choice made should be made from four choices in order to reduce guessing.)

3. Use only related materials in the same set. (This allows one set of directions to apply to all items in the matching set and allows all of the choices to be reasonable answers to the items.)

4. Place the column containing the longer statements on the left side of the page. (People tend to read an item on the left side of the page and then scan the choices on the right side of the page. Since the items on the left are only read once and the choices on the right are scanned many times, the long statements should be on the left.)

A form of matching items that goes beyond the types of items commonly found as multiple-choice items uses pictures or diagrams. Portions of the diagram are identified by letters A, B, C, etc. and the student is asked to match a statement in the left-hand column with the appropriate letter identifying a portion of the diagram.

True-false items, multiple-choice items, and matching items are all forms of recognition type items discussed earlier. They all require the student to recognize the correct answer from among a number of possible answers presented. Tests constructed of these types of items are sometimes referred to as objective tests since they can be scored consistently and fairly. Once a scoring key is developed which indicates which choice is the correct answer to each item on such a test, anyone can score the test using that key and arrive at the same score for a student.

We will now discuss recall type items which require a student to select an answer from all of the knowledge which he possesses. Tests constructed of these types of items are sometimes called subjective tests because they require judgment on the part of the scorer which is difficult to duplicate when the same scorer judges different students or when different scorers judge the same student. Recall items can be made more objective by specifying all possible correct answers before students respond to an item. Of course, this is easier said than done. These items are not recommended for use in assessment instruments used to certify task mastery. They are recommended as additional test item forms that might be used by the instructor to obtain feedback on how instruction is progressing in the classroom.

Completion Items: A completion item is a sentence containing one or more blanks which the student fills in to make a true statement. For example:

A typical automobile has a/an _____ _____ engine.
1. *internal*
   combustion

Directions for completion items typically are stated as follows:

Each of the statements below contains a blank or blanks at or near the end of the statement. You are to place the word or words in the blank spaces to the left of the statements. The first item is answered as an example.

Completion items are easy to construct but difficult to score. Students can provide a variety of answers that would complete any sentence correctly. The problem is to determine which answers are reasonable and which are not without being arbitrary. For example, the item above could be answered by inserting *"gasoline powered."* Would that answer be correct? The following are a number of hints that are helpful in constructing completion items.

1. Place the blanks at or near the end of the sentence. (The student should have all of the information needed to fill in a blank before encountering the blank. If the blank is near the beginning, the student must read the entire sentence once and then return to the beginning to try to figure out what should go into the blank.)
2. Rarely include more than two blanks.
3. Develop a scoring list of possible correct responses. (The more complete this list is, the less subjectivity will have to be exercised in judging if the answer is correct. During the scoring process this list may need to be expanded as students provide answers that are correct which you did not think of.)

Listing Items: Listing item sets call for the student to list a specific number of things. They are a way of simplifying a large number of completion items, as a matching set is a way of simplifying a large number of multiple-choice items. Each item in a listing set could be written as a separate completion item. There are no general directions for listing items since each listing item set has its own specific directions. There are two general forms of listing sets. One form asks the student to list a number of objects or things but does not require them to be listed in order. The other type asks the student to list a number of things in order. This type usually is used when testing student knowledge of procedural steps. The following is an example of a listing set in which order is not an important factor. Each response is considered an item.

List four different makes of American automobiles. The first item is answered as an example.

X. Oldsmobile	Answers:	
1. _____	Chevrolet	
2. _____	Ford	
3. _____	Chrysler	
4. _____	Rambler	

This set asks the student to list four different types of American-made automobiles but it does not call for any order in the listing. An example is given, although examples are not always required with listing items. The following set requires the student to list things in order.

List the four strokes of a four-cycle gasoline engine in order.

         Answers:
1. _____ intake
2. _____ compression
3. _____ power
4. _____ exhaust

In this case, order is important and the student is informed that he is to list the strokes in order.

As with the completion items, the listing items are difficult to score. A person should identify all possible correct answers students might provide. If the items are to be listed in a particular order, the instructor must determine how the listing items will be scored if one item is out of order or if all of the items are out of order. The following are a few helpful hints which may be useful when developing listing items.

1. The first response to be listed in the first listing set should be used as an example and should be indicated by an X, if an example is used.
2. Generally not more than six or eight things are listed within one listing set.
3. If the listing must be in order, this should be indicated in the directions.
4. Develop a scoring list of as many possible answers to the listing items as you can before administering them to students. Be ready to accept additional legitimate answers provided by students.

Essay Items: An essay item usually asks the student to present a narrative explanation or definition. For example, the student might be asked to provide the definition of validity. The student might also be asked to explain the relationship between validity and reliability. Essay type items allow the instructor to determine if the student can explain complex relationships. They are, however, very difficult to score. Many times the scoring of these items is based, to a large extent, on the experience and flexibility of the instructor. Scoring objectivity can be increased by determining the specific things that you would like students to include within the essay answer. The item can then be scored by judging how many of those things you were looking for were actually included by the student. You could also establish rules for granting credit if certain relationships are brought out by the student in the explanation and others are not. For example, if the student brings out one important concept he will be granted one point; two concepts, two points; etc. The following are a few helpful hints that might be useful when writing essay items.

1. Identify the specific concepts or points you wish to have included in the answers. Be ready to accept alternative reasonable explanations as possible correct answers.
2. Use these items only if you wish to have students explain or describe something. If you wish students to provide a listing, use a listing type item.
3. Determine definite rules to be used for granting credit while marking each essay question.

There are a number of other types of items that are sometimes used by instructors which will just be mentioned. Problems are sometimes used, especially if they can be answered with a numerical value. These items are objective items because a person can either provide the correct numerical value or cannot. At times partial points are given for correct procedure even if the answer is not correct. If this procedure is used, care must be taken to specify the basis upon which partial credit will be given. Another type of item that is sometimes used is an object test item. An object test is conducted by labeling parts of machines or tools with tape (e.g., 1, 2, 3, 4), and providing the student with a series of blanks with the same identification numbers. The student observes the piece of equipment or tool and writes the correct name down on the piece of paper in the corresponding blank. This type of test is called an object test because it uses real objects.

Assembling a Test.   Tests are generally assembled so that students encounter the easiest type of item to respond to first and the most difficult type of item to respond to last. Many educators feel that this organizational pattern produces less psychological strain on the student than if a test were organized in a reverse pattern. This does not say that the easiest item is always placed first and the most difficult item placed last. It is not possible to judge which items a particular person will find most difficult. However, it is much easier to respond to a true-false item than it is to respond to an essay type item.

The following discussion of how to organize a test will assume that the instructor wishes to include all types of test items in the test. This is not always done. It is possible to construct a test composed of all true-false items, all multiple-choice items, etc. If, however, the instructor wishes to place a number of different types of test items in the same test, they should be in the same relative order as discussed below. The suggested order is:

1. true-false
2. cluster true-false
3. multiple choice
4. matching
5. completion
6. listing
7. essay or problem

If any type of an item is not included in a test, the other types of items that are included should be in the same relative order.

A test should begin with a clear heading. The heading should fulfill at least two functions: (1) it should identify the course in which the test is being used, and (2) it should identify the content included within the test. Sometimes the date is also included so the instructor can tell the difference between one version of a test on a particular subject and another version. Other optional pieces of information are sometimes included in the heading such as the instructor's name.

Some people place a set of general directions immediately following the heading. The general directions are used primarily for administrative purposes. They inform the student about what should be done after the test is completed or any general announcements that the student should be aware of during the time he is taking the test. After the general directions, the items are placed on the test in the order described above. The items should be written along with the appropriate directions as indicated in the previous sections of this chapter pertaining to the writing of items. The items should be numbered consecutively from the beginning to the end. If the test calls for a total of 50 different responses, the items should be numbered from 1 to 50. There should only be one number 1 on a test, one number 2, etc. The example for each type of item should be indicated with an X. This makes the examples easily distinguished from the other items.

If an answer sheet is used, the answer sheet should have the same identifying information as included in the test heading. The blank spaces on the answer sheet should be numbered in the same way as the items are numbered on the test. The blanks on the answer sheet should be large enough for the student to respond adequately to a question.

Constructing Performance Evaluation Instruments

The evaluation of performance requires a different methodology from that used when writing a test. Tests usually evaluate things that cannot be seen, such as understandings of principles and ideas. Performance evaluations allow the instructor to judge performance that can be seen. Performance evaluations generally take one of two forms. They take the form of performance tests or product evaluations. Performance tests are used when the instructor is interested in determining if the student can perform the correct process as well as if the student can produce the correct product. Product evaluations are used when the instructor is primarily interested in whether the student can produce the correct product. A performance test requires the instructor to observe the student as he is completing a process and, therefore, allows the instructor to determine if the product is completed correctly. The product may be completed correctly using the correct process or an incorrect process.

From this discussion it is apparent that a performance test will provide a better evaluation of a student's ability to "do" than will a product evaluation. However, a performance test does have some drawbacks. Performance tests must be administered on a one-to-one basis. In order for the instructor to observe the performance of one student, the instructor cannot be responsive to the other students in the class. If the performance test is lengthy, this could cause serious problems in the classroom. Many students might be needing help, but the instructor could not provide assistance.

Product evaluations allow the instructor to evaluate the product which is the result of the process, but not the process itself. However, they have the advantage of allowing the instructor to evaluate the performance of students after class or during periods of time when students do not require assistance.

The basic procedure for developing performance tests or product evaluations involves three major steps.

1. Specification of the objective. The objective is usually stated as a three-part objective.
2. Specification of items to be observed.
3. Specification of criteria which form the basis for judging whether the student has satisfactorily completed each of the items to be observed.

Specifying the Objective.   As discussed in the chapter on stating objectives and in relation to constructing the learning guide evaluation blueprint, the objective should be stated as a three-part objective. The three-part objective should include (1) a statement of the conditions which are given and within which the student must perform, (2) the performance expected of the student, and (3) the performance standard against which student performance will be judged. The size of the expected performance to be included in the objective is a critical concern to the instructor when constructing performance evaluations. In any occupation there are some basic doing tasks which form the foundation for most other performances in the occupation. There are also a wide variety of tasks which require the combination of two or more of the basic elementary doing tasks to arrive at the performance of a more complex task. In constructing a performance evaluation instrument, one must be aware of the prerequisite doing and knowing skills which a student is expected to bring to the task. If an instructor can assume that students who attempt a complex task have already mastered certain elementary tasks which are part of the complex task, they need not be reevaluated. For example, an elementary task in electronics is to measure the resistance of a resistor. There is a distinct procedure that a student should follow in measuring the resistance of a resistor. This task could be taught and evaluated with a performance test or a product evaluation. A more complex task in electronics would be to analyze a circuit. One step in analyzing a circuit would be to check the quality of the resistors. If the instructor could assume that a student had already mastered how to measure the resistance of a resistor, the measuring of resistance of the resistors in the circuit could be covered as one step in the performance evaluation instrument. If the instructor could not assume that a student had mastered how to measure the resistance of a resistor before the student would be asked to analyze a circuit, the evaluation instrument for the task of analyzing a circuit would also have to include all steps that the student would have to go through in order to measure the resistance of a resistor. The instrument would not only be called upon to provide a basis for judging if a student can "analyze" the circuit, but it would also be called upon to provide a basis for judging if a student can "measure" the resistance of a resistor.

The above discussion highlights one of the largest problems which instructors have when trying to develop performance evaluation instruments. They are told that a performance evaluation instrument should be capable of providing a basis for evaluating a total performance. In many cases a total performance is a very complex task, such as analyzing a circuit. They interpret this to mean that they are to develop an instrument which includes every microperformance that a student will be called upon to perform during the completion of the task. With this interpretation, a performance evaluation instrument becomes unreasonably complex and long. The above discussion highlights the fact that any performance is generally a combination of more elementary performances. Therefore, during the sequencing of instruction it would appear reasonable to teach those basic concepts which are fundamental to many performances first. These performances can then be evaulated, and upon encountering a complex task, the instructor could assume that the student had command of the prerequisite performance. The evaluation instruments for more complex tasks could use these elementary tasks as steps and not have to concentrate on evaluating all of the microsteps. If this process is used, even a performance evaluation instrument for a complex task need not become unreasonably long. In the example of analyzing a circuit, the instructor could concentrate on the performance called for in the verb, "analyzing." The instructor could develop the instrument around the process of analyzing and assume that the performance capabilities of the students would allow them to adequately perform the fundamental performance tasks which are called upon during the process of analyzing.

It is apparent from this discussion that a performance evaluation instrument centers around the performance called for in the verb contained in the objective. Each performance evaluation should allow an instructor to judge whether the student has mastered the behavior which the verb describes or implies. Using the above example, a performance evaluation instrument developed to determine if a student can measure the resistance of a resistor would concentrate on the verb "measure." If the student masters the task he can measure. If a performance evaluation instrument is developed to determine if a person can analyze a circuit, then the performance evaluation instrument should center around the verb "analyze." This points out the great care that must be taken while selecting the correct verb.

Once the verb is selected and the student can be told the type of behavioral performance that is expected, the context of the performance should be described. This is done by specifying the "givens." The "givens" define the tools, previous prerequisite knowledges, and other machines or prerequisites which the student will be required to utilize in demonstrating the behavior. The specification of the "givens" is a very important part of specifying the objective. The procedure that a student might use in accomplishing the expected behavior might be completely different depending upon the assumed givens. The procedure that would be used in grinding a tool bit would be considerably different if one were expected to grind it with a typical pedestal grinding wheel rather than if one were expected to use an automatic tool grinding machine. The product that would be produced would probably be evaluated to the same standard, but the performance would be evaluated much differently because the machines are so much different. Therefore, a performance evaluation instrument developed to determine if a student can grind a tool bit with an automatic tool grinder would be different from the one that would be used for determining if a student can grind a tool with a pedestal grinder. The behavior and the expected performance standard would be the same but the givens would be much different.

Alternative methods of accomplishing the same end are possible in most vocational fields. If an instructor is only interested in a student accomplishing a specific end, then the givens are not really important. If an instructor is concerned that a student be able to arrive at an end using a specific procedure or a number of different procedures, then the givens become very important so that the instructor can develop performance evaluation instruments that will allow him to determine if the student can actually perform the alternative procedures correctly.

The third part of a three-part objective is the performance "standard" which will be used to judge if a student has mastered a task. In the above example of grinding a tool bit, one could indicate that the tool bit should be ground within plus or minus one degree of the angles called for in a machinist's manual. The purpose of defining the level of performance expected is to communicate the quality of performance that is expected of the student on the task. It also provides a basis for the instructor to judge the quality of the product. The standard should be established based upon the entry level job performance requirements for people entering the occupation.

Developing Performance Evaluation Items.   A performance item is one item that is observed by the instructor as he evaluates the performance. In a performance test the items are typically steps of procedure which the student must complete in order to complete the performance. In a product evaluation the items are related to aspects of the product that can be observed, which imply that the student has performed correctly. For example, if the task is to assemble a two-barrel carburetor, an instructor could evaluate this by observing the person while he assembles the carburetor, which would be a performance test; or he could evaluate the student's assembled carburetor after it was assembled, which would be a product evaluation. In a performance test the item would typically be stated as: assemble cover onto carburetor. In a product evaluation it would typically be stated as: assembled cover onto carburetor. You will notice that both items begin with a verb which indicates the behavior which the student is expected to perform. In the case of a performance test item, the verb is stated as a direct command as if it were a direction given to the student. This is because the instructor is present at the time the student is actually doing the performance. The item in the product evaluation is stated in the past tense since the instructor is evaluating the product of the performance after the performance is completed.

The procedures used to determine the items for both performance tests and product evaluations are quite similar. They both start with the definition of the objective. The next step is to determine which items should be observed during the performance or on the product. Not all performance items can be observed as product items. If the task is to prepare and give an insulin injection, one item of a performance evaluation related to this task would be to fill the syringe with insulin. If this item were in a performance test, the instructor would observe if the student filled the syringe to the correct level. If the item were in a product evaluation, the instructor would have to determine how he might judge if the student performed the item correctly after the injection was given. In this case it would be almost impossible to judge this item in a product evaluation. One could examine the insulin bottle prior to the student's administering the injection and then after the student administered the injection to determine the amount of insulin taken from the bottle. This, however, would be a crude measure since the student may have taken too much from the bottle and disposed of it prior to giving the injection.

This points out that not all performances can be adequately evaluated with both a performance test and a product evaluation. In this example, it is almost impossible to determine if the student correctly gave the injection unless the process of giving the injection is observed. Once the injection is given, there is no way to determine the adequacy of the injection by viewing the patient except by very gross methods. If the student made a drastic mistake, this would cause a drastic effect on the patient and it would be observed.

Performance Test Items: The following is an example of how the items to be included in a performance test are identified. The topic or task of the example is: drill a 3/32" diameter hole in cold rolled steel. The detailed three-part objective is: given a drill press, 3/32" drills, center-punch, cutting oil, hammer and a piece of cold rolled steel; drill a 3/32" hole in cold rolled steel; so that the hole is 3/32" in diameter and perpendicular to the surface. This objective provides the base from which the performance test is created. It defines what is going to be evaluated. In this example we are going to evaluate whether a student has mastered the task of drilling a 3/32" diameter hole in cold rolled steel given a drill press, 3/32" drills, center-punch, cutting oil, hammer, and a piece of cold rolled steel. Our problem is to identify the procedural steps that will need to be observed in order to certify that a student has mastered the task. One way to accomplish this identification of the procedural steps is to envision a circle. The circle represents the entire task to be evaluated. The instructor's job is to determine how to break the circle up into parts that can each be evaluated in such a way that when they are all evaluated they add up and totally evaluate the task that has to be certified. Figure 6-2 is an example of such a task breakdown. The circle represents the total task of drilling a 3/32" hole in cold rolled steel. The steps are identified, as indicated in the figure. When identifying and stating the steps the following rules should be observed.

1. Each step should begin with a verb.
2. Each step should be independent of the other steps. (The same performance should not be evaluated in more than one step.)
3. Each step should include only one performance.
4. If an instructor evaluates each of the steps he should have totally evaluated the performance.

If we examine figure 6-2, we will see that the steps that have been identified meet these four criteria. Each of them begins with a verb that describes the nature of the behavior that is expected. Each step is independent. For example, the student is not asked to center-punch the workpiece twice during the performance. Each step includes only one performance. For example, the first step: select the correct size drill, only

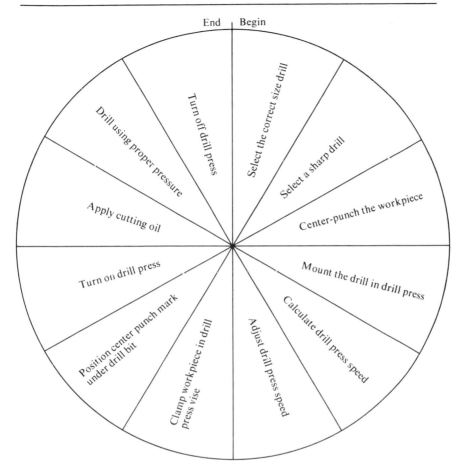

FIGURE 6-2

Sample Performance Test Task Breakdown

indicates that the student should "select" the drill. This step might have been combined with the second step to indicate that students should select a correct size drill which is sharp. If this is done, however, and the student does not complete this step correctly, it would not be possible to determine if the student did not select the correct size drill or did not select a sharp drill. Therefore, in order to develop diagnostic information which can indicate where a student did not perform adequately, it is important that each step contain a single concept so the concept that is not completed correctly can be readily identified.

After the performance steps have been identified using the above procedure, they are used along with the objective as the foundation for creating a performance test. The most common form of a performance test is a performance checklist. A performance checklist indicates the objective the student was to achieve, procedural steps the student should have gone through in order to achieve this objective, and criteria for making a judgment about whether the student completed each step satisfactorily (see sample A). The characteristic of this performance test which makes it a checklist is that the student either performs the steps satisfactorily or performs them unsatisfactorily. An instrument of this type which includes only two possible choices is called a checklist. If the instrument allowed for the categorization of a student's performance on each step into three or more categories, the instrument would be called a performance rating scale. In most cases vocational educators use performance checklists since they only require one criterion to be specified for each performance step. This criterion allows the instructor to judge the difference between satisfactory and unsatisfactory performance. If three categories are used, the instructor is called upon to develop two criteria for each performance step. The first would be used to judge the difference between the highest and middle performance categories and the next would be used to judge the difference between the middle and lowest categories.

Sample A shows how these pieces of information are combined into a performance checklist. A heading should be placed on a performance checklist just as on a written test. This allows the instructor to identify the course and the content for which the checklist was developed. The performance checklist is labeled "performance checklist" to indicate that it is different from a product evaluation. Next the three-part objective is specified which indicates the exact task the student is expected to perform and the exact task which is going to be evaluated. The procedural steps are listed as they were developed using the format described earlier. The criteria or rules for judging whether the student has completed each step correctly are identified and placed opposite the procedural steps. In sample A, the criterion for judging whether or not the student selected the correct size drill was: 3/32-inch drill. The criterion for determining if the student selected a sharp drill was: cutting edges do not reflect light. Criteria are also listed for each of the other steps.

After the basic instrument is constructed, the instructor must determine how the instrument will be scored. Generally a number of points are assigned for completing each step correctly. In the example presented in sample A, one point was given for each step completed correctly. This indicates that the instructor who developed this checklist considered each step to be just as important in the process and assigned each the same number of points. If you feel that one step should be given more weight than another step, you can assign more points to that step. If one step is twice as important as another step, that step might be given

SAMPLE A
PERFORMANCE CHECKLIST
DRILL COLD ROLLED STEEL

Course: Machine Shop

TERMINAL PERFORMANCE OBJECTIVE:

Given: A drill press, 3/32'' drills, center-punch, cutting oil, hammer and a piece of cold rolled steel

Performance: Drill a 3/32'' hole in cold rolled steel

Standard: The hole should be 3/32'' in diameter and perpendicular to the surface

Critical Items	Procedural Steps	Sat.	Unsat.	Criteria (Bases for making judgments)
*	1. Select the correct size drill	1	0	3/32'' drill
*	2. Select a sharp drill	1	0	cutting edges do not reflect light
	3. Center-punch the workpiece	1	0	punch is deep enough to allow drill to start penetrating without wandering
	4. Mount drill in drill press	1	0	tighten chuck with chuck key
	5. Calculate drill press speed	1	0	calculate using RPM formula
	6. Adjust drill press speed	1	0	adjust to closest speed adjustment
	7. Clamp workpiece in drill press vise	1	0	workpiece clamped tightly
	8. Position center punched mark under drill bit	1	0	lower drill bit onto the workpiece and center drill in punch mark
	9. Turn on drill press	1	0	switch turned on
	10. Apply cutting oil	1	0	apply a few drops on center punch mark
	11. Drill using proper pressure	1	0	pressure is firm but drill does not bend
	12. Turn off drill press	1	0	switch turned off

Total score possible = 12   Total score _____
Minimum mastery   = 11
level score

179

two points and the other step given one. After the points have been assigned, the total number of possible points is determined by adding up all the points possible on the instrument. When this is completed, the instructor should assign some minimum mastery level score which he is willing to accept as indicating that the student has mastered the performance. If 100 percent mastery is required, the student must complete each step satisfactorily. If the instructor is willing to accept a lesser number of points as indicating mastery, he must indicate the minimum level acceptable score. At times a step is considered to be a critical step. In other words, if a student misses this step he automatically has not mastered the task even though the point value he gets is greater than the minimum score. This is similar to going through a stop sign during a driver's test. In a driver's test, most items are assigned a certain number of points. If you do not perform an item correctly, a certain number of points are deducted. However, if you go through a stop sign, you automatically must repeat the test. In the example, steps 1 and 2 are labeled critical steps. If the student does not select the correct size drill or does not select a sharp drill, the instructor would stop the performance and ask the student to repeat it.

Sample B is another sample performance checklist. It was developed for the task: don a sterile gown. In this case the instructor felt that there were five steps in donning a sterile gown. These steps were identified by determining that they were independent, each measured only one concept, and there were no additional steps. Each begins with a verb. They were placed in the performance checklist indicated in sample B, and the criteria were specified. One point was assigned for each step. In this case, a 100 percent score is needed for mastery. Therefore, the student is expected to get a score of five out of five points in order to master the task.

Product Evaluation Items: A product evaluation instrument should be constructed using the same basic procedures. The same objectives would be stated as those used with performance tests. However, when identifying the steps, the steps would be identified in terms of what can be seen after the performance is completed. Each step would be constructed using the same four criteria for judging whether the steps were developed correctly as indicated earlier. However, the verb would be stated in the past tense rather than the present tense. If the task presented in sample A: "drill a 3/32″ hole in cold rolled steel," were evaluated to the performance standard indicated in sample A, there would be only two product evaluation items that could be observed. One would be whether the hole was actually 3/32-inch diameter and the other would be whether the hole was perpendicular to the surface. It would not be possible to examine any techniques or whether the correct tools were used to do the job. However, the technique of using instructor checkpoints could be used so that a prod-

SAMPLE B
PERFORMANCE CHECKLIST
DON A STERILE GOWN

Course: *Practical Nursing*

TERMINAL PERFORMANCE OBJECTIVE:

Given: A sterile towel and gown after scrubbing

Performance: Don a sterile gown

Standard: Without contaminating the gown, yourself or other sterile objects

Critical Items	Procedural Steps	Sat.	Unsat.	Criteria (Bases for making judgments)
*	1. Pick up towel and open	1	0	picks up and opens towel without touching other objects
*	2. Dry hands and arms	1	0	a. uses double thickness of towel b. dries from hand to upper arm c. uses half of towel for each arm d. discards towel without contaminating self or other objects
*	3. Pick up gown in aseptic manner	1	0	a. touches gown only b. does not allow gown to open until away from other sterile objects
*	4. Open gown in aseptic manner	1	0	a. holds onto neck edge and allows lower portion of gown to unfold b. keeps hands inside gown c. unfolds gown sliding arms into sleeves d. does not allow gown to contact other objects
*	5. Ask another person to pull gown on and tie it in back	1	0	another person pulls gown on and ties it in back

Total score possible = 5   Total score: _____
Minimum mastery
level score = 5

181

uct evaluation of this task would be more meaningful. An instructor checkpoint is used to allow the instructor to examine the product at some intermediate point prior to product completion. The student is told that when he reaches a certain step during the construction of the product (instructor checkpoint), he should stop and ask the instructor to observe the product. This allows the instructor to view a product or a machine set-up prior to the time the set-up is taken down or a portion of a product becomes no longer observable. In the case of our example, it would not be possible to view whether a person center-punched the stock, mounted the drill correctly, etc., after the product is once completed. However, if the student were asked to call the instructor when the stock is mounted and the drill press is ready to be turned on, the instructor could examine whether the student was using the correct size drill, whether the student selected a sharp drill, whether the student had center-punched the stock, etc., before the drilling took place. Then the finished product could be evaluated after the student completed the product. In this case, the stock would be evaluated to see whether the 3/32″ hole was drilled perpendicular to the stock surface. Using instructor checkpoints in this way allows for a comprehensive evaluation of the product without requiring the instructor to be constantly observing the creation of the product. This method still does not allow the instructor to observe the process of completing the product. Sample C incorporates these ideas into a modified product checklist.

As indicated earlier, the instructor checkpoint is also useful when a product is going to be assembled and certain portions of it can no longer be observed. For example, if the student is asked to assemble a two-barrel carburetor, it would not be possible to observe whether the student inserted the carburation jets correctly inside the carburetor once the cover was put on, unless the instructor disassembled the carburetor. However, if the instructor used an instructor checkpoint just prior to the student's placing the cover on the carburetor, it would be possible to view the jets. It would still not be possible to determine if the student used the correct process when inserting the jets. If you examine sample C, you can see that the items to be observed are stated in past tense. This is because they have been completed by the time the instructor observes them. The criteria are also stated in the past tense.

Specifying the Criteria. In our earlier discussion of written tests we indicated that one characteristic which a good test should have is objectivity. This meant that different instructors could score the same student's instrument and come up with the same score. This characteristic is also very important when using performance evaluation instruments. For some reason, most instructors can see the value of making their written tests objective, but many have difficulty seeing why the performance eval-

SAMPLE C
PRODUCT CHECKLIST
DRILL COLD ROLLED STEEL

Course: Machine Shop

TERMINAL PERFORMANCE OBJECTIVE:

Given: A drill press. 3/32″ drills, center-punch. cutting oil, hammer and a piece of cold rolled steel

Performance: Drill a 3/32″ hole in cold rolled steel

Standard: The hole should be 3/32″ in diameter and perpendicular to the surface

Instructor Check Points	Items to be observed	Sat.	Unsat.	Criteria (Bases for making judgments)
	*1. Selected the correct size drill	1	0	3/32″
	*2. Selected a sharp drill	1	0	cutting edges do not reflect light
	3. Center-punched the work-piece	1	0	punch is visible and about 1/32″ in diameter
	4. Mounted drill in drill press	1	0	chuck can not be loosened by hand
	5. Adjusted drill press speed	1	0	adjusted to closest correct speed
	6. Clamped workpiece in drill press vise	1	0	workpiece clamped tightly
	7. Positioned center punched mark under drill bit	1	0	drill bit centered over punch mark
☐	When stock is mounted and drill press is ready to be turned on			
	8. Drilled hole square with surface	3	0	Insert 3/32″ rod into hole and check to make sure rod sticks out at right angle with a square
☐	When stock has been drilled			

* Critical Items

Total score possible = 11   Total Score: _____

Minimum mastery

level score = 10

uation instruments should be objective. Many argue that performance is an art and therefore, it is not possible to specify highly defined criteria. If this argument were sound, there would not be a right or wrong way to do anything. In most fields an instructor would indicate quite strongly that there is a right and wrong way to do most things in the field. We contend, that if there is a right way and the instructor is able to teach it, he should also be able to define what the right way is. If he can define what the correct way is, then he should be able to define criteria for judging whether each step of the performance is done correctly or not. The rules for judging whether a student has completed a step correctly are called the criteria. One rule is called a criterion. Criteria should be specified clearly enough so that different instructors in the field could judge the same student performance in the same way. In other words, other instructors in your field should be able to read your criteria, and using them, judge a student's performance in the same way that you would judge that performance, even if the instructors would do that particular step a little differently. Adequately stated criteria allow a student to be judged fairly. A student should be judged based upon some standard and not upon the whim of the instructor who scores the performance. Many instructors use the criteria that are specified during the construction of the performance evaluation instruments as aids in teaching the performance. They are provided to the student during the teaching process so that the student can self-evaluate whether he has mastered the task, and if he has not, the criteria set a goal for the student. The following are a few helpful hints which might be used when specifying criteria.

1. Avoid using terms such as correct level, correctly, industry standards. These terms do not identify or describe criteria. Criteria are used to define these terms. (In other words, if the correct level or industry standard is to make three pies an hour; a student who makes three or more pies an hour has met the standard. If he has not, he has not met the standard. Three or more pies an hour means industry standard or correct level of performance.)
2. Criteria need not be stated as sentences but should be stated in telegraphic form using as few words as possible. (They must be reviewed often by the instructor as he judges the performance of many students. Therefore additional words just waste time.)

Generalizations About Performance Evaluation. The basic process of evaluating performance is quite a simple process, but it requires a great deal of time and energy to determine adequately the size of the steps and to identify adequately all of the steps to be evaluated during the evaluation of a performance. The size of a performance step can vary from (a) attach a clip to a resistor to (b) measure the resistance of a resistor. The size of a step is dependent upon the prior knowledge of the individual. Whether a person wants to conduct the performance evaluation through the use of a performance test or a product evaluation will be determined by the amount of time available and nature of the tasks to be evaluated. As we saw, some tasks can only be evaluated using a performance test. Other tasks can be evaluated using a product evaluation, and still other tasks can be evaluated using a product evaluation with instructor checkpoints. The exact type of instrument used will be dependent upon the task and the extent to which the evaluation of process is important. During the identification of the steps to be evaluated, it is important that the four criteria for judging steps that were discussed earlier be employed. If these criteria are used, the steps included in the performance evaluation should be meaningful and complete. The importance of the criteria should not be underestimated. Until the criteria are attached to the instrument, the instrument is nothing more than a procedural list of steps, or a list of points that can be observed. The criteria are the basis for making the evaluation because they allow the instructor to judge whether the student has performed the task correctly or incorrectly. Care must be exercised in making sure that the criteria are specific enough to allow the same teacher to judge different students fairly and in the same way, and for different instructors to judge the same student and arrive at the same score. If the instrument allows for this quality judgment, it is objective and will fulfill a very important role in the evaluation of student progress.

The following is a brief summary of the procedure that should be used during the development of a performance evaluation instrument.

1. Specify the objective.
2. Determine if you want to evaluate the performance with a performance test or a product evaluation.
3. a. List the procedural steps if a performance test is to be used.
   b. List the points to be observed after the performance is completed if a product evaluation is to be used.
   (Make sure that the steps or points are independent, contain only one performance, each begins with a verb which indicates the behavior expected of the student and all steps are listed.)
4. Identify critical items.
5. Determine if you need instructor checkpoints when using a product evaluation.
6. Determine the criteria for judging satisfactory completion of each step.
7. Establish the acceptable mastery level score for the instrument.

Constructing Attitude Evaluation Instruments

Attitude evaluation is one of the more complex types of evaluation. People have attempted to evaluate attitudes for years and have developed very complex assessment procedures which have met with minimal success.

The following discussion is limited to only "job-related" attitudes. Although the procedures discussed are somewhat simplified, they have been proven effective based on the author's experience and the experience of classroom teachers.

Most often job-related attitudes refer to those personal actions which communicate emotion toward the job, or job-related objects or people. They affect a person's ability to perform in an occupation even though he might have developed competence in both the skills and knowledge of the occupation. (You should refer to chapter 3 for a further discussion of job-related attitudes.)

The process of constructing attitude evaluation instruments is the same as that used for constructing performance tests. Usually attitudes can be assessed only by observing the person who is exhibiting the attitude. Since the construction of an attitude evaluation instrument so closely parallels that of constructing a performance test, we will assume you have read the section on performance evaluation before reading this section.

The first step is to determine the attitude which is to be evaluated. This is accomplished by specifying a three-part objective. The first part, or given, describes the environment within which you would expect a person to exhibit the attitude. The second part describes the attitude which you wish the student to demonstrate and the third part describes the observable behavior that you are willing to accept as evidence that the student has demonstrated the correct attitude. The specification of the three parts of an objective are just as critical as a base for evaluating attitude as they are as a base for evaluating performance. You would expect a person to exhibit different observable behaviors depending upon the environment within which a person is asked to react even though the attitude being assessed is the same.

Once the objective is stated, the planning of the items to be observed and the criteria for judging acceptable performance on each item is accomplished using the same approach as that used with a performance test. Envision a circle such as that presented in figure 6-3. The circle represents the total attitude which is being evaluated. The problem for the instructor is to break that attitude down into its component parts so that attitude evaluation items can be constructed. The attitude evaluation items each contain one component of the observable behavior that you would like the student to exhibit as proof that he has the correct attitude. This concept is demonstrated by breaking the circle up into non-overlapping parts. Each part should contain one observable behavior. If you add up all of the parts, you should have observed all the components which add up to demonstrate the total behavior necessary to judge if the student has the correct attitude.

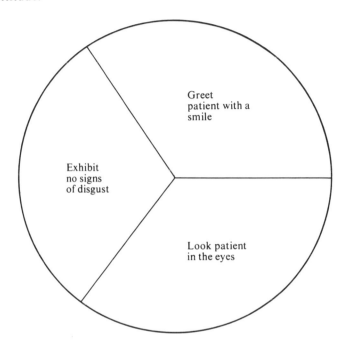

FIGURE 6—3

Components Of The Attitude:
Accept A Disfigured Patient

Figure 6-3 shows a possible breakdown of the components of the attitude: accept a disfigured patient. You will notice that this objective begins with a verb just as other objectives. It is difficult to distinguish it from the objective of a performance evaluation. This is because the attitude is highly job-related and it can be tied closely to observable changes in a person's job-related behavior. However, it is different from a performance test objective because it relates primarily to an action which is based upon a student's emotions and not necessarily upon his knowledge or skills. This will be seen later in the types of behaviors that are observed. The observable behaviors for this attitude should relate to how well a student accepts a disfigured patient. The three-part objective might be: given a disfigured patient who is not injured or seriously ill, demonstrate an accepting attitude, as specified and measured by the attitude checklist.

The three components of such accepting behavior indicated are those the instructor feels demonstrate an accepting attitude. They are: greet the patient with a smile, look the patient in the eyes, and exhibit no signs of disgust. It is assumed that if a student demonstrates adequate performance on these three items he has an accepting attitude toward disfigured patients, or he can portray an accepting attitude which is sufficient to allow him to perform adequately on the job.

These three items are then combined with the objective to form an attitude evaluation instrument. Sample D shows the components assembled into an attitude checklist. As with the performance test, it is very important that criteria be established so that the instructor can judge whether the student has or has not exhibited each of the component behaviors. In the case of the first component related to greeting a patient with a smile, the criterion would be whether the person smiled at the patient or not. The criteria for determining if a student exhibited signs of disgust would be: does not a) shudder, b) grit teeth or distort face, or c) find other things to do so attention need not be given the person. Examination of the checklist shows that each of the three items is a critical item and that in order to obtain a mastery level score the student would have to exhibit all three behaviors correctly.

As you can see, the behaviors to be observed and the criteria associated with an attitude assessment instrument are not as precise as those used in a performance test. However, the more clearly an attitude is occupationally related, the more agreement typically can be found among people in the occupation concerning the appropriate way of exhibiting the particular attitude. The attitude actually becomes a criterion for successful performance which is noticeable if not present. For example, it would be very apparent to people in the health occupations if a person could not accept a disfigured patient. Such a person would exhibit behaviors that most people in the health occupations would judge as inappropriate. This judgment would be possible because most people in the health occupations would view the self-image of a disfigured patient as being a very critical factor in helping the patient to function satisfactorily in society. If an inappropriate attitude were exhibited toward the patient, this could have serious implications for the person's ability to perform satisfactorily in society.

Most occupational programs have job-related attitudes which can seriously affect a person's ability to perform in an occupation. Only through the use of attitude checklists, or similar instruments, can an instructor certify that a student possesses the appropriate job-related attitudes.

ATTITUDE CHECKLIST

ACCEPT A DISFIGURED PATIENT

Course: Practical Nursing

TERMINAL PERFORMANCE OBJECTIVE:

Given: A disfigured patient who is not injured or seriously ill

Performance: Demonstrate an accepting attitude

Standard: As specified and measured by the attitude checklist

Critical Items	Items to be Observed	Sat.	Unsat.	Criteria (Bases for making judgments)
*	1. Greet patient with a smile	1	0	greets patient with a smile
*	2. Look patient in eyes	1	0	looks patient in eyes
*	3. Exhibit no signs of disgust	1	0	Does not: (Examples) a. shudder b. grit teeth or distort face c. find other things to do so attention need not be given the patient

*Critical Items
Total Score possible = 3   Total score: _____
Minimum mastery
level score = 3

Reporting Student Progress

A thorough discussion of the procedures and philosophy of reporting student progress when using an individualized learning system are beyond the scope of this book. There are some who argue that traditional grades (A, B, etc.) are appropriate when using such a system and some who argue for a number of alternatives to A, B, etc. Depending upon the philosophy and type of individualized learning system being used each could be correct.

However, regardless which method is adopted by a school, most would advocate the use of at least a student progress chart such as the one presented in sample E. A progress chart summarizes information on the tasks completed by each student in the program. The total list of tasks included in the program is listed across the top. The list of students in the course is listed down the left side. When a student satisfactorily masters a task, that task is checked off for that student. For example, John Doe completed the task: replace a water pump. The progress chart allows an instructor to judge quickly the progress of each student in the class. Some instructors post the progress chart in the classroom in an effort to motivate students. This procedure is useful if it does not cause a severe strain on students. The instructor should judge the advantages of posting the progress chart for his group.

Summary

The methods used to evaluate student progress in an individualized learning system must be adequately applied by an instructor in order to certify that a student has mastered a task. Student progress evaluation generally requires some assessments of what students know, can do, and job-related attitudes.

The instructor's job is first to determine what the student should be able to know, do, and the appropriate job-related attitudes. Then the instructor must determine how to evaluate whether the student can demonstrate each of these. This usually requires a written test of what the student knows, a performance evaluation of what the student can do, and an evaluation of appropriate job-related attitudes.

After the student has demonstrated that he has mastered a task, the instructor should record this on some form of progress chart.

REFERENCES

1. Bloom, Benjamin S. et al. *Taxonomy of Educational Objectives*. New York: David McKay Company, Inc., 1956.

Sample E
Sample Student Progress Chart

PROGRAM TASKS

Course: Truck Mechanics

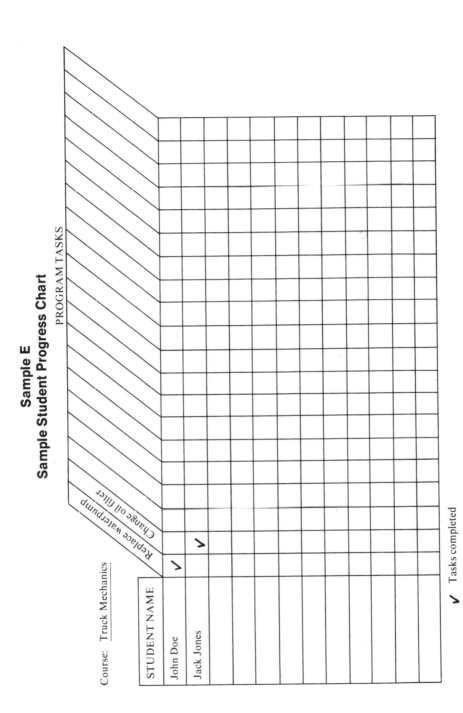

STUDENT NAME	Replace waterpump	Change oil filter													
John Doe	✔														
Jack Jones		✔													

✔ Tasks completed

Chapter 7   MANAGING THE INDIVIDUALIZED LEARNING SYSTEM

Goals and Objectives

"The greatest challenge offered to management is to reconcile and integrate human effort, resources, and facilities toward common goals, while avoiding discord and common disasters" (Mali 1972).

The real thrust of *any* educational management system is to integrate "human effort, resources, and facilities" toward the goal of educating students, or clients.

Successful efforts to individualize vocational instruction usually involve more than one person, but experience indicates that in nearly all instances there *is* one person who provides the continuing drive that makes implementation possible. This originator might be a vocational curriculum specialist employed by a state board for vocational education, a vocational teacher educator, a local director with on-going vocational instruction programs, a local director of a new institution, a local supervisor of vocational programs, a vocational instructor, or a team of vocational instructors. In brief, the scope of the undertaking is an important fact to consider when setting a goal of implementing an individualized instructional program.

The originator should also consider the motivating forces or compelling reasons why individualization is being encouraged. Some of these reasons were discussed in chapter 1. These included: (1) demands by the disadvantaged, handicapped, the poor, and children of the affluent for "open access" to all facets of public and private school curriculum; (2) general public demand for accountability, in two categories. The first category requires that educational programs deliver what they are intended to provide. In vocational technical education that means skills and knowledge leading to employability. The second demand for accountability is fiscal. The most effective means of controlling costs per successfully placed graduate of a vocational technical program is to keep all of the training stations in that program continuously occupied. A system of individualized instruction makes this possible, in that the training stations vacated by early leavers or dropouts can be immediately filled with new students working on an individualized basis. In addition, individualized instruction can be: a more efficient way to learn, a more acceptable system to contemporary learning styles, less expensive, more interesting and motivating, and more acceptable to students than the traditional group-centered instruction.

On the other hand, if the individualized system is not well-managed, it can be infinitely less effective than the traditional system in most of the areas mentioned, and in some cases, a disaster. Vocational educators must not assume that because they have made some advances toward an individualized system, that it is inherently better than the previous system.

Ingredients of a Successful System

A successful individualized learning system, whether it be one program in an institution or an entire institution or family of institutions, must have four basic ingredients:

1. *Staff* (teachers, supervisors, administrators, consultants) who are trained or are willing to be trained in development and operation of an individualized system of instruction.
2. *Instructional materials* that are relevant to the occupation and developed according to acceptable standards for the occupation in which training is being given.
3. *Facilities, equipment, and organization* that make possible the implementation of the individualized system or program.
4. *Students* who are willing and able to profit from an individualized learning structure.

Neglecting to take into consideration any of the four factors could lead to setting unrealistic objectives and to organizational frustration when these objectives are not met. For example, an instructor might set as an objective, "individualize my environmental technology program in the ten months of the next academic year." To be realistic in setting that objective the instructor should consider the following:

1. Unless the instructor has prior training, experience indicates it will probably involve fifty or more hours of learning in individualized instruction development techniques and whatever inconvenience in cost or travel this might encumber. This training might take longer if the instructor lacks creative writing and organizational skills.

2. Once trained, the development process will probably be the equivalent of an additional half-time job for that instructor for that year.

3. Specialized assistance for picture taking, development, and descriptive artwork may be needed.

4. The instructor's administrator may have to agree to double the instructional materials and audio-visual budget for that program for that year.

5. For a price ranging from $5,000 to $50,000 a satisfactory set of individualized learning packages for that program may be on the market or available from another school.

A teacher trainer or state supervisor of vocational technical education may have a goal of "increase the number of individualized programs in a vocational field up to 40 percent of the total programs in the state in two years." In setting that objective, the teacher trainer or state supervisor should consider all of the factors described for the instructor in the previous five items, but should also consider:

1. Unless there is strong support from a school director, administrator, and governing board, it is quite difficult for a new teacher in an on-going traditional institution to acquire sufficient materials and professional support to fully individualize a program. A very strong personal commitment would be needed under those circumstances.

2. Policies of some teacher organizations which do not take into consideration the professional advantages of individualized instruction to a professional teacher may not be supportive of individualized instruction.

3. If the typical mode of instruction in the general academic area of secondary and postsecondary education in that region has remained group-centered and traditional, vocational instructors moving into an individualized system will have to teach the method as well as the content of an individualized

vocational and technical program. This will be more difficult than if the students have already become accustomed to individualized instruction in their academic programs.

A director of a vo-tech institute might set as an objective, "individualize the twenty-five programs in this institute within the next two calendar years." The director should consider:

1. How would individualization influence student learning, and the instructional efficiency and productivity of the institution?
2. Are there financial resources available to increase staff costs 25 to 50 percent during that period?
3. What is the probability of acceptance by the student body?
4. What is the makeup of the existing staff? Highly traditional? Eager to change? Low turnover? Growing rapidly?
5. How much of the material might be available under a purchase, and at what cost? Would cost be commensurate with institution developed materials assumed in question 1 above?

Impact on student learning and instructional productivity and efficiency are probably the key issues in any decision to proceed with individualized instruction. The two issues are also interrelated. For example, a student in a postsecondary vo-tech institute might have the ability and interest to accelerate his instructional program in order to enter the labor market at an earlier date. In an individualized competency based system, this can be accomplished, and it will save the student money because he will pay less in tuition, and begin earning wages earlier in his work life. The public taxpayer gains to the extent that the public share for "a successfully placed graduate" is reduced. The institution gains in accountability to the public in that the cost for training a "successfully placed graduate" is reduced. Cost per graduate savings are enhanced primarily because whenever a vacancy is created, a new trainee can be moved immediately into the program to fill the training station even though it is not the end of the year, quarter, or semester.

Cost savings in individualized instruction systems do not usually occur in reductions in staff, instructional materials cost, or equipment cost. They occur through a maximizing of the use of all of the instructional resources of the vocational program so that more students can move through more rapidly, and by keeping the program at maximum student capacity. Where state regulation of a given vocational technical program dictates the length or clock hours of the program, or where the institutional policy does not permit entry at times other than the beginning of a school year or semester, these maximazation cost advantages would not apply, and individualization would have to be justified on a student benefit basis. In secondary school programs, the ability to accelerate might lessen the need for or decrease the length of postsecondary training, again providing both student and public cost-benefit.

This maximization of training efficiency is the first level benefit available to student, institution, and the public taxpayer. The second level benefit, more educationally sophisticated and perhaps more important, is directed primarily toward the student. That benefit is a choice of learning experiences which all lead to the development of competency in a given task.

A vocational program is not really "individualized" just because a student can progress through prepared learning packages at an individual rate with the instructor guiding the learning rather than providing the content input. When each subtask in the vocational technical program has more than one alternative component or learning approach in its instructional strategy, the system begins to acquire truly individualized character. When a student receives personal instructional strategy described by a computer, which considered the student's personal characteristics and learning style, but retains the right to overrule the computer and elect a new strategy, then the system can rightfully claim to have made significant progress toward a fully individualized system.

In general, financial resources have not been available to vocational educators to implement many multi-learning strategy packages for vocational task instruction. Volume in any given occupational area has not been sufficient to attract many private developers to multiple learning strategy packages either. Thus, most examples of such packages are currently found in demonstration centers or in the works of teacher educators.

Directly related to expectations of learners and teachers and the funding structure is the question, "do we select one program and carry it to its ultimate in individualized instruction, or do we use the resources we have to bring all programs under our jurisdiction toward the goal of individualized instruction concurrently over a longer period?" This is a decision being faced quite often by vocational education administrators because funds are seldom available for a crash program in all areas. Given these circumstances, we would still suggest that you try to do both. After available resources have been ascertained, institutional goals and objectives should be established which will lead to arrival at the overall objective of individualizing all programs. However, sufficient funds should be retained out of the total funding to individualize one or two programs up to the sophisticated level described previously.

That level requires providing more than one alternative learning approach to each intermediate learning objective. This one program could be an example which would accomplish several things.

First, it would provide a demonstration procedure. The developers could make trial and error mistakes on this one program rather than on all of them at the same time. Second, "time and materials experience" with the development of this exemplary program would provide more accurate budget estimates for the remainder of the programs. Third, the value of the varied learning style approaches could be measured, and if significantly better than a single learning style approach, could serve as a stimulus for the further development of other programs.

In summary, the goals and objectives for establishing an individualized vocational instruction program will vary depending on the scope and degree of control given the vocational educator. Basic considerations are staff, instructional materials, facilities, and students. Individualized instruction can be a superior system of instruction if it is competently organized and managed. The cost of personnel, time, materials, and equipment during development stages will be considerable, and the development program should not be initiated without due consideration of the demands on an individualized vocational instructional program. Early benefits will bring increased program efficiency for the student, institution, and general public. Later the more sophisticated learning materials will greatly enhance student learning opportunities.

To Buy or Build a System of Individualized Instruction

Any value judgment on the relative merits of purchasing or locally developing a system of individualized vocational instruction is subject to immediate "local-condition rejection." This means that whatever buy vs. develop guides are developed, a specific local circumstance may quickly override the wisdom of the guidelines. For example, a vocational instructor might be aware of an excellent and complete individualized instruction program in his vocational specialty, but his institution is on an austerity program. The cost of the total program may exceed the instructional materials budget for his whole institution. In that case, the instructor might be forced to develop as best he can rather than purchase the better materials. As another example, a local vocational director might perceive the development of individualized instructional materials as an excellent in-service learning experience for the staff of the vocational school. However, in early test exercises the director may find that basic creative writing and development talent is generally lacking in the staff, as well as enthusiasm for writing. Hence, the prognosis would be a long and expensive development process, probably culminating with inferior materials. Under these circumstances, purchase of materials might be the best decision if sufficient interest could be developed in the staff's *using* these materials.

The availability of professional assistance is also a factor in a buy-or-build decision. A larger institution with a learning resource development department capable of mass production of 35mm slides, 8mm films, and color video-cassettes, with professional personnel trained in learning strategies can speak more realistically of institutional development of learning materials than a small training center where each instructor is responsible for his own materials development. Sometimes a relatively small occupational training program in a comprehensive high school will also have the advantage of a fairly large resource center serving the entire high school. Similarly, in some parts of the country a number of small schools have banded together under "joint powers" to establish learning resource centers serving all of their institutions. In any case, the availability of professional assistance is an additional factor in the buy-or-build decision.

A unique opportunity for the development of an individualized vocational instructional system is the founding of a new institution. Given this situation, an administrator or team of administrators with a strong orientation to the concepts of individualized instruction can generate an individualized format and recruit instructors who have proven experience in and commitment to individualized instruction. This situation can greatly improve the success probability of developing an effective individualized instructional system. Proximity to a teacher training institution with a vocational and technical teacher training staff which is skilled in individualized instruction is also a development asset.

The political structure of the teaching staff cannot be overlooked. If the teaching staff is closely organized with an exclusive bargaining representative, it may be necessary to convince that organization's leadership of the advantages of an individualized instruction system to students *and* teachers. If they cannot be convinced, institutional development of individualized instruction at any cost might not be possible.

Perhaps most importantly, the needed content developed as described in chapters 4 and 5 must be constantly kept in mind. The best professionally developed packaged individualized instructional program is a poor buy if it does not meet the learning objectives established.

Despite the exceptions we have described, which may tend to override other logical "buy-or-build" considerations, it is possible to cite some advantages of locally developed individualized materials and some advantages of the purchase of programs or segments. Locally developed individualized instructional materials have several advantages.

1. *They are more apt to be "on target" with the performance objectives of the program.* If the local materials are developed with a reasonable level of skill, it is very likely that they will more nearly meet the learning objectives than materials which were developed at a different location without the specific objectives in mind.

2. *There is better acceptance of the materials from students.* In comparing an instructor-developed system of materials with a purchased system of materials of equal "quality," the instructor-developed individualized instruction is more likely to "succeed" with students than the purchased program. Pride in the product will not be unnoticed by students, and a determination by the instructor to "make it work" will carry the value of the materials beyond their intrinsic worth. While we have not found specific research evidence to document this, our experience indicates that when students are able to identify their instructor's hand, voice, and sometimes face in the materials, it strengthens the tie to the local laboratory and program and enhances interest. It also declares to the student that the instructor has gone to considerable effort to prepare the materials and that he must have considered them very worthwhile.

3. *There is an increased likelihood that the materials will be used by the instructor in the program.* While hard evidence does not abound on the subject, most instructors and vocational directors agree that instructors are more apt to utilize materials which they helped to develop. This is probably true in part because by having more confidence in the materials being "on target" with the objectives, they are more comfortable with them. It may also be true that all of us, having put time and effort into a project, like to see some value emerging from that project. Therefore, given a vocational program of an institution that might be emerging from group-centered instruction into an individualized system, having materials that the instructor developed might provide the extra "lick" to move the system along.

4. *They have better guarantee of continuity.* A mechanic that has built an automobile from scratch knows more about how to "patch" it when it breaks down than anyone else. When new and improved "attachments" become available, that mechanic will also be in a good position to judge where that attachment will fit best and how its performance will balance with the rest of the system. When we consider the dynamic and ever-changing nature of occupations and how vocational technical education

must change with it, it is easy to understand how a teacher that has designed and built an instructional program will be better equipped to modify it than a teacher who purchased an individualized program without benefit of knowing how and where the various concepts and rationale were assembled.

5. *There are in-service education values.* It is not possible for an instructor to develop effective individualized instructional materials without a review or additional study of the ways people learn. This is of great value to the instructor in the interpersonal work with the students so necessary in an individualized system. The materials will also be of continuing value to the instructor even if he returns to a conventional instructional program. If the instructional materials are purchased, some of these learning values to the instructor may not be realized.

6. *There is compatibility of the individualized instructional system.* If a vocational education department or institution engages in the development of an individualized instructional system, it is possible to develop a reasonably standardized format. This has the advantages of (a) facilitating interprogram and interdepartmental use of learning packages; (b) reducing the variety and quantity of support audio-video equipment required; and (c) facilitating internal instructor in-service education and communications about curriculum.

Some of the identifiable advantages of purchasing totally or partially individualized vocational instructional program materials are:

1. *Quality is usually a known quantity.* The materials can be examined as a whole as a validity check, and sometimes formal validation data are available. This is in contrast to many of the materials developed in institutions where an inexperienced instructor may invest the institution's time and money and not arrive at a usuable product.

2. *Price is a known quantity.* It is possible to look at the materials and make a judgment about whether the price is realistic. When instructors not experienced in individualized curriculum development begin a development project, it is almost impossible to give accurate estimates to the institution management as to what the total cost will be, or to estimate whether the value will be reasonably related to the cost.

3. *Purchasing is less of a strain on instructors.* Instructors who have been teaching in a conventional way for many years with little effort applied to curriculum development will probably be, at best, apprentice developers of individualized materials initially. Similarly, new instructors probably will have only a cursory acquaintance with individualized curriculum development. Our experience indicates that the ability to

develop and write individualized curriculum is a talent which is often, but not always, associated with ability to work well with students. There may be some excellent curriculum writers who are not effective in instructional work with students. It is also true that some vocational and technical instructors may be more talented in directing student contact than they are in developing and writing instructional materials.

4. *The purchase price often may be less than the development price.* If institution-developed individualized instructional materials are of good quality, it is very possible that the cost of these materials to that institution will be higher than if they were purchased. While commercial vendors may place a high markup on the materials, they do not expect to get all of their investment back in one sale. Similarly, materials may be purchased from public or private educational institutions which have developed individualized vocational instructional materials. They will usually not be charging their full cost of development against one sale. Some of these institutions seek to recover current publication costs only, having previously "written off" the development cost. This "advantage" of purchase refers to hard dollar costs only and does not consider the educational benefits to the instructor during the development process. However, the public is becoming increasingly suspicious about curriculum duplication efforts, and the program or institution that can utilize the best efforts of others at lower costs will get good marks in "accountability."

We have been discussing "buy versus build" and listing advantages of each on an "either-or" basis. It is probably most prudent to be doing some of each. The availability of relevant individualized instructional materials has to be one of the major decision factors.

Where suitable total programs or partial programs are available for purchase, the advantages of local development and the advantages of purchase described earlier in this chapter should be reviewed within the context of the known development talent within the institution and the financial resources available. This elusive quality of development talent refers to a composite of conceptual abilities which include inductive-deductive reasoning, creative writing, visual communication skills, and mental transfer of self into a learner's role. As one very gross rule of thumb developed from our experience, it is possible to say that if a one-thousand-hour program has been totally individualized, including all learning materials and audio-visual software, and it can be purchased for less than the instructor's annual salary, it is probably a reasonably "good buy."

This does not take into consideration the other advantages of locally developed vocational and technical instructional programs described previously.

If a decision to purchase is made, we would suggest two important considerations:

1. The instructors who are to be using the materials should be significantly involved in the purchase decision so that the commitment for use is present.
2. Instructors who will be using the material should receive intensive in-service training, not only in techniques of use, but also in the theory and rationale of development. They also should understand how modifications can be programmed into the system.

Materials Production, Quality, and Quantity

The urgency of local materials development in a vocational and technical program or institution depends in part on the degree of commitment of the institution to individualized instruction, and to the reasons for the move to individualization. For example, if an institution intends to remain on an annual or semester student intake system, the individualized instruction probably can be implemented gradually over a period of years. However, if the institution suddenly makes a commitment to open enrollment and a vocational instructor knows there will be new students coming in each month throughout the year whenever a vacancy occurs, the individualized instruction and development takes on some urgency.

Based on our experience it does not appear reasonable to expect a single vocational instructor to individualize materials and to teach them concurrently. The instructor must always be "ahead" of the fastest learner in the class, while taking time to give individual help to others. It is also asking a great deal of an instructor to teach a class in a conventional way, and at the same time to prepare individualized materials for that program, except over an extended period of perhaps three years.

Support can be provided in a number of ways. One area vocational technical institute in Minnesota found that two instructors with good basic writing skills, audio-visual assistance, and in-service training could do an acceptable job of individualizing a one-year vocational instructional program if given two months lead time before starting the program. This amount of lead time enabled them to get far enough ahead on materials development so that they could stay ahead during the school year. Where lead time was less or there was only one instructor, the materials tended to "run out" after two or three months, and the instructor was forced to revert to an unsatisfactory combination of conventional and individualized instruction.

Support also can be provided by having expert assistance available to instructors in the area of articulating performance objectives, writing criterion-reference exams, and the other techniques of the system. Effective usage of such specialists within an institution requires that there be reasonable consistency in individualized curriculum development procedures among the various programs and departments.

Individualized systems usually require the printing of individual learning guides for each task in each program as described in chapter 5. "Bringing up" a large number of individualized instruction programs in an institution can be a major printing, copying, collating, and binding job. Care should be taken that this function is adequately staffed. An instructor who has put great effort in materials development does not want to wait months for the return of the materials. "Outside" printing might be an asset here, but cost control factors may enter into this decision. First-time instructional learning materials nearly always require early revisions, so the initial duplicating and printing cost should be held to a minimum.

The numbers of packets printed for each program should be related to the sequencing of instruction. If it is a program requirement that all students start on Learning Guide 1, then twenty guides will have to be published for the twenty students of the program. If, however, planning enables students to begin on any of the first four guides, a lesser number will suffice.

Few vocational educators who are involved with individualized curriculum development would ever admit to making a conscious decision favoring quantity over quality. However, given a situation where adequate but limited time has been allocated for the development of individualized instructional materials for a program, it might be more prudent to strive for total individualization of the program rather than for very high quality individualization of just a few tasks. Experience also indicates an accelerating effect of materials development once a program has enough materials to function in an individualized mode. Once the instructor can be relieved of the task of information dissemination and many of the instructor's demonstrations can be accomplished through visuals, there will be more time for individual help with students, managing their learning processes, and "clean-up" of some of the instructional materials. This clean-up, in fact, becomes a part of the natural process because as the instructor works individually with students, the instructional program weaknesses will become apparent. Descriptive written materials that don't "tell," visuals that don't "show," and criterion tests that aren't valid begin to stand out and the clean-up process is underway.

Although the improvement process will be most intensive during the first two or three years, it should never end because the occupation and the students will be changing perpetually. This is one of the advantages of the individualized materials instruction system. The materials in this system *can* be changed more readily than the textbook on which a group-centered program may depend.

The Process of Educational Change

The educational literature is largely barren as to how curriculum change in our schools takes place and what the dominating influences are that affect that change.

New graduates of teacher education institutions may obtain some practice in preparation of "units" of instruction and in course organization. However, in arriving at their new place of educational employment, they often find that the texts and materials on hand do not fit their college methods class format; so they proceed either to teach the way it had been taught or to organize around the available materials. If the in-service teacher goes on to graduate school he may from time to time come up with some new curriculum ideas. However, if the new ideas require expensive materials purchase or development, or coordination with teachers of other classes or programs who have not been similarly enthused by graduate school, chances of implementation are not particularly good.

A superintendent, principal, or vocational director, may, through college course work, seminars, or professional reading, develop a strong rationale for major curriculum change. The administrator discusses the idea with the instructional staff, who may see the changes as a lot of extra work for not very clearly stated or perceivable results. They agree to "try some of the ideas," but funds for the needed instructional materials and extra staff time are not forthcoming so the "ideas" die within a year.

A controlled teaching experiment at a college teacher training laboratory school may indicate superiority of a certain type of learning material, but the results are reported primarily in college academic circles. An in-service teacher who reads about it and wants to emulate the experiment is denied funds to purchase the necessary supplies by the local vocational and technical school administrator.

To consider a model where curriculum change did take place on a large-scale basis, it would be well to review the procedures of the national science laboratory programs which emerged in the post-Sputnik era of the early 1960s. The general characteristics of the programs were:

1. Teams of specialists which included practicing mathematics and science teachers were called in and paid to develop a base curriculum, with instructional materials.
2. Over a period of several summers, thousands of teachers of mathematics and science were sent to seminars where they upgraded basic skills and also learned how to use the new materials. Their transportation, tuition, and books, plus a living stipend were paid from federal funds.
3. Instructional materials for the programs were available to local schools for only a fraction of the total cost.
4. No organizational structural changes within the schools were required—the one-hour-per-day Carnegie unit remained intact.

We would suggest that major changes in vocational and technical curriculum organization and content within ongoing educational institutions are not apt to occur unless there is:

1. A policy commitment and financial and other resource commitments from the institutional management and its governing body. The resources may be local or external in character.
2. General consensus by the staff power structure that a curriculum change is desirable in terms of benefits to students, benefits to enlightened self-interest of the staff, or both.
3. Technical and theoretical expertise either on staff or available from a proximate teacher training institution.

This is not to say that it is impossible for a determined instructor, fired up by an ideological commitment to individualized instruction in a given program. Without institutional support, however, the new individualized program will tend to lack stability and will probably end when that instructor leaves or changes assignments.

If we assume that the commitment of resources and consensus is present, what are some of the procedures that might enable an institution to make progress in an individualized process?

1. A statement of philosophy and rationale for proceeding with the individualized strategy should be originated by the chief executive officer of the staff of the vocational training institution or department, and officially approved by his board or other administrator or governing board above that level.

2. A preliminary developmental budget should be developed and approved. At this stage it is more in the realm of a "feasibility study" budget.

3. A resource speaker with individualized instruction background could be brought in to discuss the system. Negative opinions of staff should not be suppressed—in fact discussion to get these feelings out in the open should be encouraged.

4. A literature and sample collection committee should be organized and provided with clerical help to collect materials, and also to find out where exemplary individualized vocational and technical instruction programs might be operating.

5. Visitations to exemplary programs *by instructors* should be encouraged, with time off from instructing and expenses paid. Known dissidents should be *encouraged* to take these trips.

6. Professional curriculum development expertise in individualized instruction should be identified within staff, added to staff, or contracted outside of the staff.

7. An appraisal of "where we are" should be undertaken. Are there current job descriptions and/or task listings for each program? Are we starting from "scratch"?

8. Based on the results of the appraisal in number 7, there would be an assessment of the willingness of the staff to continue. Revised time and budget estimates for the individualized program development for a stated period of time would be developed and superior approval obtained.

9. Experts could begin to work with staff individually and in groups supplying philosophical background as well as technique in the development of individualized instructional materials, within the agreed time and compensation schedule. The report of the committee described in number 4 could become a resource of additional materials which may be purchased or used as a guide. Outside consultants could be called in as required.

10. Production goals for individualized materials development should be developed and presented to instructional staff for their input. A production schedule and quality control criteria would be agreed upon.

11. Provisions should be made for audio-visual support and duplication.

12. A visual progress chart reporting individual program and developmental progress should be designed, posted, and maintained.

13. Individualized learning instruction packets should be prevalidated with advisory committees.

14. Individualized learning packets should begin to be used experimentally with students.

The preceding sequential list is included to show the combination of political and practical strategies which must be included with the instructional strategies if substantial movement of an established staff toward individualized instruction is to occur. The instructional strategies are not detailed here and the reader is asked to refer to chapter 5 for these procedures.

The point being underscored is that the typical vocational and technical instructor cannot be assumed to have acquired the theory and techniques to develop and write individualized instructional materials, either in an undergraduate college or in post-service teacher training classes. Nor is the vocational instructor under any particular professional obligation to acquire such knowledge and skills. It is still possible to find professional quotations which deplore individualized instruction as a teaching method. Further, as long as a majority of vocational and technical education institutions teach using traditional methods, teacher training institutions will by necessity continue to focus primarily on teaching instructors to perform in these traditional modes.

Therefore, unless by chance the instructor becomes inbued with the desire to individualize his program, it will be up to the management of the educational institutions to arrange to motivate the instructor, to give him background in theory, to teach him the techniques, and to provide him with the extra help and materials to do the job. This still may not be enough. Given all these supportive conditions, the instructor may still not have literary qualities or the imagination to fill the role of curriculum developer. If that is the case, it may be necessary to use the option of differentiated staffing. The instructor can retain teaching duties, and outside assistance can be provided to get the individualization accomplished.

The Instructional Materials Center

An individualized system also involves the development and/or acquisition of a great deal of instructional materials, with considerable emphasis on audio-video as well as print materials. If this material is not carefully cataloged and controlled, it will disappear; it will not be available to students when needed, and the individualized system will break down.

Library-type facilities available to a vocational program vary considerably by type of institution. The facility may be one shelf in the library of a small high school. Vocational and technical materials may be cataloged in large general libraries of technical colleges or community colleges. Technical institutes may have a large central library or an instructional materials center or decentralized learning resource centers or both.

Availability is the key word for storage and control of individualized instructional materials. An auto mechanics student needing to review a sound-film-cassette tape prior to starting a brake job is not likely to walk several hundred feet down a hallway in a greasy shopcoat to a plush general library where his feet track on the carpeting and the librarian scowls while locating the needed materials.

At the other extreme we have observed certain kinds of audio-visual materials being kept right in the shop or laboratory in specially constructed receptacles. For the kind of volume of print and nonprint material required for an individualized vocational program, for a department and for an institution, it is simply not feasible that the shops and laboratories become the repositories of *all* of these materials. It would be virtually impossible to have adequately cataloged cross-referenced materials so that units applicable to more than one vocational and technical program could be available. It would also be inefficient in terms of the extra numbers of copies needed to be printed and in terms of student difficulty in finding the materials. For example, if technical mathematics were needed for five programs, it would be costly to duplicate the materials in five sets.

All facets considered, we would suggest:

1. For a single individualized program in a high school or an isolated program (or programs) in a community college, an in-house instructional materials center located within the shop, laboratory, or classroom area under the supervision and control of the instructor or instructors or instructor aide.

2. For an individualized high school vocational department, for a department with compatible programs in the community college, vocational and technical institute, or technical college, a departmental instructional materials center, staffed with one or more trained aides or clerks. Materials should be checked in and cataloged under the supervision of a person trained in library science who should retain overall responsibility for the continuing update of the facility. There also should be provision for electrified carrels, necessary audio-visual equipment, tables, and small conference rooms for those individualized activities not requiring performance in the laboratory or shop. Check-out cards should be used and should be replicated in some central location in the facility so that there is general information about individualized resources available to all in the institution.

The nature of the "stacks" contained in the resource center will depend on the format designed for the individualized materials. In some instances, shelving which will house boxes containing both the learning guide and the support audio-visual materials will be utilized and special shelving should be provided for that purpose.

Whether the institution also has a central general library will depend on its particular philosophy and goals and objectives.

Differentiated Staffing

Individualized instructional programs are uniquely adaptable to differentiated staffing, particularly if they are institution-wide. The range of positions usually includes: student aide, learning resource secretary, instructor aide, instructor, senior instructor, lead instructor, and instructional manager. Job descriptions are provided in Appendix 2. Instructor aides work with students during the instructional process under the supervision of instructors. Senior instructors are in the same compensation range as lead instructors, but they have no duties except excellent instruction and preparation of materials. It is a way of recognizing the very superior instructor. Lead instructors teach but also perform a coordinating function where there is more than one instructor teaching similar or identical programs. They provide the day-to-day leadership of student, staff, and materials deployment to obtain effective use of educational resources. These descriptions may seem to lend themselves to a "classic" or an ideal example of how the differentiated staff model can be applied, but it usually takes more management than a conventional system to make it work.

One of the management problems which can arise from a differentiated staff is the justifiable objective of the manager or supervisor to employ the "best" people that can be obtained for the system. Hence in some cases they may be able to employ fully certified, highly qualified instructors in positions designated as "instructional aides." Given this condition, they also may be tempted to organize their staffing in such a way as to utilize the full competencies of these "aides" in working with students not under ths supervision of instructors. This may be best for pupil benefit, but it does not provide the "aide" services the instructor expects, and the aides are apt to become dissatisfied because they recognize they are performing as instructors without corresponding status and compensation. Thus it is important that instructional aides be qualified for the position according to the job description. Highly "overqualified" aides may cause more problems to the instructional system than the additional qualifications are worth.

If the differentiated staffing is to function well, all participants, including the students, must be aware of their own role in the system and also understand the function of the other participants in the system.

In the individualized instructional mode, the lead and senior instructors will spend a proportionately larger share of their time working on the preparation and organization of instructional materials and less time in conveying information to students. Paraprofessionals, such as instructional aides and library clerks, will spend time putting students in contact with instructional materials, finding materials for the students, assisting with the setup of audio-visual equipment and with other laboratory and shop apparatus, and answering student questions.

Scheduling

After the student has been processed through the general assessment as described, the instructor or lead instructor of an occupational training program should conduct a preassessment based on the content of the program in which he is enrolled (see figure 7-1). This preassessment identifies more fully the tasks of a the program and gives him an opportunity to try out some of these tasks. This is a point at which an individualized instructional program makes a major departure from a traditional program. In the traditional program there is an assumption that all learners are starting from the same level of expertise in that program area, although it is known that this is not true. Many students come to vocational and technical programs with considerable differences in background in the occupation in which they are seeking training. This may have come from experience in a family business, from previous training in high school, or elsewhere. The individualized vocational instructional program should attempt to recognize those capabilities and allow the student to "test out" of those tasks at which he is already competent at the job entry level.

As a matter of procedure the instructor and newly enrolled student go over the list of tasks for the program. It is usually assumed that the student will complete all of the tasks of the program unless he identifies some that he wants to challenge immediately. Figure 7-2 is an example of a student planning form. Each program in this vocational education institution has from one to 300 tasks, and this master list is used as a planning form for the student. After the student and instructor reach agreement on the tasks to be completed, the form is duplicated. Thereafter, the student, instructor, and the central office each retain a copy. The copy going to the central office is then recorded either manually or through data processing equipment in the student's name.

When the student is ready to begin training, he is issued time cards (figure 7-3). Each day he is present for learning and each time he changes work to proceed with another task he "clocks in" and out on that particu-

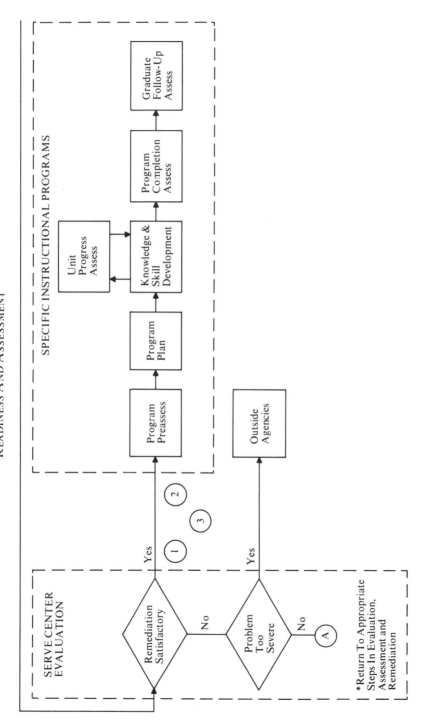

FIGURE 7–1
READINESS AND ASSESSMENT

SPECIFIC INSTRUCTIONAL PROGRAMS

Program Preassess

Program Plan

Unit Progress Assess

Knowledge & Skill Development

Program Completion Assess

Graduate Follow-Up Assess

Outside Agencies

SERVE CENTER EVALUATION

Remediation Satisfactory

Problem Too Severe

Yes

No

Yes

No

A

1

3

2

*Return To Appropriate Steps In Evaluation, Assessment and Remediation

STUDENT'S NAME	I. D. NUMBER	ADVISOR	

STANDARD PROGRAM NUMBER	PROGRAM NAME	SECTION	BLDG.

ROOM	HOURS	ENTRY DATE	ANTICIPATED EXIT DATE

CHECK TASKS TO BE COMPLETED

001 ☐	002 ☐	003 ☐	004 ☐	005 ☐	006 ☐	007 ☐	008 ☐	009 ☐
011 ☐	012 ☐	013 ☐	014 ☐	015 ☐	016 ☐	017 ☐	018 ☐	019 ☐
021 ☐	022 ☐	023 ☐	024 ☐	025 ☐	026 ☐	027 ☐	028 ☐	029 ☐
031 ☐	032 ☐	033 ☐	034 ☐	035 ☐	036 ☐	037 ☐	038 ☐	039 ☐
041 ☐	042 ☐	043 ☐	044 ☐	045 ☐	046 ☐	047 ☐	048 ☐	049 ☐
051 ☐	052 ☐	053 ☐	054 ☐	055 ☐	056 ☐	057 ☐	058 ☐	059 ☐
061 ☐	062 ☐	063 ☐	064 ☐	065 ☐	066 ☐	067 ☐	068 ☐	069 ☐
071 ☐	072 ☐	073 ☐	074 ☐	075 ☐	076 ☐	077 ☐	078 ☐	079 ☐
081 ☐	082 ☐	083 ☐	084 ☐	085 ☐	086 ☐	087 ☐	088 ☐	089 ☐
091 ☐	092 ☐	093 ☐	094 ☐	095 ☐	096 ☐	097 ☐	098 ☐	099 ☐
101 ☐	102 ☐	103 ☐	104 ☐	105 ☐	106 ☐	107 ☐	108 ☐	109 ☐
111 ☐	112 ☐	113 ☐	114 ☐	115 ☐	116 ☐	117 ☐	118 ☐	119 ☐
121 ☐	122 ☐	123 ☐	124 ☐	125 ☐	126 ☐	127 ☐	128 ☐	129 ☐
131 ☐	132 ☐	133 ☐	134 ☐	135 ☐	136 ☐	137 ☐	138 ☐	139 ☐
141 ☐	142 ☐	143 ☐	144 ☐	145 ☐	146 ☐	147 ☐	148 ☐	149 ☐
151 ☐	152 ☐	153 ☐	154 ☐	155 ☐	156 ☐	157 ☐	158 ☐	159 ☐
161 ☐	162 ☐	163 ☐	164 ☐	165 ☐	166 ☐	167 ☐	168 ☐	169 ☐
171 ☐	172 ☐	173 ☐	174 ☐	175 ☐	176 ☐	177 ☐	178 ☐	179 ☐
181 ☐	182 ☐	183 ☐	184 ☐	185 ☐	186 ☐	187 ☐	188 ☐	189 ☐
191 ☐	192 ☐	193 ☐	194 ☐	195 ☐	196 ☐	197 ☐	198 ☐	199 ☐
201 ☐	202 ☐	203 ☐	204 ☐	205 ☐	206 ☐	207 ☐	208 ☐	209 ☐
211 ☐	212 ☐	213 ☐	214 ☐	215 ☐	216 ☐	217 ☐	218 ☐	219 ☐
221 ☐	222 ☐	223 ☐	224 ☐	225 ☐	226 ☐	227 ☐	228 ☐	229 ☐
231 ☐	232 ☐	233 ☐	234 ☐	235 ☐	236 ☐	237 ☐	238 ☐	239 ☐
241 ☐	242 ☐	243 ☐	244 ☐	245 ☐	246 ☐	247 ☐	248 ☐	249 ☐
251 ☐	252 ☐	253 ☐	254 ☐	255 ☐	256 ☐	257 ☐	258 ☐	259 ☐
261 ☐	262 ☐	263 ☐	264 ☐	265 ☐	266 ☐	267 ☐	268 ☐	269 ☐
271 ☐	272 ☐	273 ☐	274 ☐	275 ☐	276 ☐	277 ☐	278 ☐	279 ☐
281 ☐	282 ☐	283 ☐	284 ☐	285 ☐	286 ☐	287 ☐	288 ☐	289 ☐
291 ☐	292 ☐	293 ☐	294 ☐	295 ☐	296 ☐	297 ☐	298 ☐	299 ☐

FIGURE 7—2

STANDARD PROGRAM PLANNING FORM

lar task. The time cards are collected regularly from all students and recorded in the central office, either manually or by data processing. At the time that a student successfully completes the criterion exams for a task, he is given an M on the card by the instructor who initials it. Or, if he tests out of a particular task, he is given a "T" by the instructor. These performance symbols are duly recorded by the instructor and the central office, so that the record always indicates the tasks mastered or tested out in total.

Utilization of the time card has four essential purposes. First it provides the student, instructor, and the institution with an ongoing record of the progress the student is making on his instructional program. We have noted great difficulty in some individualized instructional programs because the student's progress was not being monitored adequately. The student could exist for several months without anyone being aware that a problem in his progress had developed. The time card system provides an "on-line" check on student progress.

Second, as institutional experience develops, it is easier for the institutional staff to ascertain what the expected time will be for a student to complete a given task, and estimates about facility utilization become more realistic.

Third, high activity programs with effective instructors are highlighted by the student-task completion being credited to the program, and superior individualized instruction on the part of some instructors can be identified and recognized.

Fourth, a high percentage of occupations in which vocational and technical graduates will be working will require time card usage on the job and the practical experience in the utilization of the cards is helpful.

In addition to the informal instructor check on the time cards coming in and the mastery of the various tasks, if the record keeping system has been computerized, a monthly institutional printout by name of the students in the program, the tasks mastered during that month, and their percentage of completion against "regular," "handicap," and/or "disadvantaged" time is available to the instructor and to the administration. This information is valuable when making decisions concerning the management of the learning stations within the system.

Program completion by a student is accomplished when all of the tasks defined for the program have been completed and the criterion knowing and performance tests have been passed at the mastery level by the student.

Instructors in the individualized system described are accountable for a specified number of learning stations in specified locations, and for the learning of students who are occupying those stations. A student who must leave the immediate location of his program instructor in order to take related training elsewhere will need to find an opening there and "clock-in" into that new program area. The availability of stations can be managed in a variety of ways, depending on the size of the institution and its general physical arrangements. In one institution, there is a central "program box" location where instructors place program cards for each training station they have open. When all of the cards are gone, the program is filled. When one or more complete that part of their in-

STUDENT TIME KEEPING INSTRUCTIONS

General

1. The student time keeping procedure begins when the instructor and student have initially agreed upon the Instructional program plan which consists of standard program units and supplementary units.

2. The student is not required to clock on or off for breaks but must clock on and off for lunch periods.

3. All time must be recorded in hours and hundredths of hours. See conversion table below.

Procedure

1. Acquire time card stock from systems Technology department.	Instructor
2. Issue time card to student for first Instructional unit planned.	Instructor
3. Enter name, 5-digit student number assigned, standard program (and auxiliary program number if the unit is other than standard program), and unit number.	student
4. When starting to study unit insert card into time clock with the time clock guide aligned with time card "on".	student
5. At end of each day or when unit is satisfactorily completed clock "off"	student
6. Initial and provide time card to Instructor the end of last school day of each week or when unit is satisfactory completed.	student
7. Indicate under "status" the letter M for mastery or T for tested out if applicable. Initial and forward time card to systems technology department at end of last school day of each week.	Instructor
8. Repeat procedure for each instructional unit.	

Special Note:

Use unit code numbers 910 for student affairs and 920 for general practice.

MINUTES TO HOURS CONVERSION

Minutes	Hours		
5	.08	6:00 AM	0600
10	.16	12:00 Noon	1200
15	.25	1:00 PM	1300
20	.34	2:00 PM	1400
25	.42	3:00 PM	1500
30	.50	4:00 PM	1600
35	.56	5:00 PM	1700
40	.66	5:30 PM	1750
45	.75	5:45 PM	1775

FIGURE 7−3

916 AVTI TIME CARD

LAST NAME	FIRST NAME	M.I.

A3 CARD	STATUS	CLOCK	DAY-MONTH-TIME
STUDENT NO.		OFF	
		ON	
STD. PROG. NO.		OFF	
		ON	
AUX. PROG. NO.		OFF	
		ON	
UNIT		OFF	
		ON	
INITIAL		OFF	
		ON	
APPROVAL		OFF	
		ON	
		OFF	
		ON	
		OFF	
		ON	
		OFF	
		ON	

START HERE

EXAMPLE OF A TIME CARD

struction, their cards go back in the box, for another student to pick up and present to the instructor for use at that station.

Summary

In summary, demands for "open access" and "accountability" along with greater recognition of human differences are bringing increased pressure for individualizing vocational instruction programs. The development of individualized instruction programs and the operation of such programs requires a high level of management skills.

The four basic ingredients which are key factors in a successful individualized program are: staff who are trained or willing to be trained, relevant instructional materials, suitable facilities, and willing and able students. The question of staff development of individualized learning materials as opposed to outside purchase is complex and requires careful study with many considerations. Scheduling of individualized programs can also become very complicated, and care should be taken that it does not overwhelm the most important facet of the program—the student learner.

REFERENCES

1. Mali, Paul. *Managing By Objectives*. New York: Wiley-Interscience, A Division of John Wiley & Sons, Inc., 1972, p. 1.

Appendix 1   SAMPLE JOB DESCRIPTIONS

HONEYWELL

OCCUPATIONAL DESCRIPTION—EVALUATION

OFFICE & TECHNICAL OCCUPATIONS

Title SENIOR DEVELOPMENT ENGINEER   Code 11-1-001   Grade E-III
Approved By: Div. GAP   Dept. Engineering   Eff. Date 12-17-71

Primary Function

Provide the origination of that portion of a product design within his area of specialty which will satisfy the requirements of the application and be economical to produce at the rates required.

Source of Supervision

Design and Development Supervisor for full scope of supervision.

Direction of Others

Directs and coordinates the technical efforts of professional and technical personnel who may be assigned to his portion of the program.

Typical Responsibilities and Performance Requirements

The following is a list of typical responsibilities and performance requirements. For a specific job, only a few of these may be applicable in great depth or all may be applicable with a lesser depth.

I. *Technical*
   A. Identifies new business opportunities. Seeks new product ideas or applications intermittently on an assignment or opportunistic basis. Works with Engineering Department management to predict future business opportunities and to formalize and implement programs intended to capitalize on these opportunities.
      Authority: B
   B. Provides definition of product requirements. Defines, analyzes, and implements solutions to development problems which require a depth

of knowledge in his and related technical specialities. (Solutions may require innovative technical approaches or concepts.) Interprets operational requirements and defines performance criteria for his assigned tasks.

Authority: B

C. Identifies design problems of his assignment, and independently pursues their solutions with regard to related problems.

Authority: B

D. Analyzes design problems of his assignment to achieve optimal cost and technical trade-offs, and implements activities required to achieve the desired results. Requires rigorous application of engineering fundamentals with analytical solutions derived by the various means deemed necessary such as: application of theoretical analysis, physical theory, mathematical theory and analysis, engineering principles, experimental observations and other related specialized knowledge.

Authority: B

E. Applies his technical capabilities to the solution of development problems within his specialty, and assists in the definition of interfaces between his and other related technical responsibilities to facilitate formulation of design concepts requiring state-of-the-art advances or aplication of specialized technical skills.

Authority: A

F. Provides specialized technical knowledge to a project to assure optimal configuration specification. His concepts must represent the optimal solution to problems with regard to total project requirements. Selection of an optimal alternate requires complex trade-off considerations.

Authority: B

G. Prepares those portions of technical and cost proposals, or development plans, that are pertinent to his specialty and assignment, and may assist in the preparation of other, but related portions. Assures that appropriate technical documentation is prepared. This includes his portion of project progress reports, status reports, engineering drawings, and the maintenance of an Engineering Data Book.

Authority: A

H. Formulates test plans or other design verification techniques for his solutions to design problems.

Authority: A

I. Acts as the project technical authority in his specialty, if required. Provides counsel to more junior professionals or other specialists when their assignments relate to, or interface with his. Intermittently solicited for advice, mostly from within Division or participating customer representatives.

Authority: B

J. May participate in activities involving customer support, usually in a supporting role with frequent contact with customers involving detailed presentations and pre-proposal information transmittal. Presents technical reports and sells new or innovative approaches to technical problems.

Authority: B

II. *Administrative*

A. Plans and schedules his own activities and needs, including materials, services, and required technical support.

Authority: C

B. Completes his project activities within planned costs. Anticipates cost problems and initiates efforts to reduce or minimize them.

Authority: C

C. Prepares, or coordinates the preparation of oral and written reports of current status, progress, and terminal status of his or related assignments, as required by project management. Requires sufficiently detailed knowledge of a limited-scope task to allow him to effectively report status.

Authority: B

D. Directs and coordinates the technical efforts of professional and technical personnel who may be assigned to his portion of the program. Must possess sufficient confidence and sense of authority which allow him to give explanatory and coordinative instructions to individuals of same or lower grades.

Authority: C

Authority Levels

A Complete
B Act and Report
C Act after approval

Exempt   EJC/mlm

HONEYWELL

OCCUPATIONAL DESCRIPTION—EVALUATION

OFFICE & TECHNICAL OCCUPATIONS

Title   DEVELOPMENT TECHNICIAN   Code 15-1-001 Grade 07
Approved By: Div. GAP   Dept. Engineering   Eff. Date 12-17-71

Primary Function

Support engineer by performing non-routine tasks that may include design, fabrication, documentation, maintenance, operation, and testing of materials, processes, components, or systems.

Source of Supervision

Project Supervisor for full scope of supervision. Principal, Senior Engineer or Engineers for work direction as assigned.

Direction of Others

None.

Work Performed

Develops, builds, tests, or maintains a device, system, material, or process. The ability to evaluate a task of electrical, electronic, chemical, mechanical, or physical nature is necessary.

Prepares layout sketches, schematics, or plans for use by draftsmen or for further analysis on parts, or devices to which assigned. On approval of engineers, may recommend materials, parts, dimensions, and tolerances necessary for operation of completed device.

Designs, tests, operates or maintains as necessary instrumentation, machine tools, laboratory setups, environmental equipment or standards as required by the job assignment.

Proficiency required in various job areas is a combination of craft and basic engineering abilities. Applies craft and experience capability coupled with a knowledge of basic engineering principles to the physical development or testing of parts, breadboards, processes or devices where the configuration and dimensions or processing are proven on a step by step build and sketch basis. *Obtains technical guidance from senior technicians* or engineers as necessary.

Prepares reports in the form of charts, graphs, and documentation of design and development tasks for both formal and information reports consisting of engineering and scientific concepts. Verbal and written communications must be factual and concise.

Occassionally called upon to assist in the resolution of design or production deficiencies and to interface on major problems with the engineering groups concerned.

Maintenance of technical proficiency with the advancing technology is essential.

Authority Levels

A Complete
B Act and Report
C Act after Approval

Non-Exempt   EJC/mlm

Appendix 2 SAMPLE DIFFERENTIATED STAFFING JOB DESCRIPTIONS

Special Intermediate School District No. 916 for
Vocational - Technical Education
2233 North Hamline Avenue, Roseville, Minnesota 55113   (612) 636-1978

JOB DESCRIPTION AND EVALUATION
(Tentative-September 8, 1971)

INSTRUCTOR

SUMMARY:

This individual will be responsible for the occupational instruction of 15-50 full-time equivalent students depending on the nature of instruction, and number of aides assigned. This will include their work in classrooms, laboratories and LRC's.

QUALIFICATIONS:

Mandatory:

1. Must be fully-certified under the Minnesota State Plan or be able to obtain a provisional certificate and complete full certification within three years.
2. Must be willing to participate in teacher training under state and 916 auspices.
3. Must be committed to meeting individual needs of students.
4. Must be willing to work with students of variable ability and enrollment entry dates.

Desirable:

1. Demonstrated success and enjoyment in working with youth, i.e., teaching, Y.M.C.A., church youth programs, Boy Scouts, etc.
2. Demonstrated ability to use "systems" approach to instruction.

DUTIES AND PERFORMANCE EXPECTATIONS:

1. Motivate students for whom they are responsible to pursue their chosen occupational training with vigor.
2. Assist students in setting their occupational training goals.
3. Assist students in preparation of instructional plan to meet training goals.
4. Conduct task analysis and validate.
5. Derive and write performance objectives.

222

6. Develop individualized learning packages (centered around performance objectives).
7. Validate packages on target population.
8. Validate the program against total job practice (putting it all together).
9. Coordinate learning activities.
10. Motivate students on unit objectives.
11. Develop learning resources (audio-visual).
12. Develop pre-tests.
13. Develop criterion tests.
14. Demonstrate practical use of learning theory.
15. Express current philosophy of Vocational Education.
16. Demonstrate acceptable conference leading techniques.
    1. Advisory committee
    2. Small group instruction
17. Promote the health and safety of students, through supervising the learning environment.
18. Identify student learning difficulties and prescribe corrective action.
19. Knowledge of instructional equipment and existing software, in appropriate occupation.
    1. Record competencies gained
    2. Record units tested through
    3. Record time/unit
21. Assume responsibility for student progress.
22. Conduct individual, small group, and large group instruction as required.
23. Direct work of aides assigned to instructional program.
24. Prepare and/or locate and request purchase of necessary instructional materials for instructional program.

Special Intermediate School District No. 916 for
Vocational - Technical Education
2233 North Hamline Avenue, Roseville, Minnesota 55113   (612) 636-1978

JOB DESCRIPTION AND EVALUATION

SENIOR INSTRUCTOR

SUMMARY:

The senior instructor will have all the duties of the instructor, but will perform these duties at a level of excellence determined by his performance and results over a period of not less than five years.

QUALIFICATIONS:

The same qualifications as for an instructor with the following additions or changes:

1. Must be fully certified.
2. Not less than five years in instruction or supervision of instruction position.
3. Demonstrated outstanding ability in a substantial majority of instructor's duties.

DUTIES:

All of the instructor duties at a high level of excellence.

COMPENSATION:

1. Monthly range $1100 - $1550

Special Intermediate School District No. 916 for
Vocational - Technical Education
2233 North Hamline Avenue, Roseville, Minnesota 55113   (612) 636-1978

JOB DESCRIPTION AND EVALUATION

LEAD INSTRUCTOR

SUMMARY:
The lead instructor will have all the duties of the instructor. In addition will provide instructional and organizational leadership in occupational instruction where two or more instructors are engaged in the same or very similar instructional programs.

QUALIFICATIONS:
The same as for instructors with the following additions or changes:
Mandatory:
1. Full day-preparatory certification required.
2. Not less than three years in instructor or supervision of instruction position.
3. Demonstrated ability to prepare and use individualized instructional materials in the instructional process.

DUTIES:
All of the duties of an instructor plus:
1. Coordinate the tasks of the instructional team to provide maximum service to students.
2. Coordinate the development and production of appropriate instructional materials for use by the team in the instructional program.
3. Serve as primary contact with the program's instructional advisory committee.
4. Coordinate recording and processing of student progress data for area of program responsibility.
5. Recommended instructor and aide configurations to instructional manager.
6. Assist instructional manager with instructor evaluation.

COMPENSATION:
1. Monthly range $1100 - $1550.
2. All institutional fringe benefits.

Special Intermediate School District No. 916 for
Vocational - Technical Education
2233 North Hamline Avenue, St. Paul, Minnesota 55113   (612) 636-1978

JOB DESCRIPTION

MANAGER OF
INSTRUCTION, INDUSTRIAL LABORATORIES AND
MAINTENANCE DEPARTMENT

SUMMARY:

This position includes the management of instructional programs in graphics, electro-mechanical areas, industrial laboratories and construction laboratories. This manager will also be responsible for the ongoing operation and maintenance of the school plant and facilities.

QUALIFICATIONS:

Mandatory:

1. Must be qualified under the Minnesota State Plan as a supervisor or teacher of local vocational-technical programs, or; be able to obtain that certification by July 1, 1971. Applicants in doubt about their certification should contact Mr. Robert Madson, State Department of Education, Centennial Building, St. Paul, Minnesota 55101.

2. Must have not less than five years of occupational experience in one of the occupations being supervised within the last ten years, at least three of which must be in supervisory capacity, or; have been a certified vocational program supervisor for three of the past ten years.

3. Must have been in a position which required accountability for costs; either in an industrial production, or school administration structure.

Desirable:

1. Demonstrated success and enjoyment in working with youth, i.e., teaching, Y.M.C.A., church youth programs, boy scouts, etc.

2. Demonstrated ability to use "systems" approach in an industrial or or educational setting.

3. Broad base of contact in industry in one or more of program areas supervised.

4. Experience in planning educational experiences for others in school, industrial or civic organizational structure.

DUTIES:

1. Design, implement and operate a system of instruction in electro-mechanical, graphic communications, building maintenance, environmental occupations and other related occupations.

2. Make recommendations to superintendent as to the staff and equipment required for the integrated instruction and building operation program.

3. Assist in the design, implementation and operation of a system for performance appraisal and testing of incoming students, for monitor-

ing their progress while enrolled and evaluating their progress status upon their leaving the system. This system will be compatible in input with the District 916 information system.

4. Develop, within institutional guidelines, a system of staff appraisal, evaluation and compensation for all instructional and operational staff for this management center.

5. Design, implement and operate a student recruitment system for enrolling high school, post high school and adult students to keep the instructional system near capacity for training in occupations in which employment is possible.

6. Design a cost control system for appraising maintenance, heating and air conditioning efficiency to include cost per degree day, cost per square foot and other increments of measurement.

INSTITUTIONAL OBJECTIVES:

1. Provide instructional experiences for students leading to employment and/or successful occupational performance demonstration for approximately 100 part-time high school students, 190 post-high school students and 500 adult evening school students.

2. The instructional program design will allow for not less than one-third (⅓) of the typical student's time to be spent in independent study or practice in his selected occupational program.

3. The instructional program will be designed so that new student entries can be permitted at intervals not longer than every four weeks.

4. The instructional program will be designed to utilize not less than 75% of all of the operational and instructional equipment in the building and the building itself as one of its integral parts.

5. The instructional program will be designed to accommodate ranges of ability and interest from highly technical to assembly, and physically able to those confined in wheelchairs, within the reference of acceptance for employment by industry.

COMPENSATION:

1. Salary to be commensurate with proven capabilities, experience and training.

2. Fringe benefits, to be established institutionally, to include retirement coordinated with state-established programs, hospitalization, long-term disability and life insurance.

3. Employment to be on 12-months basis with four weeks vacation, with additional time off for professional improvement.

Appendix 3 NATIONAL COLLEGE VERB LIST

THE FUNCTIONAL, FORCEFUL FOUR HUNDRED FIFTY FIVE

"Creative" Behaviors

Alter	Generalize	Question	Re-group	Re-phrase	Re-write
Ask	Modify	Re-arrange	Rename	Restate	Simplify
Change	Paraphrase	Re-combine	Re-order	Restructure	Synthesize
Design	Predict	Reconstruct	Re-organize	Retell	Systematize
				Revise	Vary

Complex, Logical, Judgmental Behaviors

Analyze	Combine	Contrast	Designate	Formulate	Plan
Appraise	Compare	Criticize	Determine	Generate	Structure
Assess	Conclude	Deduce	Discover	Induce	Suggest
		Defend	Evaluate	Infer	Substitute

General Discriminative Behaviors

Choose	Describe	Discriminate	Indicate	Match	Place
Collect	Detect	Distinguish	Isolate	Omit	Point
Define	Differentiate	Identify	List	Order	Select
				Pick	Separate

Social Behaviors

Accept	Answer	Co-operate	Forgive	Laugh	Reply
Admit	Argue	Dance	Greet	Meet	Smile
Agree	Communicate	Disagree	Help	Participate	Talk
Aid	Compliment	Discuss	Interact	Permit	Thank
Allow	Contribute	Excuse	Invite	Praise	Visit
			Join	React	Volunteer

Language Behaviors

Abbreviate	Call	Indent	Punctuate	Speak	*Tell
Accent	Capitalize	Outline	Read	Spell	Translate
Alphabetize	Edit	Print	Recite	State	Verbalize
Articulate	Hyphenate	Pronounce	Say	Summarize	Whisper
			Sign	Syllabicate	Write

"Study" Behaviors

Arrange	Circle	Diagram	Itemize	Mark	Record

Categorize	Classify	Find	Label	Name	Reproduce
Chart	Compile	Follow	Locate	Note	Search
Cite	Copy	Gather	Look	Organize	Sort
			Map	Quote	Underline

Music Behaviors

Blow	Clap	Finger	Hum	Pluck	Strum
Bow	Compose	Harmonize	Mute	Practice	Tap
			Play	Sing	Whistle

Physical Behaviors

Arch	Climb	Hit	March	Ski	Swim
Bat	Face	Hop	Pitch	Skip	Swing
Bend	Float	Jump	Pull	Somersault	Throw
Carry	Grab	Kick	Push	Stand	Toss
Catch	Grasp	Knock	Run	Step	Walk
Chase	Grip	Lift	Skate	Stretch	

Arts Behaviors

Assemble	Cut	Frame	Hold	Roll	Stamp
Blend	Dab	Hammer	Nail	Rub	Stick
Brush	Dot	Handle	Paint	Sand	Stir
Build	Draw	Heat	Paste	Saw	Trace
Carve	Drill	Illustrate	Pat	Sculpt	Trim
Color	Fold	Melt	Polish	Shake	Varnish
Construct	Form	Mix	Pour	Sketch	Wipe
			Press	Smooth	Wrap

Drama Behaviors

Act	Direct	Enter	Imitate	Pantomime	Respond
Clasp	Display	Exit	Leave	Pass	Show
Cross	Emit	Express	Move	Perform	Sit
				Proceed	Turn

Mathematical Behaviors

Add	Compute	Estimate	Integrate	Plot	Subtract
Bisect	Count	Extrapolate	Interpolate	Prove	Sum

Calculate	Cumulate	Extract	Measure	Reduce	Tabulate
Check	Derive	Graph	Multiply	Solve	Tally
Circumscribe	Divide	Group	Number	Square	Verify

Laboratory Science Behaviors

Align	Conduct	Dissect	Keep	Plant	Set
Apply	Connect	Feed	Lengthen	Prepare	Specify
Attach	Convert	Grow	Limit	Remove	Straighten
Balance	Decrease	Increase	Manipulate	Replace	Time
Calibrate	Demonstrate	Insert	Operate	Report	Transfer
				Reset	Weigh

General Appearance, Health and Safety Behaviors

Button	Comb	Eat	Fill	Taste	Unzip
Clean	Cover	Eliminate	Go	Tie	Wait
Clear	Dress	Empty	Lace	Unbutton	Wash
Close	Drink	Fasten	Stack	Uncover	Wear
			Stop	Untie	Zip

Miscellaneous

Aim	Erase	Hunt	Peel	Scratch	Store
Attempt	Expand	Include	Pin	Send	Strike
Attend	Extend	Inform	Position	Serve	Supply
Begin	Feel	Kneel	Present	Sew	Support
Bring	Finish	Lay	Produce	Share	Switch
Buy	Fit	Lead	Propose	Sharpen	Take
Come	Fix	Lend	Provide	Shoot	Tear
Complete	Flip	Let	Put	Shorten	Touch
Correct	Get	Light	Raise	Shovel	Try
Crease	Give	Make	Relate	Shut	Twist
Crush	Grind	Mend	Repair	Signify	Type
Develop	Guide	Miss	Repeat	Slip	Use
Distribute	Hand	Offer	Return	Slide	Vote
Do	Hang	Open	Ride	Spread	Watch
Drop	Hold	Pack	Rip	Stake	Weave
End	Hook	Pay	Save	Start	Work

Appendix 4

A LEARNING GUIDE

TASK   *Set Up and Operate the Chief 20 Press*

PURPOSE   When the sheet size of an offset press gets larger than 11″ x 17″, we find presses using the bearer system for its cylinders. These bearers maintain the correct separation between cylinders to assure high quality printing. This package is an introduction to bearers with the Chief 20. Knowledge of the Chief 20 will apply to the Harris and Speedflex, which also use the bearer system.

Dept.	Prog.	Task	Prerequisites: Learning Packages #
09	222	618	304, 904, 902, 727

Courtesy: 916 Vo-Tech 1972.

LEARNING CONTRACT

1 STUDENT DATA

Name	Social Security Number

Length of Contract (normal time in hours)

2 TERMINAL PERFORMANCE OBJECTIVE
Given an offset metal master which has been developed with an image and a clean Chief 20 offset machine, print 500 sheets of 11″ x 17″ stock on the Chief 20 offset machine with a spoilage of less than 20%, with the remaining printed pieces of sale quality in one hour.

2a Intermediate Performance Objectives
    1. Prepare Chief 20 offset machine for operation.
    2. Operate the Chief 20 offset machine and print sheets of paper
    3. Clean the Chief 20 offset machine after printing.

3 AGREEMENT
    I, _____ agree to complete the above stated terminal performance requirement within _____ to _____. I further recognize that the conditions of the contract (performance and time agreement) report my ability to perform the requirements of the occupation and record my progress.

_____   _____
Student's Signature   Instructor's Signature
                                                        (verifies competency)

Dept.	Prog.	Task	TPO
09	222	618	618

INTERMEDIATE-PERFORMANCE OBJECTIVE #1

Prepare Chief 20 offset machine for operation.

LEARNING STEPS

RESOURCES

1. Read Chapter 22 in *ITU, Lessons in Printing*, Volume 2.
View sound-on-slide tray 124
Read Introduction Notes,
Page 1

1. *ITU, Lessons in Printing*, Volume 2, in LRC.
Sound-on-slide Tray 124.
Introduction Notes—
Attached.

2. Read Chapters I and II in the *ATF Chief 20 Instruction Manual*. Be completely familiar with all controls as described in Chapter I.
NOTE: Do not ink the Chief 20 until you have completely checked it out and have paper feeding consistently. Check with instructor as to type and weight of paper to be used.

2. *ATF Chief 20 Instruction Manual*—copies in LRC* or check with instructor.

3. Check and adjust all adjustments according to Chapter 2 in the *ATF Chief 20 Instruction Manual*.

3. *ATF Chief 20 Instruction Manual*—copies in LRC or check with instructor.

4. Go to IPO #2.
NOTE: Do not proceed with IPO #2 unless you have done above steps and feel confident with the press. Check with instructor if there are any doubts or questions regarding the Chief 20.

*Learning Resource Center

Dept.	Prog.	Task	TPO	IPO
09	222	618	618	001

INTERMEDIATE-PERFORMANCE OBJECTIVE #2

Operate the press and print sheets of paper.

LEARNING STEPS

RESOURCES

1. Read Chapter 19 in *Photo Offset Fundamentals.*
View video tape cassette #249

2. Answer Questions 2-18, and write definitions of words, p. 330. (Only words #1, 4, 6, 7, 8, 10, 12, 14, 18). Turn in your answers and definitions to the instructor.

3. Read Chapter 3, Operations of the Press, in the *Chief 20 Instruction Manual.*
NOTE: Check with instructor as to ink and fountain solution to be used.

4. Check with instructor as to quality of your printed sheets.

5. Go to IPO #3.

1. *Photo Offset Fundamentals* by Cogoli in LRC.
Video-tape cassette #249

2. *Chief 20 Instruction Manual* in LRC or check with instructor.

3. Instructor.

Dept.	Prog.	Task	TPO	IPO
09	222	618	618	002

INTERMEDIATE-PERFORMANCE OBJECTIVE #3

Clean machine after printing.

LEARNING STEPS	RESOURCES
1. Read paragraph on Cleaning the Press, last page of Chapter 3 in *ATF Instruction Manual.*	1. *ATF Chief 20 Instruction Manual.*
2. Read comments on clean-up in Introduction notes.	2. Attached.
3. Take Criterion Examination	3. See instructor.
4. Turn in examination, and after exam has been corrected request to be certified competent on this task.	

Dept.	Prog.	Task	TPO	IPO
09	222	618	618	003

INTRODUCTION NOTES

1) Bearers:

On the Chief 20A, unlike the AM 1250 and Itek 11 and 15, you will see the bearer set up for cylinder pressure. Note at the end of the blanket and plate cylinder a barrel of steel approximately ¾″ to 1″ wide. This is the bearer. The larger presses use this to maintain an even pressure between plate and blanket at all times. Even pressure is needed to assure high quality and especially when using the larger sheet sizes.

2) Plate and Blanket Packing:

With the bearer system, we must maintain proper pressure between plate and blanket by packing both the plate and blanket to bring them up to a proper height. This height is a specific amount for each press. The packing under the plate and blanket will depend upon the thickness of each. The proper amount for the packing and blanket should be .071. Therefore, if our blanket thickness measured .067, our packing should be .004 or the thickness of a sheet of 20 lb. bond. In turn, the total of plate and packing on this press is .012. Therefore, if our plate is .006, our packing will be .006 or a combined total of .012.

3) Ink Roll:

You will notice the Chief 20A has more ink rolls than the smaller presses. By using more rolls, the ink is milled much smoother and thus better lay down of solids and halftones. Also, the ink form rolls are of a different diameter, unlike the 1250 and Itek, where the ink form rolls are the same. By using different size ink form rolls, the roll recovers at different times, thus avoiding streaks when printing large solids or halftones.

4) Fountain Solution:

Normally, the fountain solution being used in the larger press is of an acid base concentrate rather than glycerin. The acid base solution makes for faster drying of the ink, but you may find the ink and water balance more critical, especially when using the glycerin base such as Repelex, on the smaller presses. Normal mixture of the fountain solution is one ounce acid etch, one ounce gum to one gallon water.

5) Rollers:

The water rollers and some of the ink rollers normally are in the roller cabinet located behind the press. The water rolls are placed here so they dry out and the rubber ink rolls so they do not develop flat spots.

INTRODUCTION NOTES
-continued-

6) Switches: The switches on the Chief 20 are different from the smaller presses. One is the inch switch, which turns the press on for a small amount of time. The reason for this is that with all the gears and rollers, it is very difficult to turn the press a small amount using the handwheel, as we can on the smaller press. The off switch has a lock on it. By turning the ring around the edge will lock the switch on off. There will be no chance of accidentally turning the machine on when the off switch is locked off. Note: there is an identical set of switches at the feeder and on the operator's side.

7) Guards: When operating the Chief 20, be sure all the guards are in place. One guard in particular is the bar on the feeder end which protects you from getting caught in the opening between the plate cylinder and blanket cylinder. Note: these cylinders both turn *in* and could be dangerous without the guard in place.

8) Clean Up: The Chief 20 has a special clean-up attachment which works very well. Check with instructor on clean-up. When cleaning up the press, it is best to remove water form rolls. Cleaner sheets are also available and can be used with or without clean-up attachment.

TASK ANALYSIS FORM   FORM C

	Frequency of *Performance* (low) (high)	*Task* *Importance* (low) (high)	*Performance* *Difficulty* (low) (high)
	1 2 ③	1 2 ③	1 ② 3

Task: Prepare Chief 20 for
              Operation

Acceptable Level of Performance: Set up the Chief 20 to print sale-
(Quality of work, time limits, etc.)   able quality pieces with dense ink
coverage with clean background
and no offsetting.

Conditions under which learner performs: Given an offset metal master with
an image, and a clean Chief 20
offset machine and 500 sheets of
11 x 17 stock

INTERMEDIATE TASKS

1. Lowers the pile board
2. Loads the feeder
3. Raises the pile board
4. Sets the tail guides
5. Sets the sheet separators
6. Adjusts feeder suckers
7. Adjusts blast adjustments
8. Places pile height governor
   in position
9. Adjusts sheet caliper
10. Adjusts sheet forwarding wheels
11. Adjusts speed wheels
12. Place guide ball holders
13. Adjust collars of hold-down bands
14. Sets side guides
15. Sets front guides
16. Sets ink form rollers
17. Sets distribution rollers
18. Sets ink ductor roller
19. Adjusts ink fountain control
20. Checks auxiliary vibrator roller
21. Adjusts washup device
22. Adjusts vibrator stroke adjustment
23. Sets lower form dampener roller
24. Sets upper form dampener roller

25. Sets water ductor roller
26. Prepares new blanket
27. Installs blanket on cylinder
28. Packs the blanket
29. Adjusts blanket tension
30. Installs plate on cylinder
31. Adjusts plate for register
32. Sets plate to blanket pressure
33. Parallels the impression and
    blanket cylinders
34. Adjusts for stock thickness
35. Sets sheet counter
36. Adjusts delivery pile
37. Sets delivery joggers
38. Sets delivery strippers

INDEX